Secrets to Writing a Series

Write Novels That Sell, Volume 3

K. Stanley and L. Cooke

Published by Fictionary Press, 2024.

While every precaution has been taken in the preparation of this book, the publisher assumes no responsibility for errors or omissions, or for damages resulting from the use of the information contained herein.

SECRETS TO WRITING A SERIES

First edition. July 17, 2024.

Copyright © 2024 K. Stanley and L. Cooke.

ISBN: 978-1738022113

Written by K. Stanley and L. Cooke.

Table of Contents

Chapter One: Introduction 1

Chapter Two: Artistic Decisions 7

Chapter Three: Types of Series 15

Chapter Four: Series Unity 25

Chapter Five: Meet Your Skeleton Blurbs 33

Chapter Six: Write Your Skeleton Blurbs 41

Chapter Seven: Meet the Story Arc 71

PART TWO: OUTLINE YOUR CLOSED SERIES 79

Chapter Eight: Meet the Closed Series Story Arc 81

Chapter Nine: Outline the Closed Series Story Arc 105

Chapter Ten: Frame Your Series Inciting Incident and Climax (Closed Series) 125

Chapter Eleven: Accept the Series Story Goal (Closed Series) 141

Chapter Twelve: The Protagonist's Worst Moment (Closed Series) 151

Chapter Thirteen: The Protagonist Gets Proactive (Closed Series) 161

Chapter Fourteen: Closed Series Structure Test 169

PART THREE: OUTLINE YOUR OPEN SERIES 177

Chapter Fifteen: Meet the Open Series Story Arc 179

Chapter Sixteen: Meet the Open Series Story Arc Patterns 185

Chapter Seventeen: Create the Open Series Story Arc Patterns .. 197

Chapter Eighteen: Open Series Structure Test 213

PART FOUR: ADD DEPTH TO YOUR SERIES 219

Chapter Nineteen: The Setup of Each Novel in a Series 221

Chapter Twenty: The Resolution of Each Novel in a Series 241

Chapter Twenty-One: Protagonist versus POV Characters 273

Chapter Twenty-Two: Backstory 291

Chapter Twenty-Three: Subplots 301

Chapter Twenty-Four: Novel and Series Titles 319

Chapter Twenty-Five: Write Your Series 331

Chapter Twenty-Six: The Series Vault 353

Chapter Twenty-Seven: Where to Next after This Book? 369

Glossary 373

Appendix: Recap of Outlining a Novel 383

Acknowledgments 385

About the Authors 387

Secrets to Writing a Series

The Creative Series Writing Method

Write Novels That Sell: Volume 3

by K. Stanley and L. Cooke

Also by K. Stanley and L. Cooke

Secrets to Editing Success: The Creative Story Editing Method

(Book #1: Write Novels That Sell)

Published February 2023

Secrets to Outlining a Novel: The Creative Outlining Method

(Book #2: Write Novels That Sell)

Published September 2023

Praise for the Write Novels That Sell Series

Praise for *Secrets to Writing a Series: The Creative Series Writing Method*

"The clear, step-by-step approach of Secrets to Writing a Series will take you from idea to epic, regardless of series length."

—Carol Fisher Saller, Editor and Author of *Maddie's Ghost*

Praise for *Secrets to Editing Success: The Creative Story Editing Method*

"One of the most frequent questions a novelist asks is, 'Does my draft contain a story?' Stanley and Cooke have written a practical guide that shows you how to answer that question. *Secrets to Editing Success* gives you actionable advice and a process to edit and revise your novel so that you can take your novel draft and turn it into a publishable book."

—Grant Faulkner, executive director of National Novel Writing Month

"*Secrets to Editing Success* is every editor's dream. Whether you're a new author reviewing your first book or a professional editor, this is without doubt the most comprehensive and detailed guide to editing I've ever had the pleasure of reading. This book will hold your hand, explain, clarify, and give you step-by-step instructions for editing your novel. Paired best when using the incomparable developmental editing software Fictionary, this guide will change your editing life. Read it. Immediately."

—Sacha Black, *Rebel Author Podcast*

Praise for *Secrets to Outlining a Novel: The Creative Outlining Method*

"A fresh, actionable, step-by-clear-step approach to creating a story outline that produces amazing results! Can't sing enough praises for *Secrets to Outlining a Novel*. Don't write your next novel without these insights, hints, and tips."

—Mary Buckham, *USA Today* bestselling author of *Break Into Fiction: 11 Steps to Building a Powerful Story*

"Writing a book is a huge (and scary) task. In *Secrets to Outlining a Novel*, Kristina and Lucy have demystified the process, breaking it down into approachable, bite-size pieces that help you understand outlining at both a macro and micro level."

—Hayley Milliman, Head of Education, ProWritingAid

Dedications

This book is dedicated to BC & Alberta Guide Dogs and Canadian Guide Dogs for the Blind. Their work has helped many people lead better lives. To the first five guide dog puppies I raised (Kinta, Jan, Candy, Sage, and Amelia), you bring purpose to my life. To my pet dogs, Chica and Farley, thank you for the daily joy you brought me.

—K. Stanley

To Ellen,

First, you were my teacher.

Then, you were my penfriend.

Now, you are missed.

—L. Cooke

PART ONE: SET UP YOUR SERIES

Chapter One: Introduction

Do you dream of writing a series of novels? Then read on.

We're about to kick off an exciting journey. We'll look at the what, the how, and the why of a series. We'll take you through an actionable process so you can set up the foundation for your series and write it as you read this book.

Secrets to Writing a Series is for anyone who wants to write a series starting from a structurally sound place. Whether you're a discovery writer (meaning you rarely outline before writing), or you love to create in-depth outlines, we'll show you a new method to set up, outline, and write your series.

What Is a Series?

Writing more than one novel does not necessarily mean you're writing a series. You can write many stand-alone novels without the novels being part of a series.

A series is a group of novels connected by common characters, plot, or settings.

This book is about the connections. Once you see them and understand how they are created, you can write any type of series.

Why Write a Series?

Perhaps you fell in love with a particular series, and that triggered your dream to write a series.

Perhaps you have a story that needs to be told in a series.

Perhaps you've seen that authors who write a series often make more money than an author who writes stand-alone novels.

Book series are big business. If you want to make big money in writing, writing a series seems to be a strong choice.

Why is that?

Readers like to read novels that entertain them, and when they find a novel they connect with, they want more. They want novels that are the same but different, and a series can give the reader exactly what they want.

In today's world, where you can order a novel at the click of a button, a series gives writers a fantastic opportunity to hook readers and get them to buy the next novel instantly.

Write a Series That Sells

Do you want to write a series that sells? If you're reading this book, we hope that's your goal.

Before creating a series, setting it up based on a strong structural foundation will help. This leads you to outline all or some of your series. After that, you get to start writing your series.

The outlining process we share in this book is no ordinary outlining process. It's new. It's creative. And it will spark your imagination. We're going to take you through a nonlinear process that leads you to a structurally sound series.

We'll start with the action of the story, because without a plot the characters have nothing to do.

SECRETS TO WRITING A SERIES

A series demands more from a writer than a stand-alone novel. Some decisions must be made before writing your series. You'll learn what these are and how to make them.

You'll learn about the different types of series and decide what type you want to write.

Series unity is a concept that makes a group of books a series. You'll learn how to find your series unity.

You'll write skeleton blurbs for your series and for the novels within your series. This is a mind-blowing exercise.

You'll learn about the difference between a story arc for a series and a story arc for a single novel. The story arc is the spine of a story and is flexible. Wait till you see what it can do for a series.

We'll look at the protagonist and the external story goal to build your series outline. By focusing on the actions the protagonist takes to achieve or not achieve the external story goal, you'll start your series on a structurally strong foundation.

We're introducing a new concept called the Series Structure Test. Before you start writing, you'll know whether your idea is strong enough to support a series, and if it's not, you'll know what to do to fix it.

Then you'll discover how you're going to open and close each novel in your series. This is important for the series to flow from one novel to the next.

We'll show you how to choose what backstory to show in each novel in the series. Backstory includes the events that happen before a novel's opening image, and backstory explains a character's motivation to reach the story goal. If a reader has read the first novel in your series, they know all the backstory already. You'll decide what parts of the earlier novels need to be included in the subsequent ones.

After that we're going to show you how to take the outline and start writing. We'll also cover subplots, and this is where you'll learn how to weave a subplot into the main plot.

And while we're doing that, we're going to build a series vault together. The series vault will be your go-to guide for all novels in your series.

How to Use This Book

Every chapter in this book gives you actionable advice that you can apply right away. If you perform the *fun series tasks* presented throughout, you'll be one step closer to becoming the author of a series.

The method we use is not genre-specific, and you can use it for any type of novel.

As you read, you can outline every scene in every novel in your series, or you can outline only the story arc scenes. You get to decide how detailed you want your outline to be. We don't want to get in the way of your creative process. We want to nourish it by giving you the flexibility to decide when you're ready to move from your idea to an outline to writing.

We'll show you examples of commercially successful series and illustrate how the story arc forces us to work harder at telling a great story—and the harder we work on creating a story, the better the story will be.

Showing you how we work is important to us. The Evolution series by K. Stanley and the My Fairy Assassin series by L. Cooke will be used to illustrate the process from start to finish. Both series started as stand-alone novels, and you'll get to see how we build them into a series.

Our book is not about giving you a formula. It's about teaching story theory that you can apply to your series. Some parts might resonate with you, which is fabulous. These parts enable you to organize your thoughts using the tools we provide. Some parts might not resonate with you, so listen to your inner artist. Not every tool in your toolbox should be used every time. You get to decide which tools work best for you.

Where to Next?

The next chapter is decision-making time. We're going to show you decisions for both series and scenes. If you make these decisions early, writing your series will be easier. So let's get started on a great adventure.

Chapter Two: Artistic Decisions

Always remember, you are an artist. As an artist who is setting off to write a series, you may have lows and highs, and our goal is to get you started with a strong series foundation and give you a process to write a commercially successful series. We want you to avoid the lows and gravitate to the highs. Isn't that what every artist wants?

This chapter shows **what** structural decisions you'll make, whether at the series level or the scene level, and later chapters show you **how** to make those decisions.

Every time you see this image of an open lock, we'll share a series secret with you.

When writing a series, you have more artistic decisions to make than when you're writing a stand-alone novel.

Every decision you make guides you along the way to a finished series. We're here to help you start from a place of strength, and by *strength* we mean a structurally sound framework. Putting in the effort now will save you time later.

Series-Level Decisions

Are you ready? This is so exciting. We're going to take the first step in writing a series. When you embark on your journey, it helps to know your destination. That destination may include a fixed number or an unlimited number of novels. This leads us to the first artistic decision.

Drumroll, please.

The **first series-level decision** is whether the series is a closed or open series.

Closed Series: Contains a fixed number of novels that tell one story. The novels are connected by the plot.

Open Series: Contains an unlimited number of novels connected by characters or settings.

The **second series-level decision** depends on whether you're writing a closed or an open series.

For a closed series, this is the moment to decide on the number of novels you want to write. You don't need this step for an open series.

For an open series, this is the moment to decide on the series' uniting factor. Will your novels be connected by character or setting?

We'll cover each of these later.

The **third series-level decision** is what each of the skeleton blurbs will show for each novel and for the whole series. And, yes, we mean more than one.

For a closed series, you'll write a skeleton blurb for the whole series and a skeleton blurb for each novel. We'll show you examples from the Hunger Games trilogy by Suzanne Collins and the Divergent trilogy by Veronica Roth. Please note: there will be spoilers.

For an open series, you'll write the skeleton blurbs for the first three novels in the series. You may even find you can write a skeleton blurb template that covers each novel. This is called a generic series skeleton blurb. We're going to show you examples of this for the Stephanie Plum series by Janet Evanovich and the Bridgerton series by Julia Quinn.

The **fourth series-level decision** concerns the main events in the story arc scenes. What are the series story arc patterns?

For a closed series, you'll outline the series story arc scenes and the story arc scenes for each novel.

For an open series, you'll create the main events for the story arc scenes of the first three novels in the series.

The **fifth series-level decision** is to decide whether your idea is strong enough to support a series. You'll learn about the **Series**

Structure Test. There is a test for a closed series and a different test for an open series.

Scene-Level Decisions

Once you've chosen the type of series you're writing, written the skeleton blurbs, performed the Series Structure Test, and outlined the story arc scenes, you have decisions to make at the scene level.

The **first scene-level decision** is what the opening and closing images will show in the setup and resolution of each novel.

The **second scene-level decision** is what type of protagonist you're going to use.

You've got three choices. The protagonist can be a single, combined, or group protagonist for each novel. In a series, you can write the novels using the same or different protagonist types. We call this the protagonist strategy.

The **third scene-level decision** is what point-of-view (POV) strategy you're going to follow.

You'll choose whether you're writing from a single POV or from multiple POVs.

The **fourth scene-level decision** is whether to write the narrative in the first, second, or third person. We call this the narrative strategy.

The **fifth scene-level decision** is what tense you're going to write each scene in. You'll write in the past or present tense. You may even write in a combination of past and present tense. That's your artistic choice.

Your Artistic Decisions

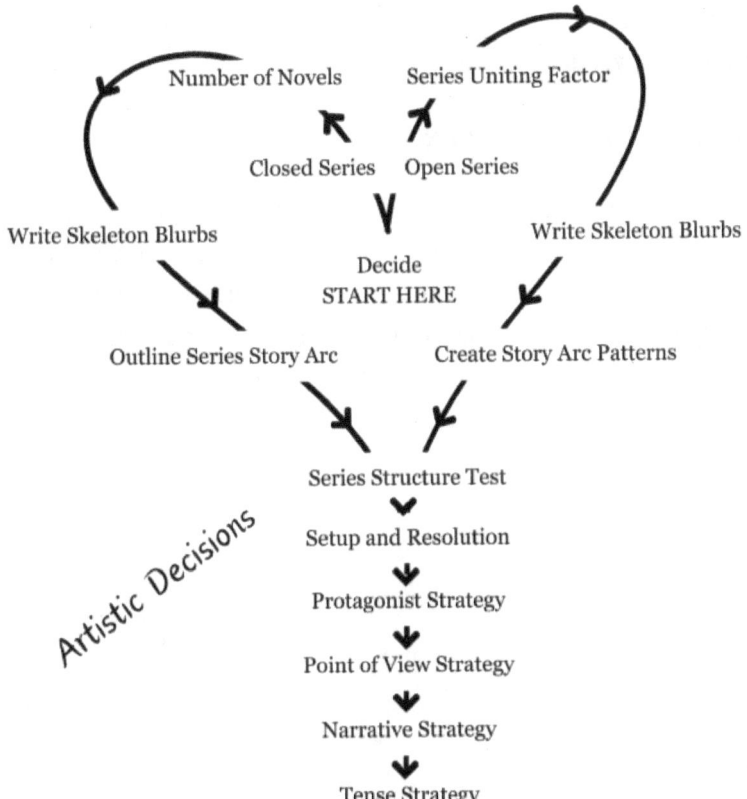

After the decisions are made and you've written the main events for the story arc scenes, we'll cover the following:

- Backstory
- Subplots

- The title of each book
- How to start writing

Series Vault

At the end of this process, you'll have built your series vault. A series vault differs from a stand-alone novel's vault (commonly referred to as a story bible). You'll use the series vault to keep track of the series and scene-level decisions.

Decisions You Don't Have to Make Yet

As you go through this process, and as your novels are published, you may find that new ideas arrive on your doorstep. Keep track of these ideas but don't let them distract you from finishing your series. At this moment you don't have to decide whether you're going to write a

- prequel
- sequel
- character spin-off
- setting spin-off

These decisions can all come later.

Your Fun Series Task

Throughout this book you'll see sections called *Your Fun Series Task*.

To get the most out of this book, complete each fun series task before going on to the next section. We really mean this. By the time you finish this book and you have completed the fun series tasks, you'll have created the foundation for your series.

After each fun series task, we'll show you how we've updated the Evolution and My Fairy Assassin series vaults, so you can build your series vault along with us.

Where to Next?

We'll take you through each of the artistic decisions, and you'll work on your series as we do this. When you've finished reading this book, you'll have created the foundation for a commercially successful series. You'll also have started writing that series. Doesn't that sound exciting?

Let's take a deeper look at series types.

Chapter Three: Types of Series

In fiction, a series is a group of novels connected by common characters, plot, or settings.

Each novel in a series uses plot, characters, or settings to tie the novels together.

Types of Novels

Before we get into the details of how to create a strong foundation for your series, let's define the types of novels. The novel types need to be categorized; otherwise, it will be difficult to move forward and write a series. Here's how we look at novels.

Stand-Alone Novel: an individual novel that is not part of a series.

Closed Series Single Novel: an individual novel that belongs to a closed series.

Open Series Single Novel: an individual novel that belongs to an open series.

You'll notice that in the definitions we used the word *novel* and not *story*. A novel is book-length narrative prose that represents a fictitious story.

Two Types of Series: Closed and Open

We're at the **first series-level decision**. Are you going to write a closed or open series? We recommend you don't move on to the next chapter until you make this decision. This one decision will influence every decision you make from here forward.

Our goal is to take the complicated art of storytelling and make it clear. Writing a series needs clarity, a process, and a goal, and that is what we'll do together. To know which decision is right for you, we'll share a detailed definition of a closed and open series.

A closed series is one story told over multiple novels.

An open series has one story told per novel in the series.

You, the artist, get to decide what you're writing, and once you do that, it's time to follow through. Many other decisions can be changed as you write your series, and we'll show you which ones.

Closed Series versus Open Series

SECRETS TO WRITING A SERIES

There are six major differences between a closed series and an open series.

The following table will help you decide whether you want to write a closed or open series. The uniting factor might be a new concept for you, and we'll cover it in "Chapter Four: Series Unity."

	Closed	Open
# of Novels	Contains a fixed number of novels.	Contains an unlimited number of novels.
Story	Is one continuous story over multiple novels.	Has multiple single stories with a uniting factor.
Story Arc	Has a distinct story arc that spans the series.	Addresses the story goal by the end of that novel.
Series Goal	Addresses the series goal in the final novel.	Addresses the story goal by the end of that novel.
Uniting Factor	Unites each novel by a plot that continues through the series.	Unites each novel to the others by characters or settings.
Reading Order	Should be read in order.	Can be read in any order.

Genre does not define whether a series is open or closed.

Closed Series: Definition & Examples

A closed series contains a fixed number of novels with a continuous plot that spans all the novels in the series. This means a single story arc represents the entire series, and a closed series entails a series story goal and series story stakes.

In a closed series, the series story goal must be addressed by the end of the series and cannot be addressed before the final novel.

Each novel in a closed series contains a complete story. This means each novel has its own story arc, story goal, and story stakes.

In a closed series, each novel's story goal must be addressed by the end of the novel.

A popular type of closed series is a trilogy. A trilogy is a series that contains three novels and tells a full story over the course of the novels. Once the decision is made to write a closed series, it's hard to change to an open series without rewriting the early novels in the series.

In this book we'll outline and start writing the Evolution series, a closed series in the murder mystery genre with a subgenre of paranormal. We'll take you through our journey of outlining this series and even share a scene with you.

We first outlined the Evolution series as a stand-alone novel. We're now taking this novel and turning it into a series. This process changed the story in many ways, and it was a surprise and delight to see how outlining a series brought us to a new story.

Examples always help clarify an idea, so here are some of our favorites.

Closed Series:

Young Adult Dystopian: Divergent (three books) by Veronica Roth

Young Adult Dystopian: Hunger Games (three books) by Suzanne Collins

Adult Fantasy: Broken Earth (three books) by N. K. Jemisin

Adult Fantasy: Game of Thrones (five books) by George R. R. Martin

Adult Political Thriller: Jason Bourne (three books) by Robert Ludlum

Adult Horror: The Realm (three books) by L. Marie Wood

Open Series:

Adult Historical Regency Romance: Bridgerton by Julia Quinn

Adult Amateur Sleuth: Stephanie Plum by Janet Evanovich

Adult Cozy Mystery: Agatha Raisin by M. C. Beaton

Adult Romance: The Wedding Date by Jasmine Guillory

Adult Romance: Cottonwood Cove by Laura Pavlov

Adult Thriller: Jack Reacher by Lee Child

Open Series: Definition & Examples

An open series consists of an unlimited number of single novels. Often an author doesn't know how many novels will be in the series when they start writing it.

An open series can be read in any order. A reader can pick up any novel in the series, read only that novel, and understand the story fully.

Each novel contains a complete story. There is a story arc for each novel in the series with a story goal and story stakes. Each story goal must be addressed at the end of each novel. The protagonist may be the same in each novel but doesn't have to be. Likewise, the setting may be the same in each novel but doesn't have to be.

The novels in an open series constitute a series because they are connected by common elements. Usually this means they follow the same character or take place in the same setting.

In an open series, there is no series story arc, series goal, or series stakes, although these can follow a pattern throughout the series called the generic series story arc.

Once you start writing an open series, it will be difficult to change it to a closed series, because you have not set up a series story arc like you would for a closed series.

The list of open series below shows the number of novels in each series (as of the writing of this book). Later we'll show you the uniting factor for some of these series and why the group of novels is considered a series.

The Bridgerton series by Julia Quinn is an example of a romance genre open series with eight novels.

The Stephanie Plum series by Janet Evanovich is an example of a mystery genre open series with thirty novels.

The Agatha Raisin series by M. C. Beaton is an example of a cozy mystery genre open series with thirty-five novels.

The Chestnut Springs series by Elsie Silver is an example of a romance genre open series with five novels.

The Jack Reacher series by Lee Child is an example of a thriller genre open series with twenty-nine novels.

The Roy Grace series by Peter James is an example of a detective genre open series with nineteen novels.

In this book, we'll outline and start writing the My Fairy Assassin series by L. Cooke. It is an open series in the young adult fantasy genre.

Your Fun Series Task

You have enough information to decide whether you're writing a closed or an open series. We recommend you decide this before moving forward. Over to you...

1. Decide if your series is open or closed.
2. Add that decision to your series vault.

This task may seem small, but it's important, because you're going to build your series vault as you read this book, and each task will bring you one step closer to writing a commercially successful series.

Evolution & My Fairy Assassin Series Vaults

Here's the start of the series vault. You're going to love how much this helps you write your series. As we progress, we'll keep each of our series vaults updated.

We've decided that Evolution is a closed series, and My Fairy Assassin is an open series. Below you see the vault heading along with what we decided for Evolution and My Fairy Assassin.

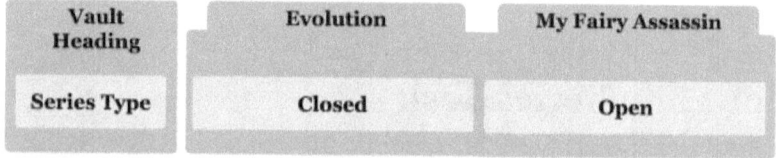

Where to Next?

You've decided whether the series you're writing is a closed or open series. Next you'll learn what factor unites your series.

Chapter Four: Series Unity

What Is Series Unity?

A series is a group of novels that are connected in some way. Series unity comes from the elements of story that make a group of novels a series.

For a closed series, the plot is the uniting factor.

For an open series, the characters or settings are the uniting factors.

Subplots can strengthen series unity for both closed and open series.

The unity in the Hunger Games closed series comes from the main plot. The series unity is strengthened by a subplot. One subplot in the Hunger Games series is the romance between Katniss and Peeta.

The unity in the Stephanie Plum open series comes from the character. Stephanie Plum, a bounty hunter, is the protagonist in every novel in the series. The series unity is strengthened by the subplot, which is the love triangle between Stephanie, Joe, and Ranger. At the time of writing, this subplot has engaged readers for thirty novels. That's quite an accomplishment for a subplot.

The unity in the Bridgerton open series comes from the setting. The societal constraints mean that in every story the reader comes back to find out how each character navigates the societal constraints. Another part of the series unity occurs because each member of the Bridgerton family is the protagonist for a single novel, and the main plot is a romance. The reader comes back to the series to see whether each protagonist will find their one true love when society is set up to make them fail.

When we—as readers—read a series, we don't think about series unity, as we trust the writer. When we—as writers—write a series, series unity should be at the forefront of our minds.

A series with structural unity built in from the start exudes confidence. A reader trusts a story because the author has demonstrated control over the series.

A series, whether it is closed or open, must have unity or it is not a series.

Closed Series Unity: Plot

In a closed series, the plot is the obvious uniting factor. There will be a plot that starts at the beginning of book one and ends at the end of the final book in the series. The plot is the series protagonist trying to achieve the series story goal.

At the end of each novel in a closed series, the reader should be left wondering whether the protagonist will achieve their overall series goal. In each novel, the climax scene must show the reader whether the protagonist achieved the story goal for that novel, but not the series story goal.

Because we know what the end of each novel must do, we need to decide how many novels we will have in our closed series.

There are two ways to make this choice.

The first is to research genre expectations. Are trilogies what readers prefer in your genre? That is great. Then meet your readers' expectations with a series that fits their desires.

The second is to write the number of novels that your story demands. Go with what resonates with you as a writer.

Open Series: Character-Based Unity

An open series based on character unity is a series where each novel is connected by a character or characters.

The Stephanie Plum series written by Janet Evanovich is an open character series. The protagonist is Stephanie Plum, a bounty hunter who solves a crime in each novel.

Because this is such a tight series, we can create a generic series skeleton blurb that works for each novel.

A series skeleton blurb looks like this:

> [A protagonist] must [do something]; otherwise, [something bad will happen].

The following skeleton blurb can be applied to every novel in the Stephanie Plum series:

> Stephanie must catch a crook on the run; otherwise, she won't make money as a bounty hunter.

In an open series, the protagonist may or may not change much by the end of the series. Stephanie Plum doesn't change much from novel to novel. In fact, many readers follow the series because she is humorous and always gets into trouble. This keeps the reader engaged with the character.

The Roy Grace series by Peter James is an open character detective series.

The Jack Reacher series by Lee Child is an open character thriller series.

In the Stephanie Plum and the Roy Grace series, the secondary series unity is based on setting. In the Stephanie Plum series, the setting is her hometown. The hometown could be changed and the series would still be about Stephanie Plum. In the Roy Grace series, the setting is in Brighton. Any other city in England would do for the series to work. Because the setting can be changed, setting is not the primary uniting factor.

In the Jack Reacher series, setting is not a secondary series uniting factor, because Jack Reacher, being a drifter, ends up in a new location in every novel in the series.

Open Series: Setting-Based Unity

A setting series is a group of novels set in the same location.

The Bridgerton series by Julia Quinn is an open series historical romance connected by setting. The Regency society that the Bridgerton family lives in unites the stories in the series.

Our analysis of the Bridgerton series is based on the original published version. The original novels all include one prologue and one epilogue. Julia Quinn later updated the novels to include a second epilogue because her fans wanted to know more about the characters. We chose to analyze the original version because that version made the series commercially successful.

We also wrote a generic series skeleton blurb for the Bridgerton series.

> *A Bridgerton family member must overcome societal obstacles; otherwise, they won't find true love.*

The secondary series unity for the Bridgerton series is character unity. Each novel revolves around one of the Bridgertons. This is secondary because, without the Regency society, the series doesn't work.

The Dublin Murder Squad series by Tana French is a setting-based series in the psychological mystery genre. The mysteries all take place in Dublin. This series does not have a secondary series unity. The protagonists are different members of the Dublin Murder Squad.

In a setting-based series, readers love to come back to a series for the emotional impact of the locations. They come back because the writer made the fictional world real.

Your Fun Series Task

You've already decided whether you're writing an open or closed series. Now we're going to add to that.

Remember: The **second decision** depends on whether you're writing a closed or an open series.

For a closed series, this is the moment to decide on the number of novels you want to write. If you don't know the number, choosing to write a trilogy is a good place to begin.

For an open series, this is the moment to decide on the series uniting factor. To find the uniting factor, we're going to work on the first three novels in the series. For both a character-based and a setting-based series, the first three novels in the series are enough to show how to create the uniting factor for a longer series.

The **second decision** for a closed series:

- Decide on the number of novels in your series.
- Add that number to your series vault.
- Set the uniting factor to plot in your series vault.

The **second decision** for an open series:

- Decide whether the series' uniting factor will be character or setting.
- Add that decision to your series vault.

Evolution and My Fairy Assassin Series Vaults

Deciding that Evolution is a closed series means the uniting factor is the plot. There will be one story that starts at the opening image of book one and ends at the closing image of the final book in the series. We've also decided the Evolution series will be a trilogy.

We decided My Fairy Assassin is an open series, and the uniting factor will be character. We don't know how many novels will be in the series.

Vault Heading	Evolution	My Fairy Assassin
Series Type	Closed	Open
Number of Novels	3	Unlimited
Uniting Factor	Plot	Character

Where to Next?

Now you know the basic foundation for your series. The next chapter shows how to create skeleton blurbs for the novels in the series and for the series as a whole. It will be difficult to do that without knowing whether your series is closed or open and what the series' uniting factor is, so it's critical to complete your fun series task for this section.

Chapter Five: Meet Your Skeleton Blurbs

Are you still deciding whether you're writing a closed or open series? As they say, "Stop the presses!" We really, really, really recommend that you make that decision before moving forward. Without that decision, you won't know what skeleton blurbs to write.

What Is a Skeleton Blurb?

A skeleton blurb is one sentence that reminds you who the protagonist is, what their goal is, and what's at stake if they don't achieve the goal.

It looks like this:

> *[The protagonist] must [strive for a goal]; otherwise, [something bad will happen].*

A closed series needs a series-level skeleton blurb; plus each novel needs its own skeleton blurb.

An open series can have a generic series skeleton blurb, and each novel needs its own skeleton blurb.

Why You Need Skeleton Blurbs

The skeleton blurb is your first creative expression, a promise to yourself that your story has potential, and it kicks off outlining and writing each novel in your series.

If you're a discovery writer, the skeleton blurb will give you the tool to determine whether each scene you write is related to the story you want to tell. Without a skeleton blurb, it's hard to know what the story is, and you may end up writing scenes that don't belong in the story.

For writers who love to outline, the skeleton blurb lets you evaluate whether every scene belongs in the story before you even write it. Without a skeleton blurb, you might find it hard to outline quickly.

After you've written your novels, you can use the skeleton blurb to write the story blurb that goes on the back cover of your novel. Skeleton blurbs are your friends. They are a tool for you to use until you submit your novel for publication.

If you're writing a closed series, it will be a tremendous help if you create a skeleton blurb for each novel and for the series itself. The number of novels will determine how you're going to structure the series story arc and determine how many skeleton blurbs you need to write.

If you're writing an open series, you don't need to create a skeleton blurb yet for every novel in your series, But we recommend you create the skeleton blurb for at least the first three novels. We're going to challenge you with writing a generic series skeleton blurb that could be applied to each novel.

We recommend using an external story goal, as this creates action. For readers to connect with the protagonist, the protagonist must do something; otherwise, they're boring. The protagonist cannot just be doing anything. They must do something because of something they want to achieve. That's the story goal. And there must be consequences if the protagonist doesn't achieve the story goal; otherwise, there will be no tension in the story.

The further you get into outlining or writing the series, the harder it becomes to change the story. It's easier to experiment with new ideas earlier in the process.

This is more important for a series than a stand-alone novel, because if you write book one in a series without knowing where you want the series to go, it's going to be hard to change book one, especially if you've published it. By the time you get to book three, you'll have new ideas you want to include, but unless you thought of it ahead of time, book one won't have set up the world or story to support the new ideas.

A closed series is the most inflexible, so having the whole story promise for each novel outlined beforehand will stop the series-writing process from becoming an unmanageable undertaking.

A setting-based open series has more flexibility. That being said, by creating a series-level skeleton blurb and skeleton blurbs for the first three novels, you can create a series unity that shows the reader you're a great storyteller.

Difference between a Series and a Single Novel Skeleton Blurb

The main difference between a series skeleton blurb and a single novel skeleton blurb is that you have more choices to make. You're an artist, and these choices are fun. Bring it on!

The Protagonist

Let's start with the protagonist. You must know who the protagonist is; otherwise, you can't know who the story is about. If you don't know who the story is about, it will be hard to write that story. When you come to writing your series, we recommend the five story arc scenes be written from the protagonist's POV. This means it's important to know who the protagonist is before you start writing.

The first choice depends on your protagonist strategy. Will you have

- the same protagonist for each novel in the series?
- different protagonists for each novel in the series?

You may not be sure yet, so don't get stuck here. Refer to the character using the word *Protagonist* until you have a strategy.

There is more information about the protagonists in chapter six.

The Series Goal

In a closed series, the protagonist will have an external goal for the series and a different external goal for each novel. The external goal for the final novel may be the same as the goal for the series. You'll find that out later. The external goal for each novel must drive the external goal for the series.

For a closed series skeleton blurb story goal, you'll know it's strong when that goal is addressed in the climax scene of the final novel in the series. Either the protagonist achieves the series goal or not. This just showed what the main event in the climax scene of the final novel must do. Without a series skeleton blurb, it's hard to know what the main event in the climax scenes should be.

The series' skeleton blurb story goal also provides the conflict for the series—and not just any conflict, but conflict that will make it hard for your protagonist to reach their story goal. Without a series skeleton blurb, it's hard to see whether the conflict is related to your story.

For an open series, you'll have a skeleton blurb goal for each novel in the series. You might even have a generic skeleton blurb goal that fits every novel in the series. The Stephanie Plum series has this.

The Series Stakes

The series stakes show what happens if the protagonist doesn't achieve the series goal. This creates tension in your story. And just like the conflict, this is not just any old tension. Its tension is related to the protagonist and what they are trying to achieve. This type of tension keeps the reader engaged.

For a closed series, the stakes for each novel must be stronger than those for the previous novel. You've probably just guessed that this is going to help us with a series story arc. You'll also have stakes for the series and stakes for each novel.

For an open series, each novel will have stakes if the goal is not achieved.

Put It All Together

Without a series skeleton blurb, it's hard to evaluate whether the tension will keep the reader engaged.

In a closed series, you can use this to check that the stakes increase with each novel in the series. Try to write your series skeleton blurb first. Then write each of the single novel skeleton blurbs.

In an open series, the stakes are part of the uniting factor, and the generic series skeleton blurb is a fabulous place to check to see whether this is working for the series. It will be easier if you write the skeleton blurbs for the first three novels. After that, if you can find the uniting factor in the blurbs, write your generic series skeleton blurb.

Your Fun Series Task

For both an open and a closed series, you'll eventually create a skeleton blurb for each novel in the series. You may not know what to write in a skeleton blurb yet. We're looking for placeholders, so as you write your series, you'll always have these to refer to until the series is written.

For a Closed Series:

By the end of the next chapter, you'll have created a skeleton blurb for the series and for each novel.

Add the following placeholders to your series vault:

1. A heading for the series skeleton blurb
2. A heading for a skeleton blurb for each novel in the series, whether it's three novels or twelve

For an Open Series:

We recommend you create a skeleton blurb for at least the first three novels you want to write. This way you can see what connects the novels in your series. You may even find that you can write the same skeleton blurb for each novel.

Add the following placeholders to your series vault:

1. Book one skeleton blurb
2. Book two skeleton blurb
3. Book three skeleton blurb
4. Generic series skeleton blurb

Where to Next?

We're going to build the series and single novel skeleton blurbs together. We'll use the Hunger Games trilogy by Suzanne Collins and the first three novels in the Stephanie Plum series by Janet Evanovich to show examples of commercially successful novels.

We'll continue to use Evolution and My Fairy Assassin to show how to create a foundation for a series that hasn't been written yet.

Chapter Six: Write Your Skeleton Blurbs

To create skeleton blurbs, we'll start by choosing a protagonist, then set the series goal, and finally create the series stakes. You can do this for both a closed and an open series.

A skeleton blurb contains the protagonist, the external story goal, and the story stakes. The blurb must answer three questions:

1. Who is the protagonist?
2. What is the external story goal?
3. What is at stake?

In a full sentence, it looks like this:

> [The protagonist] must [strive for a goal]; otherwise, [something bad will happen].

Series Skeleton Blurbs: The Series Protagonist

From the many writers we've taught how to write a series, we learned that writers often don't have a series protagonist in mind. This is the start of the blurb process. Later on, when you know more about your series, you'll create a protagonist strategy. But first you need to understand the series protagonist and how that will influence your series.

A series protagonist?

Yes, we say in unison. Your series is going to need a protagonist. We'll show you options, so when you come to that part of the process, you'll create a strategy.

We love to think of a protagonist as an entity. There are three types of protagonist entities:

1. A single protagonist: **one** main character on **one** adventure.
2. A combined protagonist: **two** main characters on the **same** adventure striving for the **same** story goal.
3. A group protagonist: **three or more** characters on **different** adventures striving for the **same** story goal.

If you want to show one character's struggles with the story goal, a single protagonist is a strong choice. If you want to show the duality of characters striving for the same story goal, a combined protagonist might be best. If you want to show how a community must come together to achieve their story goal, then a group protagonist might be for you.

For now imagine the combined or group protagonist as a single protagonist entity with a single goal. This will help you create a structurally sound skeleton blurb. It will also help you decide what your protagonist strategy is after you've created your skeleton blurbs.

Here are the options for a series protagonist:

- A single protagonist
- A combined protagonist
- A group protagonist
- A combination of the above

For each novel in the series, you can have the following:

- The same protagonist: This can be a single protagonist, a combined protagonist, or a group protagonist. The Hunger Games series uses a single protagonist (Katniss), and the Game of Thrones series uses a group protagonist (the humans).
- A different protagonist: The Bridgerton series follows this strategy. Each novel is written with a different family member as the protagonist.
- Different protagonist entity types: For example, one novel in the series could have a single protagonist, and the next novel a combined protagonist. The Divergent series follows this strategy. Tris is a single protagonist in *Divergent* (book one) and *Insurgent* (book two). Tris and Tobias are a combined protagonist in *Allegiant* (book three).

All three options are good. It's an artistic choice you get to make.

You'll use the series protagonist strategy to determine your POV strategy. You may not be ready for this yet. If not, for now use the words *Series Protagonist* in all your skeleton blurbs.

You can always change your protagonist strategy later, even after you've published one or two novels in a series. If you've published book one and two and there is the same single protagonist for both books, you may decide that book three needs a combined protagonist. You might do this if in the first two books there is a strong secondary character begging to be given a larger role in the third book.

Let's go one step deeper and look at the POV characters.

Point-of-View Characters

We won't decide on the POV characters or a POV strategy yet. We want you to know what's coming in case you already know this and want to include the information in your series vault now.

The POV character is the character that the reader will experience the scene through.

In stories with multiple POV characters, the POV character does not have to be the protagonist in every scene.

If you choose a single POV for the entire novel, you're deciding the reader will know only what that character knows.

If you choose to write your story from multiple POVs, you're deciding the reader will know more than the protagonist knows. This creates knowledge gaps, which in turn can create tension.

This is a larger decision when you're working on a series. You have to ask yourself whether you have a large enough story to keep the reader engaged from one character's POV, or whether you need multiple POVs.

The Hunger Games trilogy by Suzanne Collins uses a single POV character for all three novels. Katniss Everdeen carries the story.

The Game of Thrones series by George R. R. Martin has multiple POV characters in each novel. The group protagonist is the humans who are fighting the White Walkers (a group antagonist).

The Hunger Games trilogy and Game of Thrones series are at extreme ends of the POV spectrum. What they have in common is the author chose a style and stuck to it.

In general, people don't like change. Writing one novel from a single POV in a series and then writing the next one from multiple POVs may alienate readers. They loved your first novel enough to buy the second, and they will be expecting that same tone, style, and structure. If you choose to change the POV strategy, make sure you understand why.

Choosing a Series Protagonist Type

Knowing the protagonist entity for your series will make it easier to write the series.

A series can use more than one type of protagonist entity. The following examples of commercially successful series all use protagonist entity types differently:

- Divergent by Veronica Roth: single, single, combined
- The Dark Tower by Stephen King: single, group, group...
- Game of Thrones by George R. R. Martin: group, group, group...

Evolution and My Fairy Assassin

For the Evolution series we've decided Jaz Cooper will be the single protagonist for the three-book closed series.

We've added "Protagonist Type: Single" to Evolution's series vault.

We've also decided Liv Wright is the single protagonist for the My Fairy Assassin open series with an undetermined number of novels.

We've added "Protagonist Type: Single" to My Fairy Assassin's series vault.

Keep in mind that as we outline the novels in both a closed and an open series, we may find that a different protagonist strategy works better. Either way, by the time we start writing, we'll know what type of protagonist we're going to use.

At this point you have either decided on a protagonist strategy or you haven't. Either way, we recommend you move to the next step. Sometimes it's easier to determine who the protagonist is after you create the story goal and the story stakes.

The next step is to create the goals and stakes for the series and for the novels. We'll show you how this works for the Hunger Games and the Stephanie Plum series. Then we'll show you how we built this for Evolution and My Fairy Assassin series.

Series Skeleton Blurbs: Goals

Let's get to work on the second part of the series skeleton blurb: the goal.

The Hunger Games Trilogy by Suzanne Collins

Our favorite example of a **closed** series is the Hunger Games trilogy. We wrote the following series skeleton blurb for the trilogy:

Katniss Everdeen must become the leader of the rebellion and overturn the Capitol; otherwise, everyone outside of the Capitol dies or is doomed to a life of misery.

Now that we have the series skeleton blurb, let's look at the single novel skeleton blurbs. This is what we wrote for each novel in the Hunger Games series.

The Hunger Games (book one): Skeleton Blurb

SECRETS TO WRITING A SERIES

Katniss Everdeen must win the Hunger Games; otherwise, she dies.

Catching Fire **(book two): Skeleton Blurb**

Katniss Everdeen must find a way to keep Peeta alive; otherwise, Peeta dies and can't protect her family.

Mockingjay **(book three): Skeleton Blurb**

Katniss Everdeen must become the leader of the rebellion and overturn the Capitol; otherwise, everyone outside of the Capitol dies or is doomed to a life of misery.

Stephanie Plum series by Janet Evanovich

We wrote skeleton blurbs for the first three novels in the Stephanie Plum open series.

One for the Money **(book one): Skeleton Blurb**

Stephanie Plum must catch Joe Morelli, who is wanted for murder; otherwise, she will lose her job as a bounty hunter.

Two for the Dough **(book two): Skeleton Blurb**

Stephanie Plum must catch Kenny Mancuso, who shot his best friend; otherwise, she will lose her job as a bounty hunter.

Three to Get Deadly **(book three): Skeleton Blurb**

Stephanie Plum must catch Mo Bedemier, Trenton's most beloved citizen, who was charged with carrying a concealed weapon and skipped bail; otherwise, she will lose her job as a bounty hunter.

The stakes for each novel remain the same. If Stephanie doesn't catch the accused person, she will lose her job.

The goal for each novel in the series is to catch a runaway criminal. This gives each novel a goal that links the novels. This series has both character and setting unity. The character unity is having Stephanie Plum be the protagonist for every novel. The setting unity is having Stephanie Plum perform the same job in the same city for the same company for every novel.

By writing the skeleton blurbs for three novels, we can see the series unity clearly, and from that, we can write a generic series blurb.

> *Stephanie Plum must catch a runaway criminal; otherwise, she will lose her job as a bounty hunter.*

Evolution and My Fairy Assassin

We'll show you later in this chapter how we built the skeleton blurbs in full for Evolution and My Fairy Assassin. You may want to read this entire chapter before you attempt to build your skeleton blurbs, or you may want to start now.

Series Skeleton Blurb: Stakes

You already know the protagonist and what their goal is. That's two-thirds of the series skeleton blurb written. Let's look at the stakes and see what they can do for you. Stakes do the following:

- Give the character the motivation to achieve the story goal.
- Create reader empathy for the protagonist.
- Help you keep every scene focused on conflict and tension.

Stakes for a Closed Series

We've taught many writers how to write a series, and we learned as instructors that it's hard to create story stakes where the stakes increase with each novel. We're going to help you deal with that problem.

Once a reader has read the climax scene in book one, they are acclimatized to that level of drama. This means that to keep them engaged, the stakes must be higher for the next book in the series; otherwise, readers won't feel the tension.

The tension rises in a single novel from the opening image to the climax scene. The tension must rise in a series for each novel too. This can't happen if the stakes don't increase for each novel.

For a closed series, the highest stakes are in the series skeleton blurb and, usually, in the skeleton blurb for the final novel. The stakes for the series and the final novel can be the same.

If you know your series skeleton blurb, then you know that the main event in the climax of the final novel must show the protagonist addressing the series goal. No matter how many novels you write, the final novel shows the reader whether the protagonist achieved or didn't achieve the story goal set out in the series skeleton blurb.

The stakes in the skeleton blurbs also show you whether each climax scene can be written so that they are each unique. Ask yourself, Does each novel have a different climax scene? They must. It's easy to fall into a pattern of writing climax scenes that seem different but are really too similar to be interesting to the reader.

The Stakes for the Hunger Games Series

The series goal for the Hunger Games trilogy is that Katniss Everdeen must become the leader of the rebellion and overturn the Capitol.

If that's all you knew, you would ask yourself what would happen if Katniss didn't achieve the story goal. The answer is that everyone outside of the Capitol dies or is doomed to a life of misery.

To determine the stakes in your series skeleton blurb, look at your series goal. What bad things will happen if the protagonist doesn't achieve the goal?

In *The Hunger Games* (book one), the stakes are Katniss's life.

In *Catching Fire* (book two), the stakes are Katniss's and Peeta's lives.

In *Mockingjay* (book three), the stakes are the lives of everyone Katniss loves.

It's important to note the stakes are higher in each novel, and the stakes of book three are also the stakes of the series.

This makes the structure strong, because the climax scene for the series can be the same as the climax scene for *Mockingjay* (book three). And this means it has double the power.

Stakes for an Open Series

For an open series, the stakes are in the series' skeleton blurb and can relate to the novel's genre.

For example:

The stakes in a romance novel can be related to finding true love.

In a mystery, the stakes can be related to the murderer killing the protagonist.

In a thriller, the stakes can be related to the protagonist's life being at risk.

In a fantasy, the stakes can be related to the magical world's existence.

In a dystopian novel, the stakes can be related to the evil society winning.

In a horror novel, the stakes are about death.

In an open series, the reader is looking for more of the same but different. And the stakes should be of equal weight in each novel.

No matter how many novels are in your series, each novel must show whether the protagonist was successful at achieving that novel's story goal. The generic series skeleton blurb is a framework to ensure the readers' expectations are met in every novel.

The reader comes back to a series because they know what they are getting in the next novel. By looking at the stakes in each novel as you write them and keeping an eye on the generic series skeleton blurb, you ensure the reader will remain loyal.

In an open series, because the story goal is new in each book, the increase in tension created by higher stakes is not needed, as it is in a closed series.

Let's look at a romance series that doesn't have unity in the series stakes.

Book One: If couple A doesn't get together, they will never find true love.

Book Two: If couple B doesn't get together, they will never find true love.

Book Three: If couple C doesn't get together, they will die because the fairies will be annoyed at not getting an invitation to the wedding.

Book Four: If couple D doesn't get together, they will not find their true love.

Book Five: If couple E doesn't get together, they will not find their true love.

As you can see, book three's stakes are larger than those of the other books and stick out like a sore thumb. Most likely the reader won't come back to book four and five, as they had fallen in love with the structural pattern in books one and two. Book three does not address the same stakes. Death by fairies is not the stakes they were expecting from the series, and that might cause them to not buy the next book.

The Stakes for the First Three Books in the Agatha Raisin Series

Catching the murderer is a genre expectation in a cozy mystery. The protagonist will do so in the climax scene, akin to the happy-ever-after moment in a romance novel.

We can determine the stakes from the series goal. What is the problem that occurs when a murder is not solved? The murderer could kill again, especially someone who is close to solving the mystery. This brings us to the stakes for the first three novels in the Agatha Raisin series.

In *Agatha Raisin and the Quiche of Death* (book one), the stakes are Agatha's life.

In *Agatha Raisin and the Vicious Vet* (book two), the stakes are Agatha's life.

In *Agatha Raisin and the Potted Gardener* (book three), the stakes are Agatha's life.

It's important to note the stakes are the same in each novel. This is a possible pattern for an open series. Each novel's stakes can be the same. When the stakes are the same, this increases the series' unity.

The generic series goal for each novel in the Agatha Raisin series is that Agatha Raisin must solve the murder.

Now we come to what happens if Agatha Raisin does not solve the murder. Does a murderer get away with the crime? Yes! The reader does not want a murderer to be at large and have gotten away with killing someone. The reader wants the murderer to be held accountable.

We wrote the generic series skeleton blurb to be the following:

> *Agatha Raisin must solve the murder that happened in her Cotswold village; otherwise, she might be killed.*

Skeleton Blurbs for Commercially Successful Closed Series

The Hunger Games

We'll start with the series and novel blurbs. We wrote these, and Suzanne Collins may have written something completely different.

The Hunger Games Series Skeleton Blurb

Katniss Everdeen must become the leader of the rebellion and overturn the Capitol; otherwise, everyone she cares for will die.

The Hunger Games (book one) Skeleton Blurb

Katniss Everdeen must win the Hunger Games; otherwise, she dies.

Catching Fire (book two) Skeleton Blurb

Katniss Everdeen must find a way to keep Peeta alive; otherwise, Peeta dies and he can't protect her family.

Mockingjay (book three) Skeleton Blurb

Katniss Everdeen must become the leader of the rebellion and overturn the Capitol; otherwise, everyone outside of the Capitol dies or is doomed to a life of misery.

The Protagonist

Suzanne Collins chose to write the trilogy with Katniss Everdeen as the protagonist for each novel.

The Story Goals

In *The Hunger Games* (book one), Katniss wants to survive the games. She doesn't know yet that she will be the leader of the revolution.

In *Catching Fire* (book two), Katniss wants to save Peeta's life even if it means she dies. In this book Katniss still doesn't know she'll become the leader of the revolution, but we bet Suzanne Collins knew. Katniss has changed as a character. She is willing to die so Peeta can live.

In *Mockingjay* (book three), Katniss reluctantly accepts the role of the leader of the revolution. She has grown from wanting to save her own life and Prim's, to saving Peeta's, to saving the life of anyone who isn't part of the Capitol.

With her growth in each book, the stakes get higher.

The Stakes

In *The Hunger Games* (book one), the stakes are Katniss's life.

In *Catching Fire* (book two), the stakes are Peeta's life.

In *Mockingjay* (book three), the stakes are the lives of everyone Katniss loves.

The stakes of book three are the same as the stakes of the series.

Here again we see a strong structure, because the climax scene for the series is the same as the climax scene for book three.

The Divergent Trilogy

Divergent by Veronica Roth is also a closed series. Here are the blurbs we wrote.

Divergent Series Skeleton Blurb

Tris must find out what is behind the factions; otherwise, all those she cares about will lose their identity.

Divergent (book one) Skeleton Blurb

Tris must hide that she's a divergent; otherwise, she will be killed.

Insurgent (book two) **Skeleton Blurb**

> Tris must find out what those outside of Chicago intend; otherwise, she won't be able to protect her friends.

Allegiant (book three) **Skeleton Blurb**

> Tris and Tobias must work together to stop the outsiders; otherwise, the population of Chicago will have their memories erased and the city will cease to exist.

Skeleton Blurbs for Commercially Successful Open Series

Here we'll take a look at two series, one where the series is linked by character and one where the series is linked by setting.

The Stephanie Plum Series

We wrote skeleton blurbs for the first three novels in the Stephanie Plum series by Janet Evanovich.

One for the Money (book one) Skeleton Blurb

> Stephanie Plum must catch Joe Morelli, who is wanted for murder; otherwise, she won't make money as a bounty hunter.

Two for the Dough (book two) Skeleton Blurb

Stephanie must catch Kenny Mancuso, who shot his best friend; otherwise, she won't make money as a bounty hunter.

Three to Get Deadly (book three) Skeleton Blurb

Stephanie must catch Mo Bedemier, Trenton's most beloved citizen, who was charged with carrying a concealed weapon and skipped bail; otherwise, she won't make money as a bounty hunter.

For the Stephanie Plum series, it's her job that links the series.

A generic skeleton blurb works to showcase the promise of each novel in the series and how the series links together.

Stephanie Plum Generic Series Skeleton Blurb

Stephanie Plum must catch a runaway criminal; otherwise, she won't make money as a bounty hunter.

To make the novels in the series similar but different, Stephanie must catch a different criminal in a unique way.

The Bridgerton Series

The Bridgerton series comprises Regency-set novels based on the Bridgerton family.

We wrote the skeleton blurbs for the first three novels in the Bridgerton series by Julia Quinn.

The Duke and I (book one) Skeleton Blurb

Daphne must show Simon he's worthy of a full family life; otherwise, she won't find true love with Simon.

The Viscount Who Loved Me (book two) Skeleton Blurb

Anthony must overcome his fear of early death; otherwise, he won't find true love with Kate.

An Offer from a Gentleman (book three) Skeleton Blurb

Benedict must overcome the social judgement due to Sophie's birth; otherwise, he won't find true love with Sophie.

The Bridgerton Series Generic Skeleton Blurb

A Bridgerton family member must overcome obstacles; otherwise, they won't find true love with love their interest.

Each novel has different obstacles that create a different reason why the love interests can't be together in a happily-ever-after way.

The unity for this series is the time period and the family. The family is large enough to create individual love stories around different family members. This is fabulous for romance and historical romance series.

Skeleton Blurbs for Evolution

Let's create the skeleton blurbs for the Evolution series, which started its life as a stand-alone novel. To change it from a stand-alone novel into a series, we need a series skeleton blurb.

Originally, the first book was written in a single POV, first-person narrative. We're not sure whether that will be true for the series. We're going to discover this as we work through our process.

The idea for the series took a bit of brainstorming. How could we extend the stand-alone novel into a concept that would be large enough for a series?

We decided the antagonist should be an organization that's after Jaz's dead husband's research. We also decided that Jaz couldn't be the only person with the ability to see into a dog's mind, so Jaz's daughter is born with the ability. Others close to Jaz will get infected too.

For the series, we know the following:

Protagonist: Jaz Cooper.

The Goal: Keep the ability to see into a dog's mind a secret.

The Stakes: Jaz and those with the ability will be experimented on and possibly die.

The following is our starting point for the series skeleton blurb:

> *Jaz Cooper must keep the ability to see into a dog's mind a secret; otherwise, she and those with the ability will be experimented on and possibly die.*

The high-level plot for each novel is to show the following:

Book One: Jaz discovering her ability to see into a dog's mind and that her daughter inherits the ability.

Book Two: Jaz protecting her daughter because others want access to the ability.

Book Three: Jaz using the ability to bring down the organization bent on destroying those who have the ability.

This gives us enough to create a skeleton blurb for each novel.

Book One: Jaz Cooper must find out who killed her husband, using her ability to see into a dog's mind; otherwise, she might die.

Book Two: Jaz Cooper must find out who is trying to take her daughter, using her ability to see into a dog's mind; otherwise, her daughter will be stolen by the testing organization.

Book Three: Jaz Cooper must discover and eliminate the experimentation center, using her ability to see into a dog's mind; otherwise, she and anyone with the dog-vision ability will be experimented on and possibly die.

When we reviewed the story stakes for the three novels, we realized the stakes for the second book were not as bad as the stakes in the first book. We changed the book two skeleton blurb to be the following:

Book Two: Jaz Cooper must find out who is trying to take her daughter; *otherwise, her daughter will be stolen by the testing organization and possibly killed.*

With the change, the stakes get higher with each book. In book one, only Jaz's life is at stake. In book two, her daughter's life is also at stake, and in book three, anyone who can see into a dog's mind could die.

The stakes grew from Jaz's life to her daughter's life to the lives of multiple people.

After writing the three skeleton blurbs, we think the series skeleton blurb isn't quite right yet. Keeping a secret is too vague and hard to relate to the single novels in the series.

We're going to make the series skeleton blurb the same as the book three skeleton blurb.

Series Skeleton Blurb:

*Jaz Cooper must **discover and eliminate the organization testing the ability on humans**; otherwise, Jaz and all the others who have the ability might be killed.*

Each of the single skeleton blurbs must relate to the series skeleton blurb.

In book one, if Jaz fails to find out who killed her husband, she won't be able to find the organization behind the person who killed her husband. She needs this step to happen in her journey if she's to achieve the series goal.

In book two, if Jaz can't keep her daughter's ability secret, her daughter might be taken from her. This gives her the motivation for book three, where she must destroy the testing organization.

We'll add the skeleton blurbs to the Evolution series vault.

Skeleton Blurbs for My Fairy Assassin

Let's work on My Fairy Assassin.

For an open series, we need a skeleton blurb for the series and for the first three novels in the series. This is a character-based open series.

When the My Fairy Assassin series was a stand-alone novel, it was written from a single-POV, first-person narrative. As with the Evolution series, we're not sure whether that will be true for this open series. Let's find out.

The series theme is about how time travel can change the future.

In the Evolution series, we didn't name a specific antagonist. With the My Fairy Assassin series, we're more opinionated. We decided the antagonist will be Liv's stepfather, who wants to destroy the fairy world and take back what he has lost. We also decided that one of the subplots will be the love affair between Liv and a fairy. There might be scope to look at adding in a love triangle, so another love interest could be introduced.

We are going to write the skeleton blurbs for the first three novels in this series.

The following are the goals for each novel:

Book One: Liv's goal is to save her sister by navigating the fairy world and using the time portal.

Book Two: Liv's goal is to save her mother by navigating the fairy world and using the time portal.

Book Three: Liv's goal is to save her aunt by navigating the fairy world and using the time portal.

Now we'll add the stakes and create the skeleton blurbs.

Book One:

> *Liv Wright must use the fairy time portal to save her fairy assassin sister; otherwise, a scientist will destroy the world.*

Book Two:

> *Liv Wright must use the fairy time portal to save her fairy saboteur mother; otherwise, a druid will destroy the world.*

Book Three:

> *Liv Wright must use the fairy time portal to save her fairy enforcer aunt; otherwise, an alchemist will destroy the world.*

In an open series, the idea is that the reader wants to come back to a world where they have more of the same, but different.

The level of the stakes stays the same because the reader knows that the end of the world is going to happen if Liv does not achieve her story goal.

After writing the three skeleton blurbs, we know the series unity of saving the family members is important to the generic series skeleton blurb. There is a new world in each novel because of the time travel, and this must also be addressed.

For the My Fairy Assassin series, we know the following:

Protagonist: Liv Wright.

The Goal: Use the fairy time portal to save a family member.

The Stakes: This world's worst person will end the world.

In a full sentence, the following is the generic series skeleton blurb:

> *Liv Wright must use the time portal and save a family member; otherwise, this world's worst person will end the world.*

Each single blurb relates to the series skeleton blurb.

In book one, if Liv does not kill the scientist, her sister will die and the world will end. This is the origin story where we find out how Liv knows about the fairy world.

In book two, if Liv does not kill the druid, her mother will die and the world will end. Liv will save the world but not free her mother, creating a bittersweet ending. Her ongoing search for her mother can become a subplot for the series.

In book three, if Liv does not kill the alchemist, her aunt will die and the world will end.

We think we've got enough of a unifying strategy to move forward with My Fairy Assassin. We don't want to get stuck here, and we don't want you to get stuck either. You can come back at any time and rewrite or update the skeleton blurbs based on what you discover as you move forward.

Your Fun Series Task

It's your turn to decide the type of protagonist you want to use for each novel in your series. You're not going to decide on a POV strategy yet. This will come later, when you outline each novel on a per-scene basis.

For a series with the **same protagonist entity type** in all novels in the series, add the following to your series vault:

- Protagonist Type: single/combined/group
- Protagonist Name(s): [If you don't know the name, just use *Protagonist*.]

You can always change this later. The goal now is to move forward. Don't get stuck here if you don't know the answers yet. Placeholders—memos titled "Placeholder" saying the information is not known yet—will remind you to do this when your muse wakes up and provides the information.

For a closed series:

1. Create the overall series skeleton blurb with a goal that will be addressed in the climax scene of the final novel in your series.
2. Create a skeleton blurb for each novel in the series.
3. Add all skeleton blurbs to your series vault.

For an open series:

1. Create the skeleton blurb for the first three novels in your series.
2. Create the generic skeleton blurb.
3. Add the blurbs to your series vault.

You've just created the skeleton blurbs for your series. Well done!

Evolution and My Fairy Assassin Series Vault

Vault Heading	Evolution	My Fairy Assassin
Series Type	Closed	Open
Number of Novels	3	Unlimited
Uniting Factor	Plot	Character
Protagonist Name	Jaz Cooper	Liv Wright

SECRETS TO WRITING A SERIES

Vault Heading	Evolution	My Fairy Assassin
Series/Generic Skeleton Blurb	Jaz Cooper must discover and eliminate the organization testing the ability on humans; otherwise, Jaz and all the others who have the ability might be killed.	Liv Wright must stop the world's worst people by time traveling; otherwise, the world will end.
Book One Skeleton Blurb	Jaz Cooper must find out who killed her husband using her ability to see into a dog's mind; otherwise, she might die.	Liv Wright must use the fairy time portal to save her fairy assassin sister; otherwise, a scientist will destroy the world.
Book Two Skeleton Blurb	Jaz Cooper must keep others from discovering her daughter can see into a dog's mind; otherwise, her daughter might be killed.	Liv Wright must use the fairy time portal to save her fairy saboteur mother; otherwise, a druid will destroy the world.
Book Three Skeleton Blurb	Jaz Cooper must discover and eliminate the organization testing the ability on humans; otherwise, Jaz and all the others who have the ability might be killed.	Liv Wright must use the fairy time portal to save her fairy enforcer aunt; otherwise, an alchemist will destroy the world.

Where to Next?

The story arc is the magic behind a well-told story. Its genius is that it gives you a solid frame for your story but is still flexible. You can have such fun making artistic choices around the story arc. But it gets even better. The story arc for a series is more flexible than for a single novel. Artistic choices abound, and these choices will make your story unique to you.

Chapter Seven: Meet the Story Arc

Let's begin our story arc journey with a little theory. You get a break here, as there is no fun series task again until "Chapter Nine: Outline the Closed Series Story Arc."

Why Believe in the Story Arc?

We studied the story arc for years, looking for a way to express the key scenes of a story in the simplest way possible so writers could use it across all genres to make their story better.

Based on this research, we chose five story arc scenes, not to reduce a story to a mere five scenes but to provide a framework for writers to use while they create their unique stories.

Over time, successful commercial fiction has followed the basic form of the story arc. This form provides the underlying structure for popular stories regardless of the genre. You can build in genre expectations on top of the basic form of a story.

Let's go back in time to Aristotle's *Poetics*. Aristotle's famous observation about stories is that every story has a beginning, a middle, and an end. The beginning is the setup of the story, the middle is the confrontation, and the end is the resolution.

The beginning, middle, and end are not flexible in their placement. The beginning of a story always happens at the beginning, the middle always happens in the middle, and the end always happens at the end. This is how a reader experiences a story. This seems obvious, but it's important in the context of the story arc.

We'll take you through our thought process for using five scenes in the most basic story arc. Pay attention to the bolded items in the lists below, and you'll see each of the story structure theories contains the five story arc scenes.

In our search for simplicity, we wanted to know the minimum number of story arc scenes required to create a structurally sound story.

Joseph Campbell

Joseph Campbell wrote *The Hero with a Thousand Faces* (popularly referred to as *The Hero's Journey*) in 1949. Many great stories have been written that follow this journey. The hero's journey consists of twenty plot points:

1. Departure, Separation
2. World of Common Day
3. **Call to Adventure (the Inciting Incident)**
4. Refusal of the Call
5. Supernatural Aid
6. **Crossing the First Threshold (Plot Point 1)**
7. Belly of the Whale
8. Descent, Initiation, Penetration
9. Road of Trials
10. **Meeting of the Goddess (Middle Plot Point)**
11. Woman as Temptress
12. Atonement with the Father
13. Apotheosis
14. The Ultimate Boon
15. **Refusal of the Return (Plot Point 2)**
16. The Magic Flight
17. Rescue from Without
18. **Crossing the Return Threshold (Climax)**
19. Master of the Two Worlds
20. Freedom to Live

SECRETS TO WRITING A SERIES

Christopher Vogler

In 1998, along came Christopher Vogler with *The Writer's Journey: Mythic Structure for Writers*. This book reduced the complexity of *The Hero with a Thousand Faces* and made it easier to apply the theory to writing a novel.

1. Ordinary World
2. **Call to Adventure (Inciting Incident)**
3. Refusal of the Call
4. Meeting with the Mentor
5. **The Crossing of the First Threshold (Plot Point 1)**
6. Test, Allies, Enemies
7. Approach to the Inmost Cave
8. **Ordeal (Middle Plot Point)**
9. Reward
10. **Return (Plot Point 2)**
11. The Road Back
12. **Resurrection (Climax)**
13. Return with the Elixir

John Yorke

In 2013, John Yorke wrote *Into the Woods: A Five-Act Journey Into Story*.

This story structure includes five acts instead of the standard three. Act 2 starts right after what we call the inciting incident. Act 3 starts right after what we call plot point 1. Act 4 starts right before what we call plot point 2. Act 5 starts at the climax. This also contains the five story arc scenes required to create a structurally sound story.

1. No Knowledge
2. Growing Knowledge

3. **Awakening (Inciting Incident)**
4. Doubt
5. Overcoming Reluctance
6. **Acceptance (Plot Point 1)**
7. Experimenting with Knowledge
8. **Key Knowledge (Middle Plot Point)**
9. Experimenting Post Knowledge
10. **Doubt (Plot Point 2)**
11. Growing Reluctance
12. Regression
13. **Reawakening (Climax)**
14. Acceptance
15. Total Mastery

K. M. Weiland

In 2013, K. M. Weiland published *Structuring Your Novel*. This structure also contains the five story arc scenes we know we need.

1. Hook
2. Setup
3. **Inciting Event (Inciting Incident)**
4. The Build-Up
5. **First Plot Point (Plot Point 1)**
6. First Pinch Point
7. **Midpoint (Middle Plot Point)**
8. Second Pinch Point
9. **Third Act Plot Point (Plot Point 2)**
10. **Climax (Climax)**
11. Resolution

Kristina Stanley

By 2016, we had researched many of the story structures and determined that these five story arc scenes are required to create a structurally sound story.

1. Inciting Incident
2. Plot Point 1
3. Middle Plot Point
4. Plot Point 2
5. Climax

The five story arc scenes—inciting incident, plot point 1, middle plot point, plot point 2, and climax—are the minimum scenes necessary to create a structurally sound story.

Types of Novels

The story arc has different roles for a single novel and for a series. We are going to look at novels in the context of the story arc, a closed series, and an open series.

For a stand-alone novel, a closed series single novel, and an open series single novel, we recommend that the story arc scenes be placed within the ranges listed below.

Inciting incident: before the first 15 percent of the story (this includes inciting incidents that happen before page one).

Plot point 1: between 20 percent and 30 percent of the story.

Middle plot point: between 45 percent and 55 percent of the story.

Plot point 2: between 70 percent and 80 percent of the story.

Climax: between 85 percent and 95 percent of the story.

What Happens If a Story Arc Scene Is Missing?

If even one of the story arc scenes is missing, there is no story. That is so important that we're going to repeat it.

If even one of the story arc scenes is missing, there is no story.

This is an excerpt from *Secrets to Outlining a Novel: The Creative Story Outlining Method.*

The main purpose of the inciting incident is to shake up the protagonist's ordinary life.

If there is no inciting incident, there is no story, because all we're reading about is a protagonist's ordinary life.

The main purpose of plot point 1 is to show the protagonist accepting the story goal.

If there is no plot point 1, meaning the protagonist doesn't accept the story goal, then there is no story, because the protagonist doesn't do anything.

The main purpose of the middle plot point is to show the protagonist changing from reactive to proactive.

If there is no middle plot point, the protagonist doesn't drive the story forward and cause problems, and there is no story.

The main purpose of plot point 2 is the protagonist learns the final piece of information they need to address the story goal. This can be internal or external and will drive them to the climax. This is also where the protagonist is at their lowest point in the story.

Without the new information, the protagonist cannot address the story goal. If they can never address the story goal, the story never ends. There is no story if there is no plot point 2.

The main purpose of the climax scene is to show whether the protagonist achieved the external story goal.

If there is no climax scene where the protagonist achieves the story goal or doesn't, there is no story, because the story isn't over. The story is over when the story goal is addressed by the protagonist.

Where to Next?

The following chapter introduces the story arc in the context of a closed series. After we cover the closed series, we'll move on to the open series.

PART TWO: OUTLINE YOUR CLOSED SERIES

Chapter Eight: Meet the Closed Series Story Arc

A closed series will have a series-level story arc that starts in book one and ends in the final volume.

In an open series, there is no overarching story arc across the series. Part three of this book covers the open series story arc.

The story arc is a flexible tool. We asked a group of story editors to list the five story arc scenes for the first novel in the Hunger Games trilogy. Not all editors chose the same scenes. They were close but different. Each editor brought their own experiences to the task and saw different things in the story. Every reader brings their own experiences too. This shows they will experience your story in their own way.

The story arcs you're working on are for you, the author. They give you the framework for your series. You must know they exist in the right place, performing their duties. The reader doesn't need to know your behind-the-scenes strategy.

For single novels within a series, we know the recommended placement for the five story arc scenes is as follows.

The inciting incident occurs somewhere before the first 15 percent of the story. We say before 15 percent because it can even occur before the start of book one. This happens in the Jason Bourne series. Jason is shot before the story starts. He loses his memory because he was shot, and that is the inciting incident for the series and for book one of the Bourne series.

One could also argue that with free samples on online publishing sites, it's important to place the inciting incident before the end of the free sample. The samples usually end somewhere around 10 percent into a novel. Having the inciting incident in the sample will hook the reader and encourage them to click the buy button. If the inciting incident occurs before the story starts, an option is to place that information in the published story blurb or book description. That way the reader knows about it and is already hooked on the story.

Plot point 1 occurs between 20 percent and 30 percent of the story. If it comes too late, the story will drag. The reader expects the protagonist to accept the story goal. If it comes too early, the story may lack depth, causing the reader to skim.

The middle plot point occurs between 45 percent and 55 percent of the story. It is the middle, after all, and a middle goes in the middle.

Plot point 2 occurs between 70 percent and 80 percent of the story. The placement is for the same reason as plot point 1. Too late and the story drags. Too early and it lacks depth.

The climax occurs between 85 percent and 95 percent of the story. This leaves enough space for the protagonist to get from plot point 2 to the climax at a high pace, and it leaves enough space after the climax for a resolution that will satisfy the reader.

We use percentages above because with e-books there is no way to get a consistent page count. These percentages are guidelines and not strict rules. The story arc is elastic and meant to be played with. We're giving you a starting point. You, as the artist, get to decide whether you want to wander outside the boundaries of novels that traditionally are commercially successful.

Where Are Story Arc Scenes Placed in a Series?

Now that we all know where the story arc scenes are placed in a single novel in a series, we need to know where to place these scenes across a closed series.

A story arc for a closed series starts at the beginning of the first novel and ends at the last page of the final novel.

The percentages of where these scenes are placed are more flexible when you're looking at the story arc for a closed series. This is because the word count is longer, there are multiple story arcs, and there is an overarching story arc.

We're going to work through an example using the Evolution series. The three novels in a trilogy are similar to act 1, act 2, and act 3 in a single novel.

To make it easy to follow, our total word count goal for this three-book series is three hundred thousand words, and we want each novel to be one hundred thousand words. Nobody writes this exact, but again, it simplifies our example.

For a single novel, the following image shows where to place the story arc scenes.

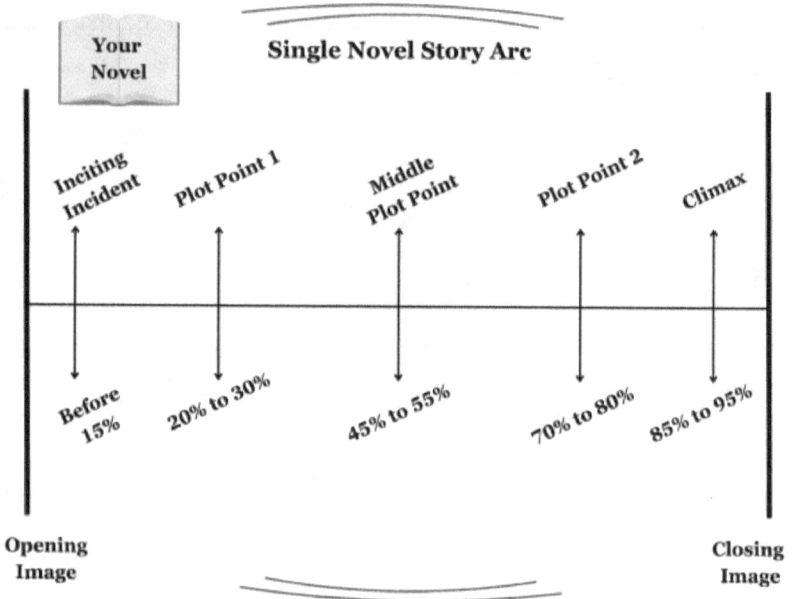

The End Goal

Let's look at the end goal. Here we've taken the story arc for three single novels in a trilogy and placed them in one diagram.

The diagram shows one possibility of how to overlay a series story arc on a trilogy, placing single novel and series story arc events in the same scene.

Not all trilogies follow a series story arc that matches the story arc scenes for the single novels. We're showing you the simplest form in the hopes it gives you ideas for the first outline of each novel in your series.

The diagram shows one way to place the story arc scenes.

- Book one and the series inciting incident
- Book one plot point 2 and series plot point 1

- Book two and series middle plot point
- Book three and series plot point 2
- Book three and series climax

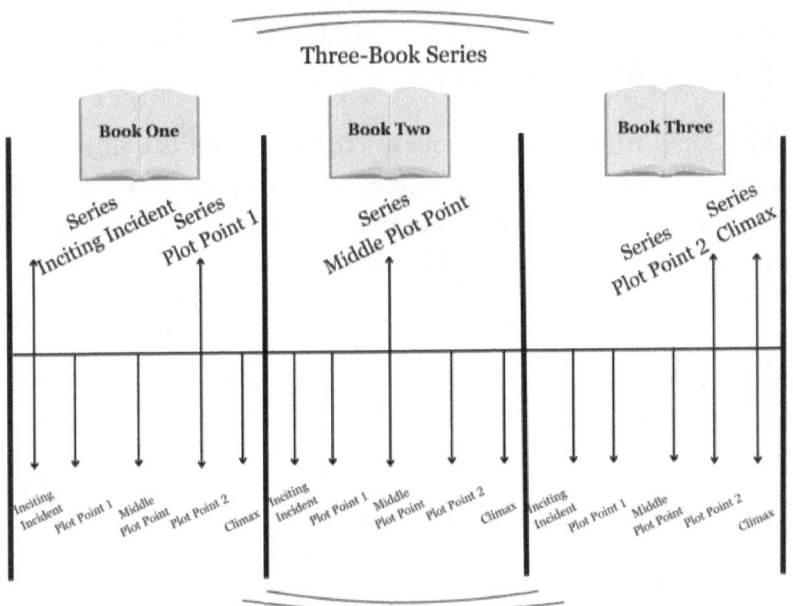

A Scene Main Event

Before we move forward, it's important to recall what a main event in a scene is.

The main event is the action that happens in a scene that is caused by a character (or characters) or causes a character (or characters) to react.

The main event is the "what," not the "how" or the "why" of the event. This concept is going to help us create a structurally sound outline for our series.

For example, the main event for the inciting incident in *The Hunger Games* (book one) and for the series is "Katniss volunteers for the Hunger Games." The main event is simple and clear. When you're creating the main events for each scene in your story, try to write them without the "how" or the "why." You don't need to know yet how or why the character is taking the action.

We're going to use main events to create the foundation for your series. Working with us, you'll create the main events in the story arc scenes first. Then we'll look at the important concept of multiple story arcs. You'll have multiple novels in your series, so you'll need multiple story arcs.

Before moving on, we'll look at the story arc for single novels that are the first novel in a trilogy.

Closed Series Single Novel Story Arc Examples

We have chosen two commercially successful closed series to analyze. These are the Hunger Games trilogy by Suzanne Collins and the Divergent trilogy by Veronica Roth.

The first novel in each of these series demonstrates how flexible the story arc is.

The Hunger Games (book one) Story Arc

The Hunger Games (book one) follows the story arc closely.

SECRETS TO WRITING A SERIES

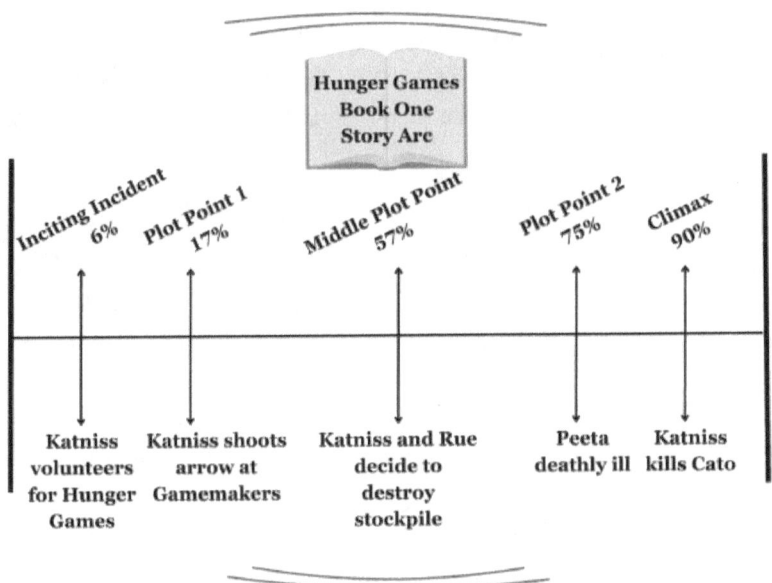

Inciting Incident: Katniss volunteers for the Hunger Games. Her ordinary world has just changed. This same inciting incident disrupts Katniss's ordinary world for both *The Hunger Games* (book one) and the series. The inciting incident is performing two duties.

A protagonist must react to the inciting incident, or the incident isn't strong enough. Katniss must react to volunteering for the Hunger Games. She's just given herself a death sentence. We think that's strong.

Plot Point 1: Katniss shoots an arrow at the Gamemakers. She's just decided she's going to accept the story goal of surviving the Hunger Games.

It's important to note that plot point 1 couldn't have occurred without the inciting incident. This shows us another way the inciting incident is strong. If Katniss hadn't volunteered for the Hunger Games, there would be no story and no story goal to accept.

Middle Plot Point: This is the moment Katniss gets proactive. Together with Rue, she makes a plan to destroy a stockpile of the other competitors' food. She is now proactively trying to win the Hunger Games.

Plot Point 2: Peeta is deathly ill. This is Katniss's lowest point, as she's discovered how strong her feelings for Peeta are, and if she doesn't do something drastic, she'll lose him. Her strong feelings for Peeta are the information she needs to rally herself and survive the Hunger Games.

Climax: Katniss kills the final competitor. The Hunger Games are over because she and Peeta will no longer fight.

Divergent (book one) Story Arc

Divergent (book one) pushes the boundaries for the location of plot point 1, plot point 2, and the climax. Plot point 1 occurs at 10 percent into the story. Plot point 2 occurs at 90 percent of the story. We're showing you this example to illustrate that the story arc is a flexible tool.

SECRETS TO WRITING A SERIES

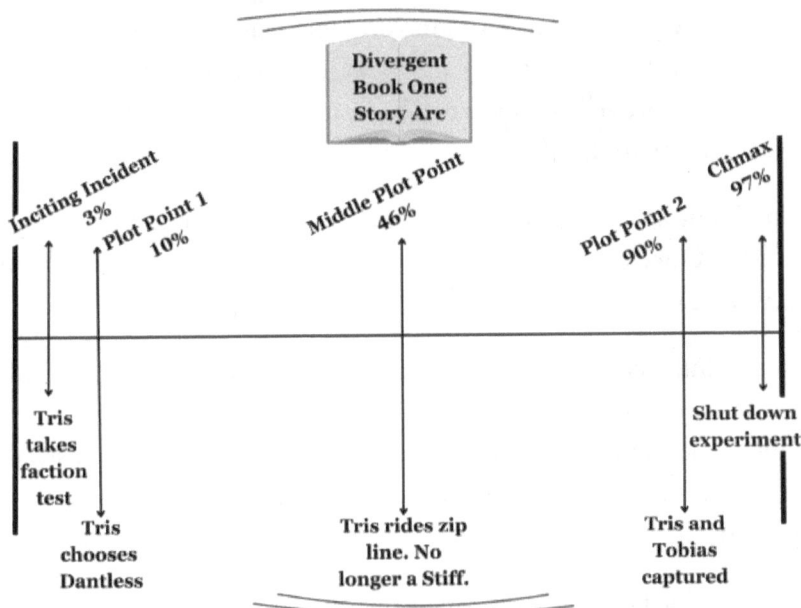

Inciting Incident: This is the first shakeup in Tris's world. She takes a test to find out what faction she belongs to, and the results are inconclusive. She expected a clear result, and now she has to figure out what faction to choose.

Tris is the POV character for each of the story arc scenes. And that means the main event in each scene impacts her specifically. The main event in the inciting incident has not started the story yet. That will happen in plot point 1.

Tris must react to not getting a clear result when she is tested to determine what faction she belongs to. This doesn't mean she's passive. There is a difference between reactive and passive. A passive protagonist is boring.

This same inciting incident disrupts Tris's ordinary world for both *Divergent* (book one) and the series. Again, the inciting incident is performing two duties.

We'll show you later that the inciting incident for *Allegiant* (book three) occurs at the end of *Insurgent* (book two). This means it happens before *Allegiant* starts. The flexibility of the story arc makes it an amazing tool.

Plot Point 1: Tris chooses the Dauntless faction over her family's faction. Once she makes the choice, she can't go back to her own faction or to her family.

Plot point 1 couldn't have occurred without the inciting incident. This means the inciting incident is strong. If Tris's results clearly chose a faction for her, she would have chosen that faction. Instead, her test result was inconclusive, so she could choose the faction she wanted.

Middle Plot Point: This is Tris's false victory. She rides the zip line with the Dauntless initiates and feels the Dauntless faction is where she belongs. She becomes proactive in trying not to get cut from the faction.

Plot Point 2: Tris is about to get executed, and Tobias is injected with a serum that makes him want to kill her. She gets the final piece of information she needs to succeed in the climax scene. She learns that Tobias will confuse enemies and friends. She needs this knowledge to bring him back to her in the climax.

Climax: Tris and Tobias shut down the program controlling the Dauntless, so they stop killing Abnegations. The Dauntless try to kill her and fail.

Both series were commercially successful even though the placement of the story arc scenes for each is quite different.

Multiple Story Arcs for a Series

The story arc gets more interesting in the context of a closed series.

A closed series must have an overarching story arc and a story arc for every novel in the series.

In a trilogy, for all three novels there will be an overarching series story arc told as one story. This means a three-book series needs four story arcs:

1. Series Story Arc
2. Book One Story Arc
3. Book Two Story Arc
4. Book Three Story Arc

Below is one possible structure for a series story arc for a trilogy. Note the series story arc doesn't have to map directly to the single novel story arc scenes.

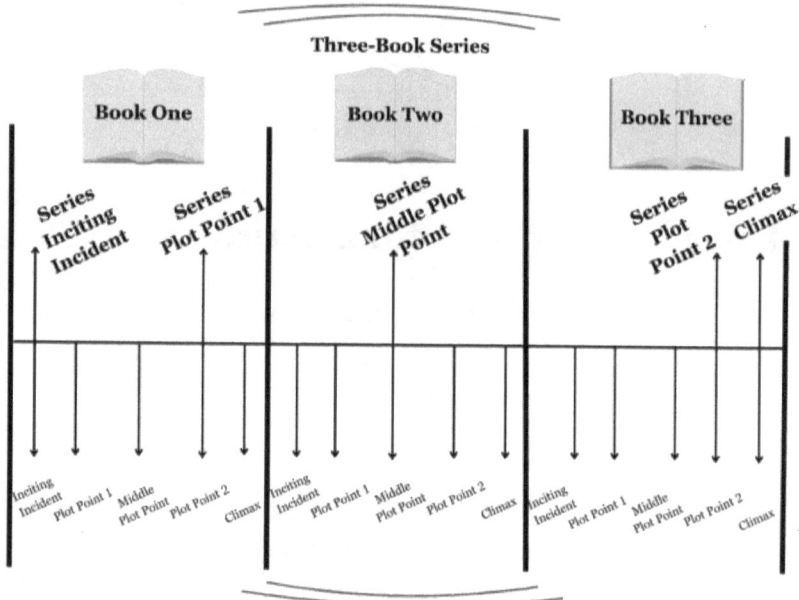

This structure is a starting point. It shows one possible link between each novel story arc and the series story arc scenes. Right after this, we'll show you an example of a commercially successful series that is a little different from this diagram.

Why? Because we want you to see how flexible the story arc is when it's the foundation of a series.

The Five Story Arc Scenes in the Context of a Series

The previous two examples gave you a strong understanding of the story arc placement in a single novel. Let's look at the five story arc scenes in the context of a series.

We'll continue with the Hunger Games trilogy as an example.

Series Inciting Incident

Role of Inciting Incident in a Closed Series

The inciting incident must shake up the protagonist's ordinary world in the context of the series.

The inciting incident in book one of a series can be the same as the inciting incident for the series. If it is, the same main event for book one must be strong enough to kick off the series too.

As a reminder, here are the blurbs we wrote for the Hunger Games series.

The Hunger Games Series Skeleton Blurb

Katniss Everdeen must become the leader of the rebellion and overturn the Capitol; otherwise, everyone outside of the Capitol dies or is doomed to a life of misery.

The Hunger Games (book one) Skeleton Blurb

Katniss Everdeen must win the Hunger Games; otherwise, she dies.

Series Inciting Incident

The inciting incident for *The Hunger Games* (book one) and for the series is the same event.

By volunteering for the Hunger Games, both goals in the skeleton blurbs are addressed. If she doesn't volunteer, she can't win the Hunger Games or go on to lead the rebellion and overturn the Capitol.

Series Plot Point 1

Plot point 1 is where the protagonist accepts the skeleton blurb goal. The story goal will be different for the first novel and for the series.

You wrote a skeleton blurb for your series and for each novel, so you know they are different. The only skeleton blurbs that can be the same are the skeleton blurbs for the series and for the final novel. This means the placement of the series plot point 1 is going to vary depending on the length of your series.

In plot point 1 of *The Hunger Games* (book one), Katniss must accept the goal of trying to win the Hunger Games. This happens when she shoots an arrow at the Gamemakers. In plot point 1 of the Hunger Games series, Katniss must accept the goal of becoming the leader of the rebellion and overturn the Capitol. This happens after the climax scene in book one, when Katniss and Peeta show they are willing to eat the poisonous berries.

Series Middle Plot Point

The middle plot point for the series will occur somewhere in the middle of the series. It may fall somewhere around the middle plot point of a single novel. Remember, the action is in relation to the series skeleton blurb goal.

The middle plot point for a single novel will show the protagonist changing from reactive to proactive for that novel's story goal. The middle plot point for the series will show the protagonist changing from reactive to proactive for the series' story goal.

The middle plot point for *Catching Fire* and for the Hunger Games series is the same scene.

Catching Fire (book two) Skeleton Blurb

Katniss Everdeen must find a way to keep Peeta alive; otherwise, Peeta dies and can't protect her family.

SECRETS TO WRITING A SERIES

In *Catching Fire* (book two) at the middle plot point, Katniss understands the arena is structured like a clock. She can now proactively fight to keep Peeta alive. Here she is addressing the story goal for book two.

The second part of the middle plot point is that she figures out that some of the tributes are working together to keep her alive. This moves her toward becoming the leader of the revolution and foreshadows that others believe in her ability to save them and the districts. This foreshadows that Katniss will become the leader of the revolution and take down the Capitol.

The scene works beautifully as a middle plot point for both the series and book two.

Series Plot Point 2

If you choose to make plot point 2 the same scene for both the final novel and for the series, it means the protagonist will get the final piece of information they need to address the skeleton blurb goal for both the series and the single novel in the same scene. It also means that the protagonist will be at their lowest point for the series and for the final novel. This is an easier option than what the Hunger Games series does.

The series plot point 2 occurs at the end of *Catching Fire* (book two). This happens when Peeta is taken by the Capitol and District 12 (Katniss's home) is destroyed.

Plot point 2 for *Mockingjay* (book three) happens when Katniss's sister is killed. Katniss volunteered for the Hunger Games in book one to save her sister's life. She completely failed.

Series Climax

There can be only one climax in a novel. This is the scene that answers the skeleton blurb goal. The series skeleton blurb goal is addressed in the final novel of the series as well as the final novel blurb goal. This shows us that the final novel climax scene is also the series climax scene.

In *Mockingjay* (book three), Katniss and the rebels take the Capitol. Katniss has the opportunity to kill President Snow. However, at the last moment, she kills President Coin instead, believing that she was responsible for Prim's death and that she would be just as tyrannical as Snow. This is the climax for both the series and for the final novel in the series.

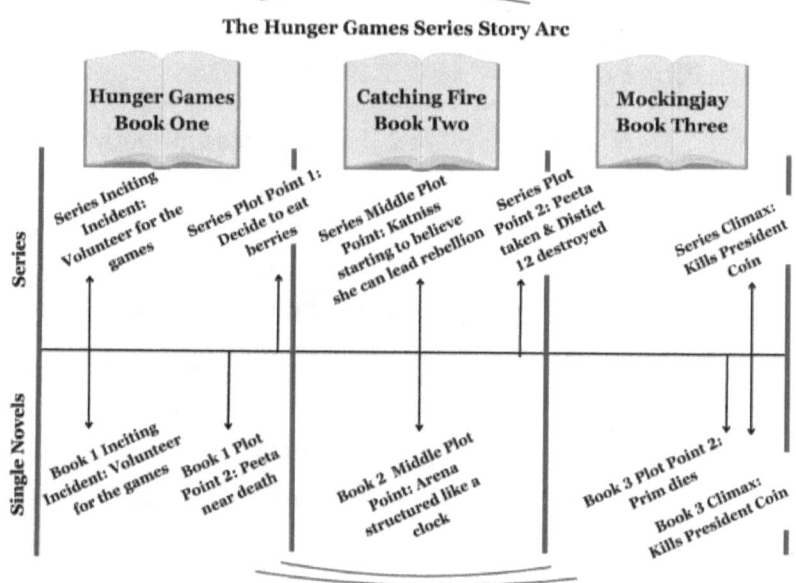

Story Arc Duties: Single Novel Versus Closed Series

The following compares the duties of the five story arc scenes for a single novel in a series and the series as a whole.

All Story Arc Scenes	Closed Series Single Novel	Closed Series
POV	Protagonist has the POV.	Protagonist has the POV.
Protagonist Role	Shows the protagonist leading the action.	Shows the protagonist leading the action.
Action	Changes the story direction.	Changes the story direction.
Action	Raises the stakes.	Raises the stakes.
Tension	Is full of tension.	Is full of tension.
Style	Is written in active form.	Is written in active form.
Skeleton Blurb	Is related to a single novel skeleton blurb.	Is related to a series skeleton blurb.

Inciting Incident	Closed Series Single Novel	Closed Series
Main Event	Before 15% into a single book.	Disrupts the protagonist's world and causes them to react in the context of the series story goal.
Placement	Disrupts the protagonist's world and causes them to react in the context of a single book story goal.	Near the end of a previous book and before 15% into its book.
Mirror	Single book climax.	Series climax.
Required?	Yes.	Yes.

Plot Point 1	Closed Series Single Novel	Closed Series
Main Event	The protagonist accepts the story goal.	The protagonist might be unaware they are accepting the series goal.
Placement	20 to 30% into a single book.	Series plot point 2.
Mirror	Single book plot point 2.	From single book plot point 2 through to the inciting incident of the following book.
Required?	Yes.	Yes. Can be the same as single book plot point 2 or exist on its own.

Middle Plot Point	Closed Series Single Novel	Closed Series
Main Event	Climax in a single book.	Climax in the series.
Foreshadow	Protagonist moves from reactive to proactive in relationship to the single book goal.	Protagonist moves from reactive to proactive in relation to the series book goal.
Placement	45 to 55% into a single book.	45 to 55% into the series.
Required?	Yes.	Yes. Can be the same as the single book middle plot point, or exist on its own.

Plot Point 2	Closed Series Single Novel	Closed Series
Main Event	Protagonist is at their lowest point in a single book.	Protagonist is at their lowest point in the final book in the series and in the series.
Placement	70 to 80% into a single book.	Contains the final piece of information to address the series goal.
Information	Contains the final piece of information to address the single book story goal.	It is the same scene as plot point 2 for the final book and is placed for the single book.
Mirror	Single book plot point 1.	Series plot point 1 and book one plot point 1.
Required?	Yes.	Yes.

Climax	Closed Series Single Novel	Closed Series
Main Event	Address a single book story goal.	Address the series story goal and the final book story goal.
Placement	85 to 95% into a single book.	Contains the final piece of information to address the series goal.
Information	Can hint a the next book in the series.	No new information.
Mirror	Single book inciting incident.	Book one inciting incident (same as series inciting incident.
Required?	Yes.	Yes. This is the same as climax scene in the final book of the series.

Where to Next?

We're going to create the main events for the five story arc scenes in a closed series. Create your main events along with us, and you'll have created the first level of your series foundation.

Chapter Nine: Outline the Closed Series Story Arc

In this chapter, we'll outline the story arc scenes in a closed series. A closed series has a fixed number of novels with a story arc that starts in the first novel and finishes at the end of the last novel in the series.

An open series has no story arc that starts in the first novel and finishes at the end of the last novel. We'll cover an open series in "Chapter Fifteen: Meet the Open Series Story Arc."

You've created skeleton blurbs for your series and for each novel in your series, so have those handy as you work through this chapter.

Next, you're going to create the main events for your series story arc scenes. Story arcs can be intimidating for a series, and we're going to make it simple. As with all our processes, we are going to give you actions for each step. Before we can do that, let's remind ourselves of the theory.

The minimum number of scenes needed to create a story arc is five:

- Inciting incident
- Plot point 1
- Middle plot point
- Plot point 2
- Climax

We want to remind you we are looking at the action plotline for a series. We are not working on internal character arcs or subplots. Our goal is to create the main events for the story arc scenes for each novel and for the series itself. You'll build the rest of the story around the main events.

The order you outline or create the main event for each story arc scene will depend on where you are in your process. Because we have already outlined the first book in the Evolution series, we're going to use the inciting incident of book one and the skeleton blurb of the series to find the climax of book three.

If you haven't outlined your book one yet, we suggest outlining plot point 1 in book one first. This is where your protagonist accepts the story goal, and the main event is easy to find. After plot point 1, you define the main event for the inciting incident.

Let's review the duties of an inciting incident in the context of a single novel.

The inciting incident for a single novel must do the following:

- Be told from the protagonist's POV.
- Be written in active form.
- Cause the protagonist to react to the action. The reaction is the start of the protagonist's journey.
- Be related to the story goal stated in the single novel skeleton blurb.
- Mirror the climax scene in the same novel.

In addition to the single novel duties, the main event in the inciting incident of a series scene must

- Be related to the story goal stated in the series skeleton blurb.
- Mirror the climax scene... but what climax scene, you ask? We'll get to that.
- Be strong enough to support the series.

Now we need to look at this in the context of the series.

If one scene addresses the inciting incident for both book one and the series, the main event must be related to the goal in both the book one skeleton blurb and the series skeleton blurb. It can also mirror the climax scene in book one and in the series.

Mirroring Scenes

Humans like symmetry. And mirroring scenes is a way to give a novel symmetry. When the opening and closing scenes mirror each other, this will give the reader closure. They will feel satisfied with the story.

Scenes that mirror each other can either be opposite or complementary in action. You can also mirror scenes at an emotional level. For each of the scenes that should be mirror scenes of each other, decide whether they are complementary, opposite, or a combination.

Effective scene mirrors keep the reader engaged in the story. A mirrored opening image and closing image will give closure to the reader. The ending will be satisfying, and the reader will feel the story is over. They know they are at the end.

Imagine how much stronger this is for mirroring the opening image of the first novel with the closing image of the series.

Later, we'll show you the opening and closing images for popular published closed and open series, and for Evolution and My Fairy Assassin.

For each novel, these are the scenes that mirror each other:

- Opening image and closing image
- Inciting incident and climax
- Plot point 1 and plot point 2

In a series, the following are the scenes that can mirror each other:

- Book one opening image and series closing image
- Book one inciting incident and series climax
- Book one plot point 1 and series plot point 2

This is a starting point for places to look for opportunities to mirror scenes.

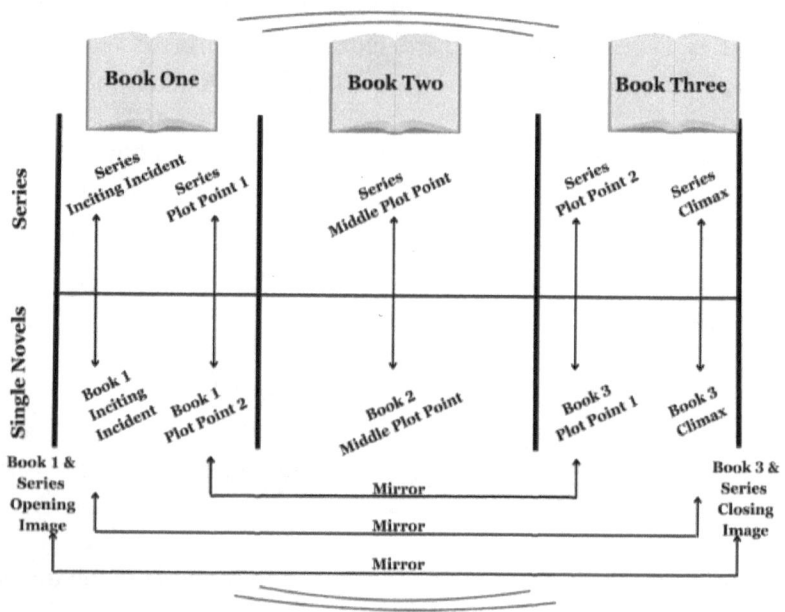

Divergent Scene Mirroring Example

In the Divergent series by Veronica Roth, the book one inciting incident mirrors the climax in the series. In *Divergent* (book one) the inciting incident occurs when test results are inconclusive. Tris has no clear faction, and she is lost. Here comes a spoiler, and it's big. In the *Allegiant* (book three) climax, Tris dies, and she is lost again.

The mirroring is poetic and helps make Tris's death less painful for the reader. It's a big decision to kill a series protagonist, and the author had to find a way to do this without alienating her readers. She did this with mirroring. The inciting incident gives the first hint that Tris is going to leave her mother. In death, she returns to her mother.

Outlining a Series Novel

When we outline a single novel, we outline the story arc scenes in the following order:

- Main event in plot point 1
- Main event in the inciting incident
- Main event in plot point 2
- Main event in the climax
- Main event in the middle plot point

For the series, we'll start the outline with the following:

- Book one plot point 1
- Book one inciting incident
- Series climax (not the book one climax)

We'll get to the rest of the order as we proceed.

Outlining the Closed Series Evolution

We're going to use the following structure for the Evolution series to illustrate outlining and writing a series. This is our starting point, and we'll build on this as we work our way through this book.

We've decided the following main events occur in the same scene:

- Book one and the series inciting incident
- Book one plot point 2 and the series plot point 1
- Book two middle plot point and the series middle plot point
- Book three plot point 2 and the series plot point 2
- Book three climax and the series climax

The image below shows you how we're going to create a foundation for the Evolution series.

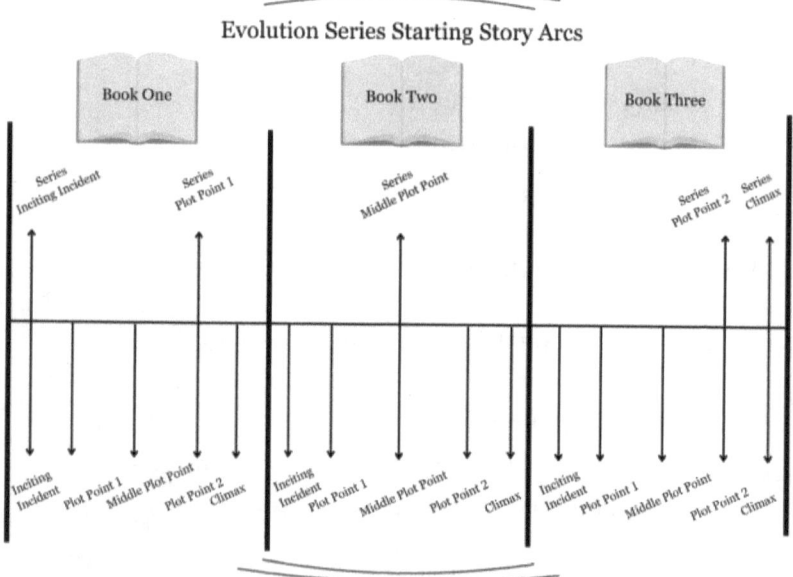

SECRETS TO WRITING A SERIES 111

If you haven't made any decisions about the placement of your story arc scenes for the series, use the same decisions we made. It's the easiest way to start. When you're writing your series, you may decide that the scenes you planned to combine should be written as two separate scenes. You'll know if you need to do this only after you outline and write a draft.

Evolution Series Story Arc Example

Each novel in the Evolution series will be one hundred thousand words, and the series is a trilogy that will be three hundred thousand words.

We'll talk about percentages not because the story arc is about precise mathematics, but because a framework forces us to be creative within boundaries. It forces us to work harder at telling a great story.

For the Evolution series, we've decided the story arc for each novel will look like the following:

- Inciting incident: 10 percent
- Plot point 1: 25 percent
- Middle plot point: 50 percent
- Plot point 2: 75 percent
- Climax: 90 percent

Note that this might not be what we end up with. It's only a framework at this point. This gives us three story arcs in a row plus the series story arc shown on the diagram above.

The percentage goals we recommend for the story arc scenes for a single novel do NOT apply to a closed series story arc. The series story arc must adapt to the single novels.

When you write the series, you'll build scenes around the story arc scenes. After the first draft is written, you'll check to ensure the story arc scenes are generally in the right place.

The series story arc might not have all five story arc scenes. For example, a long series may not need a series middle plot point. This is a similar concept to the story arc scenes for subplots. Not all subplots will contain all five story arc scenes.

In our example, there will be an inciting incident, plot point 1, the middle plot point, plot point 2, and the climax for the series. These scenes will be related to the series skeleton blurb, just like the story arc scenes in each novel are related to the skeleton blurb for each respective novel.

The five story arc scenes for a series have additional duties that are not part of the single novel story arc scene duties.

Series Inciting Incident

We'll start with the series inciting incident. We know the main purpose of the inciting incident is to shake up the protagonist's ordinary world.

Each novel in the series will show a new ordinary world for the protagonist.

The first ordinary world of the protagonist happens during the setup of book one in a series. Once there has been a disturbance in the protagonist's ordinary world, the protagonist's ordinary world is not shown again. If it is, it means the story is moving backward and not forward.

This shows us the main event in the inciting incident can be the same for book one as it is for the series. If this is the case, the inciting incident must perform double duties. It addresses the skeleton blurb for book one and for the series.

Note that when you get to book two, a new ordinary world will be shown. Book one will have changed the protagonist's ordinary world, so they have a new starting point, and you must show that to the reader before the book two inciting incident. This holds true for every book in a closed series.

Series Inciting Incident Placement: In our example, this scene (or scenes) occurs at ten thousand words or 10 percent into book one. This is about 3 percent into a three-hundred-thousand-word series. The image below shows where the scene is placed in the context of the first novel in the series and in the series as a whole.

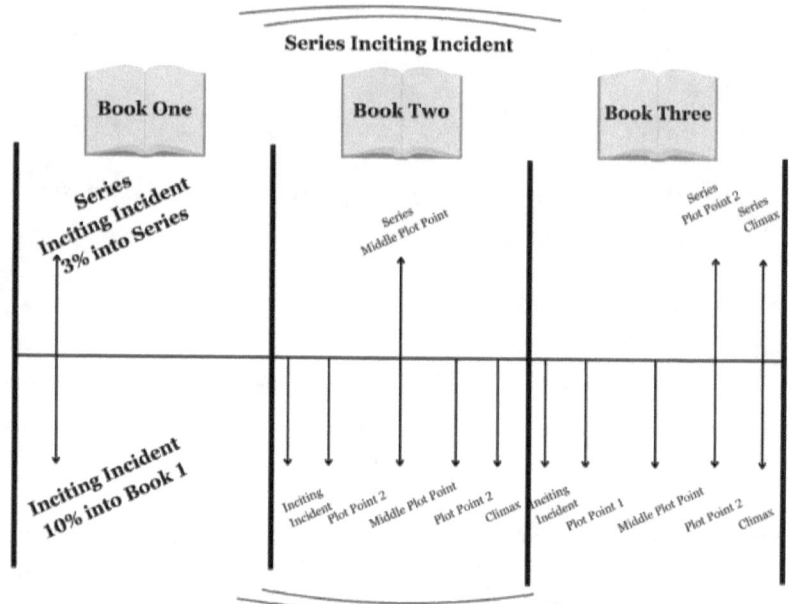

And now the fun really starts. In our example, plot point 1 of the series is also going to be plot point 2 of book one. This means plot point 2 of book one has double duties to perform. It must be both plot point 1 for the series and plot point 2 for book one.

Book One Plot Point 2 and Series Plot Point 1

Book One Plot Point 2

The main purpose of book one plot point 2 is to show the protagonist learning the final piece of information they need to address the story goal in book one's skeleton blurb. This can be internal or external and will drive them to the climax. This is also where the protagonist is at the lowest point in book one.

Series Plot Point 1

The main purpose of plot point 1 is to show the protagonist accepting the story goal stated in the series skeleton blurb.

For the series, the same scene must show or hint at the protagonist accepting the story goal in the series skeleton blurb. The protagonist doesn't need to know this is what they are doing, but the author does.

Series Plot Point 1 Placement: In our example, this occurs at seventy-five thousand words or 75 percent into book one, and seventy-five thousand words or 25 percent into the series. There is a symmetry created by this placement, but you don't have to do this. Plot point 1 of the series is the beginning of act 2 of the series.

Act 2 of the series is kicked off when the protagonist accepts the series story goal. This is typically between book one plot point 2 and early in the second novel in the series.

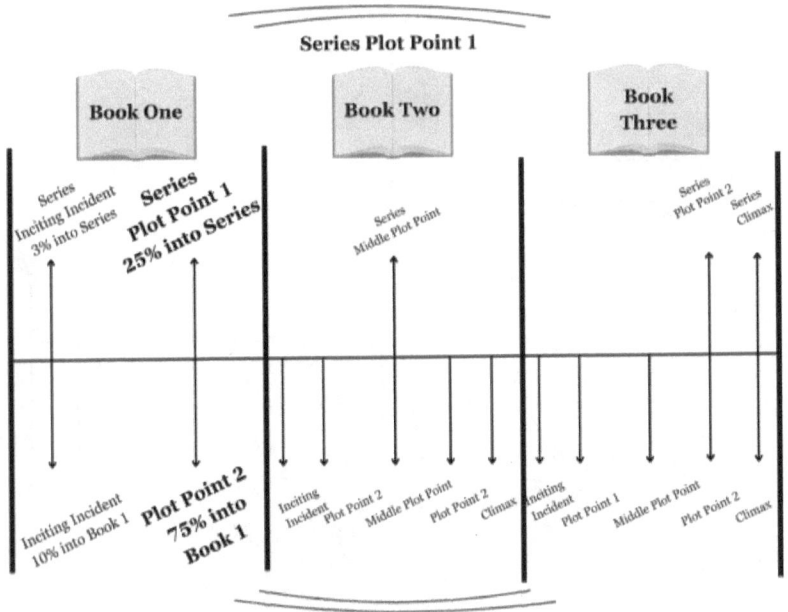

The Middle Plot Point

The main purpose of the middle plot point is to show the protagonist changing from reactive to proactive. The middle plot point for the series can be the same as the middle plot point for book two in a trilogy. The protagonist will be moving from reactive to proactive related to the story goal in book two and the series goal in the skeleton blurbs.

This is an interesting story arc scene because it doesn't have to exist in a series, but it can. The protagonist has already moved from reactive to proactive in the middle plot point of book one in the series. This may be enough.

Series Middle Plot Placement: This occurs at fifty thousand words or 50 percent into book two, and one hundred and fifty thousand words or 50 percent into the series.

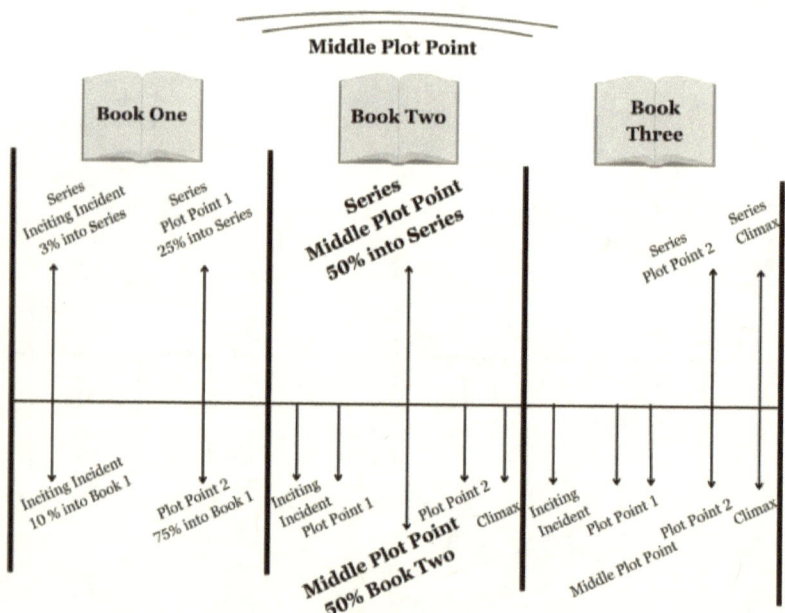

Series Plot Point 2 and Book Three Plot Point 2

We chose to make plot point 2 of book three and plot point 2 of the series occur in the same scene. The scene (or scenes) addressed relate to the book one skeleton blurb and the series skeleton blurb. There are other ways to do this. The Hunger Games series does this well.

For the series plot point 2, we find ourselves looking at another plot point that must perform double duties related to the book three skeleton blurb and the series skeleton blurb.

The lowest point in book three for the protagonist will also be the lowest point for the protagonist in the series. It must be worse than the book one and book two plot point 2 scenes.

Series Plot Point 2 Placement: This occurs at seventy-five thousand words into book three, and 275,000 words into the series. This means plot point 2 will be 91 percent into the series.

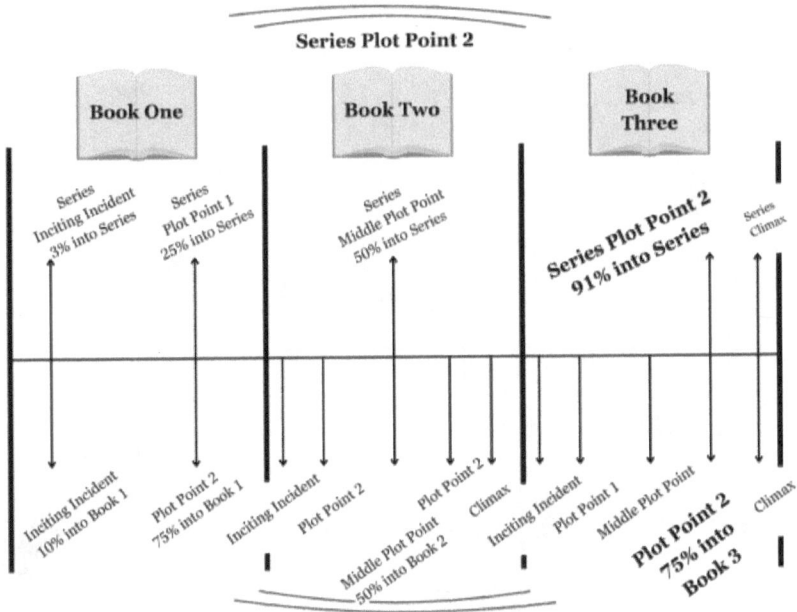

The Series Climax

The series climax scene is going to occur late in the series but between 85 percent and 95 percent into novel three. This works because the reader has just finished three books and is ready for the story to end. A long resolution may cause problems. This also shows that the climax of book three can't come any later than 90 percent. It could even come earlier. If you want the climax scene of the series to be at 90 percent into the series, then this would be placed at seventy thousand words into book three, which is a bit early. Here again, you get to play with the story arc and decide how it works best for your series.

Series Climax Placement: This occurs at ninety thousand words into book three, and two hundred and ninety thousand words into the series. This means the climax will be placed at 90 percent into book three and 96 percent into the series.

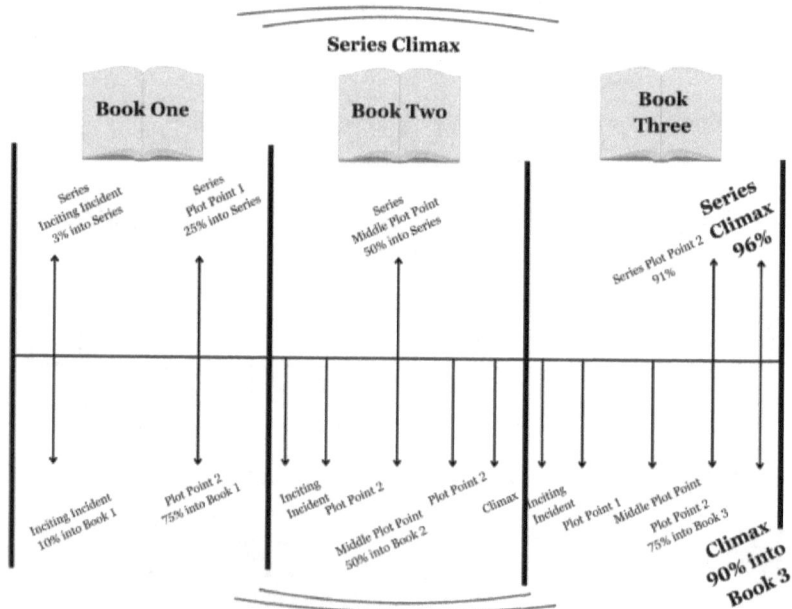

Evolution Series Story Arc

We are already at the place where we can list high-level main events for the story arc scenes for the series. The following image gives us the framework for how we are going to structure the Evolution series. We bet you didn't think you'd be at this level so early in the journey, and we hope you're excited.

We're going to build on this throughout this book, just as you'll build the structure for your series.

We chose the main event from the main action that happens in each of the story arc scenes. See "Chapter Seven: Meet the Story Arc" if you need a refresher.

The image below shows you the generic main event for the story arc scenes for the Evolution series as follows:

Series Inciting Incident: Disruption to Jaz's world.

Series Plot Point 1: Jaz accepts the series story goal.

Series Middle Plot Point: Jaz moves from reactive to proactive.

Series Plot Point 2: Jaz is at her lowest point and discovers the final piece of information.

Series Climax: Jaz achieves the story goal.

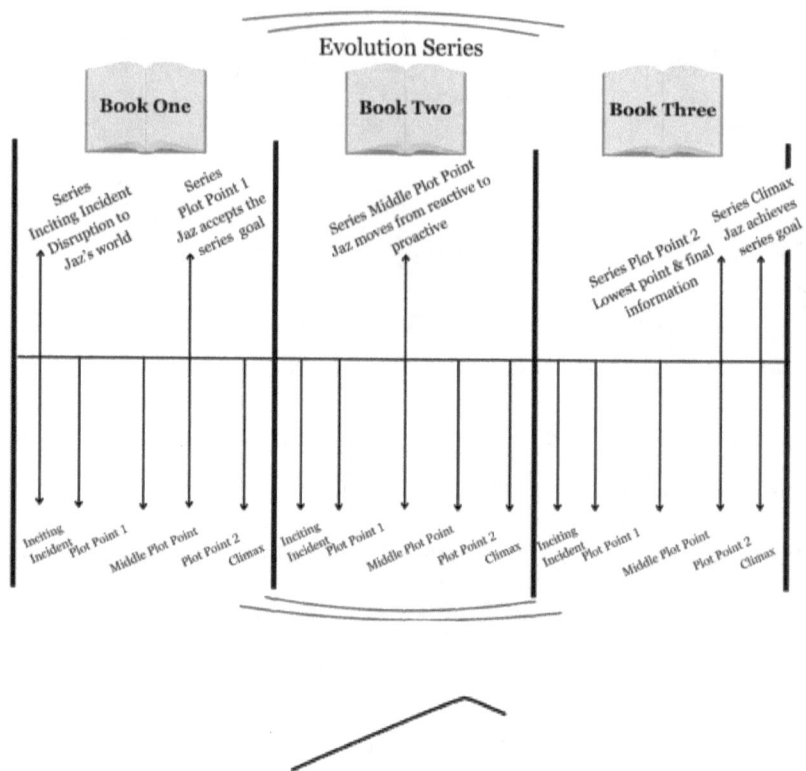

Your Fun Series Task

We're going to keep building our series vault and add the main events for the five series story arc scenes. The main events will be generic for now. We've given you what you need to accomplish in each story arc scene for the series versus each novel in the series.

Add the main events for the series story arc scenes to your series vault.

- Series Inciting Incident: Disruption to protagonist's world.
- Series Plot Point 1: Protagonist accepts the series story

goal.
- Series Middle Plot Point: Protagonist moves from reactive to proactive.
- Series Plot Point 2: Protagonist is at their lowest point and discovers the final piece of information.
- Series Climax: Protagonist achieves/fails to achieve the story goal.

Evolution Series Vault

We've added the following to the Evolution series vault. We're going to update the main events with more specific main events as we work our way through this process.

Vault Heading	Evolution
Series Inciting Incident	Disrupts Jaz's world and causes her to react in the context to the single novel and series story goal.
Series Plot Point 1	Jaz accepts the series story goal.
Series Middle Plot Point	Jaz moves from reactive to proactive in relation to the series story goal.
Series Plot Point 2	Jaz is at her lowest point in the final novel and series. She discovers the final information she needs to reach the series climax.
Climax	Jaz achieves the series and final novel story goal.

Where to Next?

You have a generic structure for your series story arc, and we're going to work together to make it specific. We'll start by creating the main events for the series inciting incident and the series climax.

Chapter Ten: Frame Your Series Inciting Incident and Climax (Closed Series)

We're going to create specific main events for the five series story arc scenes for Evolution. You can create your main events along with us. This chapter covers the series inciting incident and series climax, so we can frame the series.

We found the easiest way to create the main events for the five story arc scenes in a series is to start with the book one plot point 1. We'll use that to find the book one inciting incident, and that is going to help us discover the book three climax.

We'll address book two last. When we outline a stand-alone novel, we outline the middle plot point last, and we'll follow a similar process for a series.

If you know the main event in any of the series story arc scenes, start with that event and work your way to the next logical scene.

It's easiest to start with book one plot point 1 because we know the main event is the protagonist accepting the series goal, and we know the series goal.

We'll outline them in this order:

1. Book One Plot Point 1
2. Book One Inciting Incident
3. Series Inciting Incident
4. Series Climax
5. Book Three Climax

For the Evolution series, we'll create the main event in book one plot point 1 from the book one skeleton blurb. We'll use that to create the main event for the book one inciting incident.

Because the inciting incidents for book one and for the series are the same scene, their duties increase a bit, and we'll remind you how. You don't have to write these as the same scene or scenes. Later in the process, your story may demand separate scenes. For now, this is the easier way to get started.

The series climax scene will be stronger if it mirrors the series inciting incident, so knowing the series inciting incident makes it easy to create the main event for the series and book three climax scenes.

This generic image below shows how to create the main events for the series story arc to ensure structural integrity. We're going to use Evolution to take you through steps 1 through 11. You'll create your series story arc along with us.

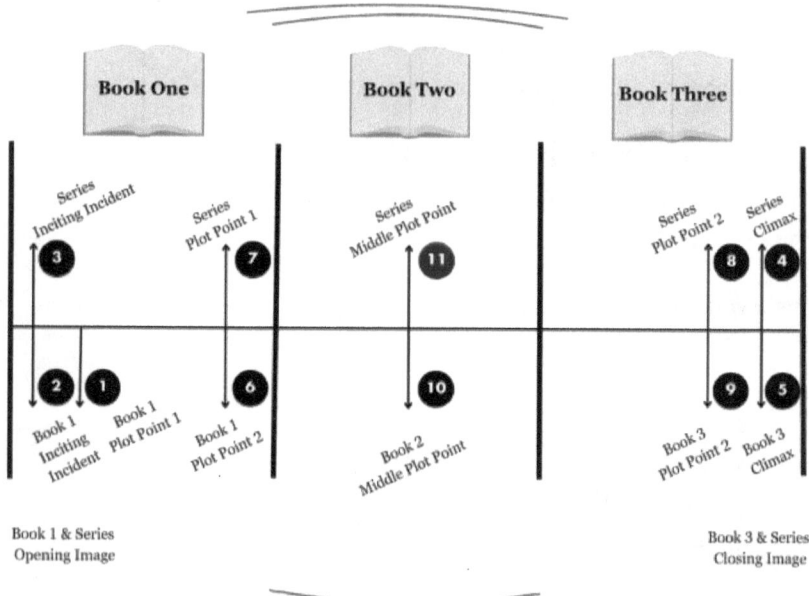

You can see we've created a structure we can use to create the main events for the series. We've framed the series by the series inciting incident and the series climax.

How to Find the Inciting Incident and Plot Point 1

Step 1: Plot Point 1 Book One

Here's how this works. We know the series skeleton blurb for the first book in the Evolution series. You know the series skeleton blurb for book one in your series.

Refer to that now and follow along. You've recorded it in your series vault for easy reference.

Do you have it? Let's proceed.

Evolution Series (book one) Skeleton Blurb:

Jaz Cooper must find out who killed her husband, using her ability to see into a dog's mind; otherwise, she might die.

We know in plot point 1 that the protagonist accepts the story goal. There are two parts to the story goal. Part one is Jaz finding out who killed her husband. Part two is using a dog's visions.

At the start of the story, Jaz doesn't know her husband was murdered. She thinks his death was an accident.

We decided the main event in plot point 1 of book one is that Jaz uses a dog's vision and finally believes her husband was murdered.

Here you see a scene name, "Murder Established," for plot point 1 added to our story arc outline.

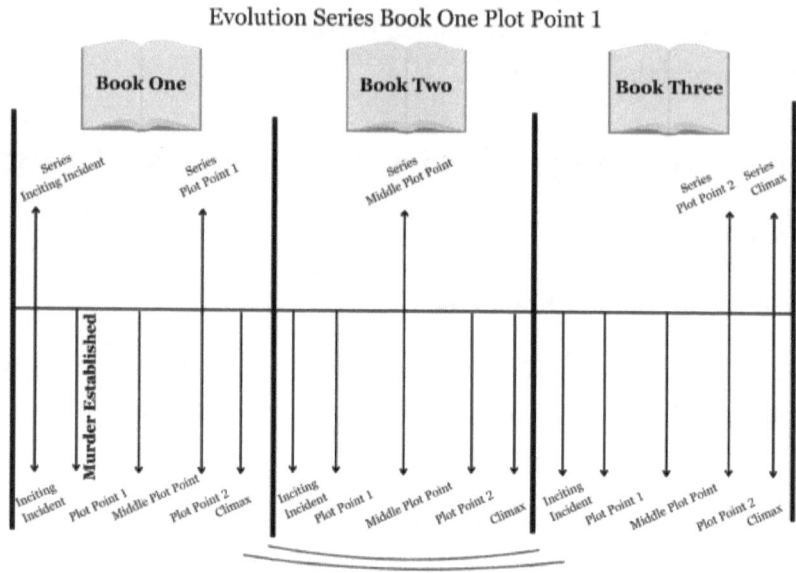

Steps 2 & 3: Inciting Incident for Series and Book One

Using the main event in plot point 1 and the skeleton blurb for both book one and the series, we can determine the inciting incident main event for both book one and the series. The inciting incident must lead to plot point 1.

Refer to your series vault and read your series skeleton blurb.

For the Evolution series, the following is the series skeleton blurb:

> *Jaz Cooper must discover and eliminate the organization testing the ability on humans; otherwise, Jaz and all the others who have the ability might be killed.*

The main event in the inciting incident will change Jaz's ordinary world for book one and the series. She will not go back to the world that existed before this inciting incident. The dog visions are key to the story and must be in the inciting incident.

We decided that the following is the main event in the inciting incident in book one: Jaz saves a dog's life and gains the ability to see into the dog's mind.

Here you see a scene name, "Jaz Gains Visions," for the inciting incident has replaced the generic scene name in our story arc outline for both book one and the series.

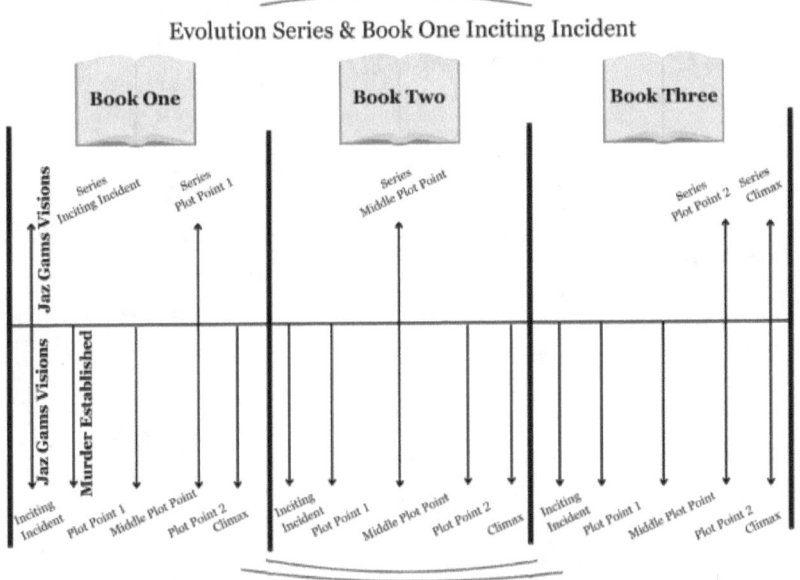

You'll have noticed we gave the inciting incident for the series the same name as the inciting incident of book one because it's the same scene. It's fun to watch the series build. As we go, we'll continue to replace the placeholders with specific names.

Let's remind ourselves what a climax scene must do.

There can be only one climax in a novel. This is the scene (or scenes) that addresses the skeleton blurb goal. The series skeleton blurb goal and the final novel blurb goal are addressed in the final novel of the series. This shows us that the final novel climax scene is also the series climax scene.

Climax	Closed Series Single Novel	Closed Series
Main Event	Address a single book story goal.	Address the series story goal and the final book story goal.
Placement	85 to 95% into a single book.	Contains the final piece of information to address the series goal.
Information	Can hint at the next book in the series.	No new information.
Mirror	Single book inciting incident.	Book one inciting incident (same as series inciting incident.
Required?	Yes.	Yes. This is the same as climax scene in the final book of the series.

The climax scene for the series must address the story goal in the series skeleton blurb. It must show whether the protagonist achieved the series story goal.

The series goal cannot be addressed in any of the novels prior to the final novel. Once the series goal is addressed, the story is over.

How to Find the Climax Main Event

Let's look at how to find the main event in the climax of the series.

Decide whether the protagonist is going to achieve the series goal. This gives you the first clue to what the main event is in the series climax.

The climax scene mirrors the inciting incident for the series. This gives you another clue to the main event in the series climax, because you already know the main event in the series inciting incident.

We're going to show you how to find the main event in the climax.

Steps 4 & 5: Climax for the Series and for Book Three

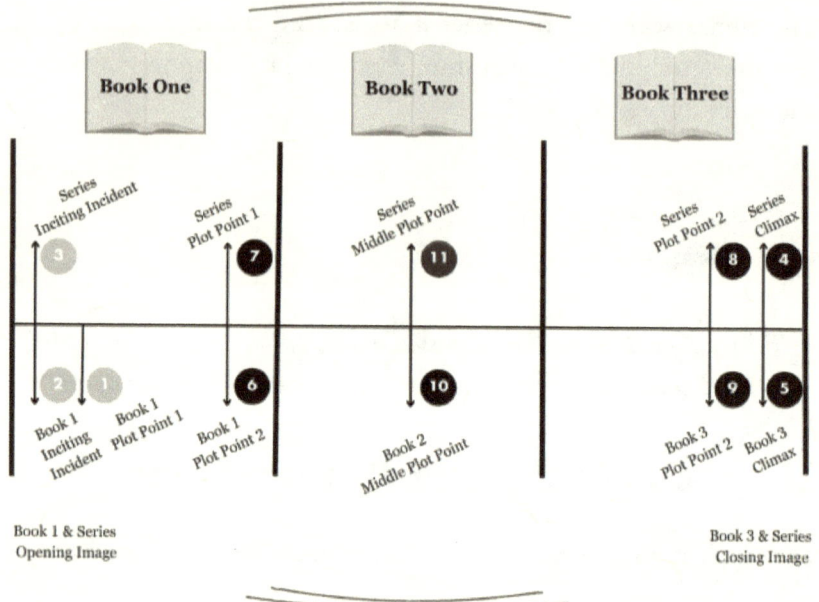

In the section on mirroring, we stated that the inciting incident and the climax scenes will be stronger if they mirror each other.

For the first book in the Evolution series, the main event in the inciting incident and the series inciting incident are the same scene. The book three climax and the series climax are also the same scene.

The main event in the climax scene must show if the protagonist achieved the story goal.

We know the following:

1. The story goal for the series (from the series skeleton blurb)
2. The story goal for book three (from the book three skeleton blurb)
3. The main event in the inciting incident
4. That Jaz achieves the series story goal

With these four pieces of information, we can create the main event for the book three climax and the series climax. Refer to your series vault so you have this information ready.

For the Evolution series, we know the following:

Inciting Incident: Jaz saves a dog's life and gains the ability to see into the dog's mind.

We know Jaz achieves the story goal that is in the skeleton blurb for book one. We also know she must use a dog visions. This shows us the main event in the climax scene is the following:

Climax: Using a dog's vision, Jaz discovers who murdered her husband.

Because Jaz saved the dog's life and gained the ability to see into its mind, she was able to save her own life in the climax when she discovered who murdered her husband.

The following is the skeleton blurb for the series and for book three.

Jaz Cooper must discover and eliminate the organization testing the ability on humans; otherwise, Jaz and all the others who have the ability might be killed.

We've decided that Jaz is going to achieve the series story goal and the book three story goal.

This means that in the main event of the climax scene in book three and in the series Jaz must do the following:

- Use a dog vision
- Eliminate the organization testing on humans

We think that in book three we need an earlier scene where Jaz discovers the organization testing on humans, and that discovery will drive her to the climax. This could even be the inciting incident in book three.

We decided the main event in the **series climax** is the following:

Jaz uses her ability to see into a dog's mind to eliminate the testing organization.

Isn't that amazing? We just discovered the main event in the climax scene of book three, and we discovered a second main event. We may make the discovery of the evil organization in book three, or we may decide that it needs to be shown at the end of book two. We'll wait and see how that turns out.

Let's look at mirroring the inciting incident of book one and the climax of the series.

The inciting incident of the series and book one: Jaz saves a dog's life and gains the ability to see into the dog's mind.

The climax of the series and book three: Jaz uses her ability to see into a dog's mind to eliminate the testing organization.

The mirror happens because Jaz saves a life in the inciting incident, and she is either going to end a life or end an organization in the climax of the series. For now we don't need any more detail. We'll fill in more details as we outline and write the trilogy. What we don't want to do at this stage is box ourselves into one storyline. We are still exploring our options.

Here you see a scene name, "Jaz Eliminates Organization," for the climax added to our story arc outline.

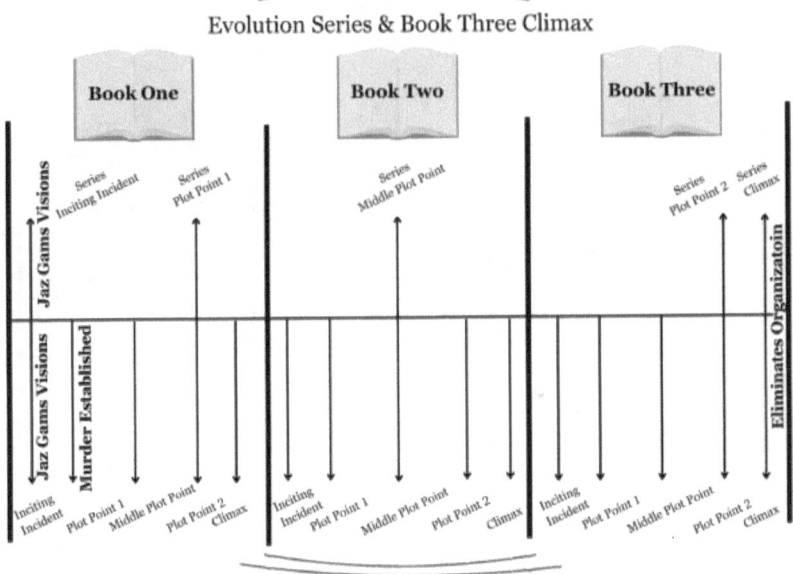

Evolution Series & Book Three Climax

You'll have noticed we gave the climax for the series the same name as book three, as it's the same scene. Here is a way to see just the inciting incident and the climax scenes.

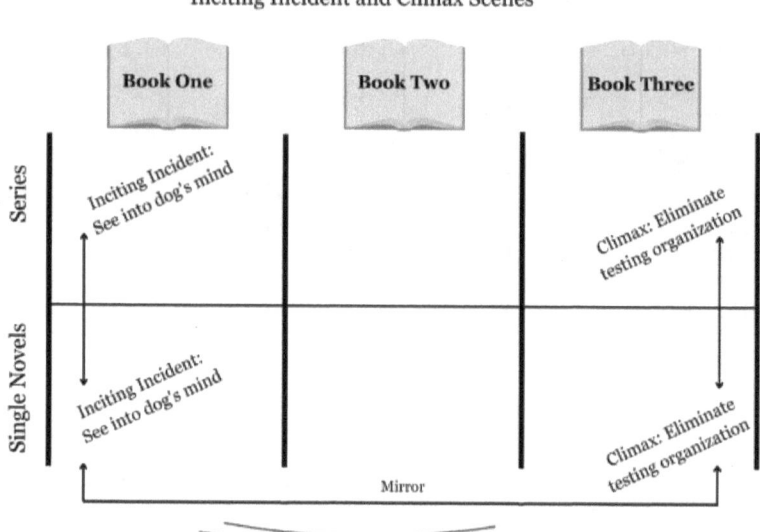

We now have the end points of our framework to base our series on. Everything we outline and write will lead us to the series and book three climax.

Before we outline the next scenes, let's take a look at the Hunger Games series' inciting incident and climax.

The Hunger Games Example

In the Hunger Games trilogy, the series inciting incident occurs when Katniss volunteers for the games, taking the place of her sister, Prim. This is the same as the inciting incident in book one.

In *Mockingjay* (book three), Katniss and the rebels take the Capitol. Katniss has the opportunity to kill President Snow. However, at the last moment, she kills President Coin instead, believing that she was responsible for Prim's death and that Coin would be just as tyrannical as Snow. President Coin was planning on holding a new

SECRETS TO WRITING A SERIES

type of Hunger Games, where the children of the Capitol would be the participants.

We'll draw the Hunger Games trilogy together in a diagram to make it clear. We'll start with the series inciting incident and the series climax and show you how these two scenes frame the series.

It's brilliant, really. The inciting incident for the series and the climax for the series mirror each other. In the inciting incident, the Hunger Games are kicked off. In the climax, they are stopped for good.

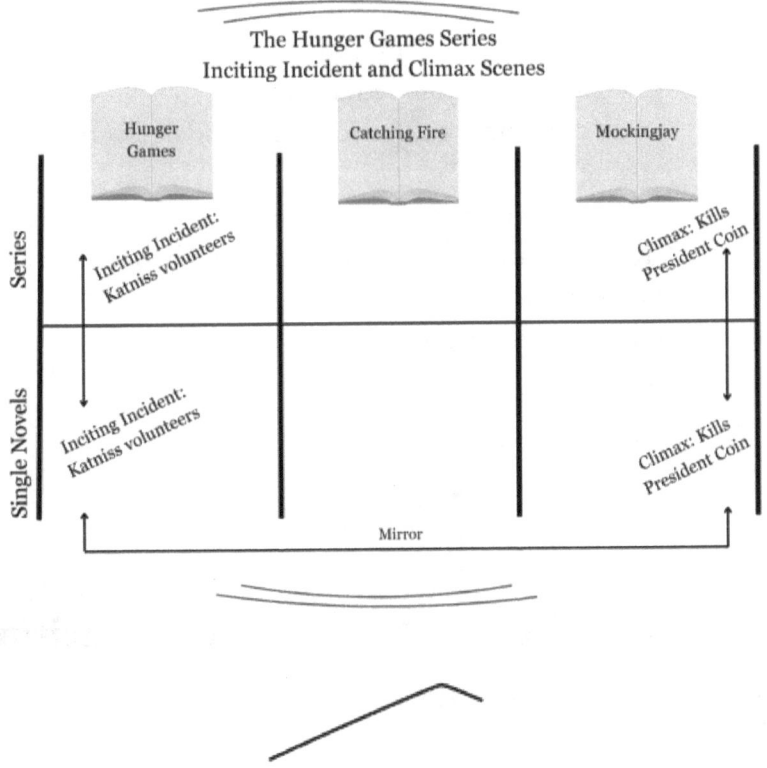

Your Fun Series Task

This is where you get to start outlining the story arc for your series. In your series vault, add the following headings:

- Book One Story Arc Scenes
- Inciting Incident
- Plot Point 1
- Book Three Story Arc Scenes
- Climax

Next, do the following:

1. Create the main event for your book one plot point 1.
2. Add that event to your series vault.
3. Create the main event for your series and book one inciting incident.
4. Add that event to your series vault.
5. Create the main event for your series and book three climax.
6. Add that event to your series vault.

Evolution Series Vault: Series inciting Incident & Climax

Vault Heading	Evolution
Series Inciting Incident	Jaz saves a dog's life and gains the ability to see into the dog's mind.
Series Plot Point 1	Jaz accepts the series story goal.
Series Middle Plot Point	Jaz moves from reactive to proactive in relation to the series story goal.
Series Plot Point 2	Jaz is at her lowest point in the final novel and series. She discovers the final information she needs to reach the series climax.
Climax	Jaz uses her ability to see into a dog's mind to eliminate the testing organization.

Vault Heading	Evolution
Book One Inciting Incident	Jaz saves a dog's life and gains the ability to see into the dog's mind.
Book One Plot Point 1	Jaz uses a dog vision and finally believes her husband was murdered.
Book Three Climax	Jaz uses her ability to see into a dog's mind to eliminate the testing organization.

Where to Next?

Now that you've framed your series, you can work on the series plot point 1. This will be the moment the protagonist accepts the series goal. This is not the same as the plot point 1 scene you just created the main event for. Most likely the series plot point 1 will come later in book one.

Chapter Eleven: Accept the Series Story Goal (Closed Series)

In the previous chapter, you created the end points for the frame of your series story arc. The protagonist will have a series story goal, and that goal must fit into book one in the series and the series as a whole.

The main event for plot point 1 is the action that causes the protagonist to accept the story goal for book one in the series.

This led us back to the main event in book one's inciting incident. The action in the inciting incident shakes up the protagonist's world. You made sure this action relates both to the book one story goal and to the series goal.

Now we'll show you how to create the main events for book one plot point 2 and the series plot point 1. The following illustration shows where these scenes sit on the story arc.

We're going to address steps 6 and 7 in the following image.

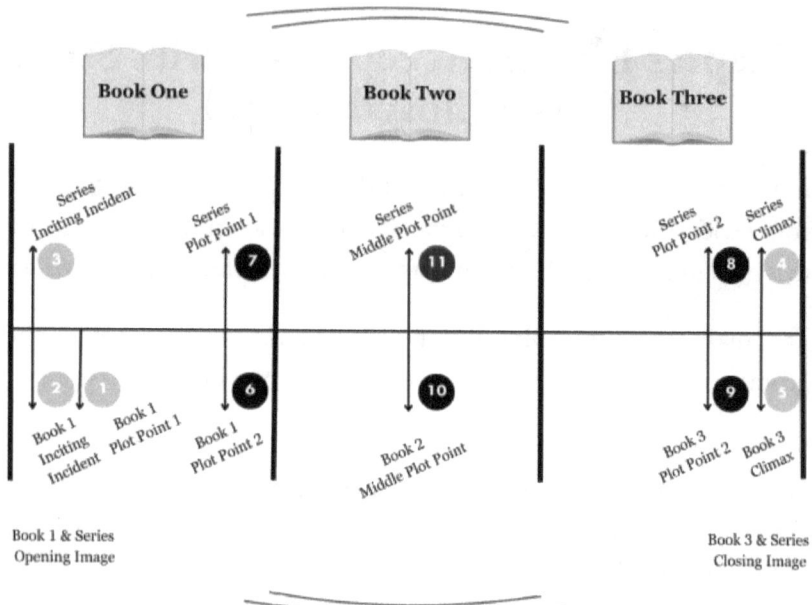

As we stated in the previous section, we are doing this for outlining the series story arc so we have a framework to work from. When we write the series, these may end up being different scenes. The goal is to create the series story arc without getting stuck.

The scene that contains book one plot point 2 and the series plot point 1 must:

- Cause the protagonist to be at their lowest point of the story so far in book one.
- Share the final piece of information the protagonist needs to address the book one story goal.
- Create a sense of urgency in book one.
- Mirror book one plot point 1.
- Cause the protagonist to react to the action in the scene.
- Cause the protagonist to reactively accept the story goal for the series.

- Mirror the series plot point 2. This will be in book three.

Evolution: Accepting the Series Story Goal

For the Evolution series, we're going to create the main event in plot point 1 of the series using plot point 2 of book one.

So far for Evolution, the series skeleton blurb is the following:

*Jaz Cooper must **discover and eliminate the organization testing the ability on humans**; otherwise, Jaz and all the others who have the ability might be killed.*

Book one skeleton blurb:

*Jaz Cooper must **find out who killed her husband, using her ability to see into a dog's mind**; otherwise, she might die.*

Book three skeleton blurb:

*Jaz Cooper must **discover and eliminate the organization testing the ability on humans**; otherwise, Jaz and all the others who have the ability might be killed.*

Inciting Incident (Book One and Series): Jaz saves a dog's life and gains the ability to see into the dog's mind.

Series Climax: Jaz uses her ability to see into a dog's mind to eliminate the testing organization.

First, we need to determine plot point 2 for book one in the Evolution series. Here is an excerpt from *The Secrets to Outlining a Novel: The Creative Outlining Method*.

So far, we know:

> *Inciting Incident: Jaz saves a dog's life and gains the ability to see into the dog's mind.*
>
> *Plot Point 1: Jaz uses a dog's vision and finally believes her husband was murdered.*
>
> *If we want plot point 2 to mirror plot point 1, and we do, then death seems like a good action that would mirror plot point 1 and bring Jaz to her lowest point. We also know that, to stay true to the skeleton blurb, Jaz must use the dog's visions to get her from the middle plot point to plot point 2.*
>
> *We decided the main event for plot point 2 is:*
>
> *Jaz's actions cause someone close to her to die.*
>
> *This means Jaz is at her lowest point as she loses someone close to her because of her actions. The skeleton blurb shows us Jaz is trying to figure out who murdered her husband. Chasing this goal puts her life in danger, but she loses someone else instead. It all comes back to the skeleton blurb.*

For the Evolution series, we decided the main event in book one for plot point 2 is:

> *Jaz's actions cause someone close to her to die.*

This might not be enough to support the series. It deals with the first four duties in the context of plot point 1 in book one. Now the main event in the scene must also do the following:

- Cause the protagonist to react to the action in the scene.
- Cause the protagonist to reactively accept the story goal in the series.
- Mirror the series plot point 2, because the scene is also plot point 2 of book one.

The first point is easy. Someone close to Jaz has died. Of course she will react to this. We now need to hint at the story goal for book three. The story goal for book three is to discover and eliminate the organization testing the dog-vision ability on humans.

Even though she doesn't know about the testing organization, we're going to foreshadow that it exists. The final piece of information Jaz gains in book one plot point 2 will lead her to the climax of book one and will set her up for accepting the series goal.

Book one plot point 2 will show Jaz how serious it can be if others find out about her ability.

Let's update the main event for plot point 2 in book one so it performs its duties.

We decided the **main event for the series plot point 1** is an extension of the main event in book one plot point 2:

> *Jaz's actions cause someone close to her to die. That person is killed by the book one antagonist. The antagonist belongs to the testing organization. Although Jaz doesn't know it, this is where she accepts the story goal of destroying the group.*

Here you see a scene name, "Jaz's Friend Dies," for the book one plot point 2 added to our story arc outline. We've also added the scene name, "Jaz's Friend Dies," for the series plot point 1 main event.

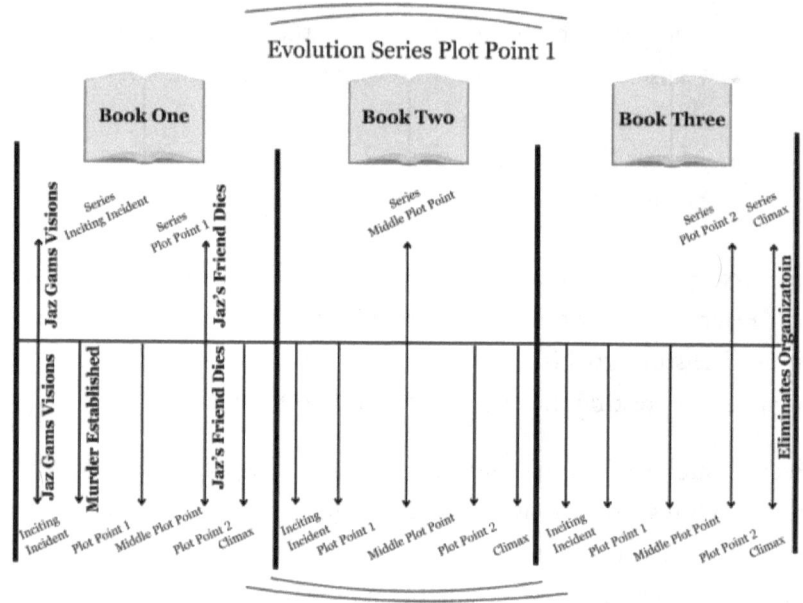

The Hunger Games Example

In *The Hunger Games* (book one), Katniss accepts the series goal when she chooses to defy the Capitol and eat poisonous berries instead of killing Peeta. Katniss doesn't know she's just accepted the series goal, but the author does.

This means plot point 1 for the series is placed between the climax of book one and the opening image of *Catching Fire* (book two).

This creates an exit hook for the reader. The hook is what will happen to Katniss and Peeta because they defied the Capitol on a live broadcast. The reader knows there will be repercussions. They just don't know what those repercussions will be.

You'll see later that we recommend placing an exit hook at the end of a novel after the climax scene. *The Hunger Games* (book one) smartly combines the series plot point 1 and the exit hook.

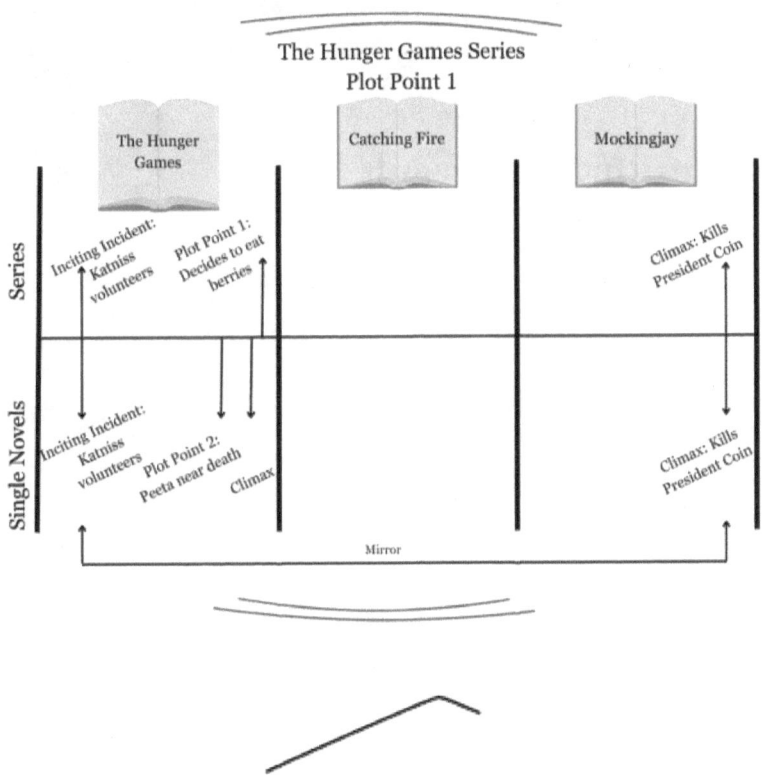

Your Fun Series Task

In this section we added more main events for the series and single novel story arc scenes.

Your task is to keep working on your series vault.

1. Create the main event for the series plot point 1.
2. Add that event to your series vault.

3. Update book one plot point 2 in your series vault.

Evolution Series Vault

Vault Heading	Evolution
Series Inciting Incident	Jaz saves a dog's life and gains the ability to see into the dog's mind.
Series Plot Point 1	**Jaz's actions cause someone close to her to die. That person is killed by book one's antagonist. The antagonist belongs to the testing organization. Although Jaz doesn't know it, this is where she accepts the story goal of destroying the group.**
Series Middle Plot Point	Jaz moves from reactive to proactive in relation to the series story goal.
Series Plot Point 2	Jaz is at her lowest point in the final novel and series. She discovers the final information she needs to reach the series climax.
Climax	Jaz uses her ability to see into a dog's mind to eliminate the testing organization.

Vault Heading	Evolution
Book One Inciting Incident	Jaz saves a dog's life and gains the ability to see into the dog's mind.
Book One Plot Point 1	Jaz uses a dog vision and finally believes her husband was murdered.
Book One Plot Point 2	**Jaz's actions cause someone close to her to die.**
Book Three Climax	Jaz uses her ability to see into a dog's mind to eliminate the testing organization.

Where to Next?

We're heading to the protagonist's worst moment in the series. This is also the place where they receive the final piece of information they need to reach the climax.

Chapter Twelve: The Protagonist's Worst Moment (Closed Series)

You've created the main events for the following scenes:

- Book one inciting incident
- Book one plot point 1
- Book one plot point 2
- Series plot point 1
- Book three climax
- Series climax

Remember the mirroring concept. We're going to use the main events for the series plot point 1 (in book one) to create the series plot point 2 (in book three). We've chosen this scene next because we know that for the best structure, plot point 1 of the series mirrors plot point 2 of the series.

We're going to address steps 8 and 9 in the following image.

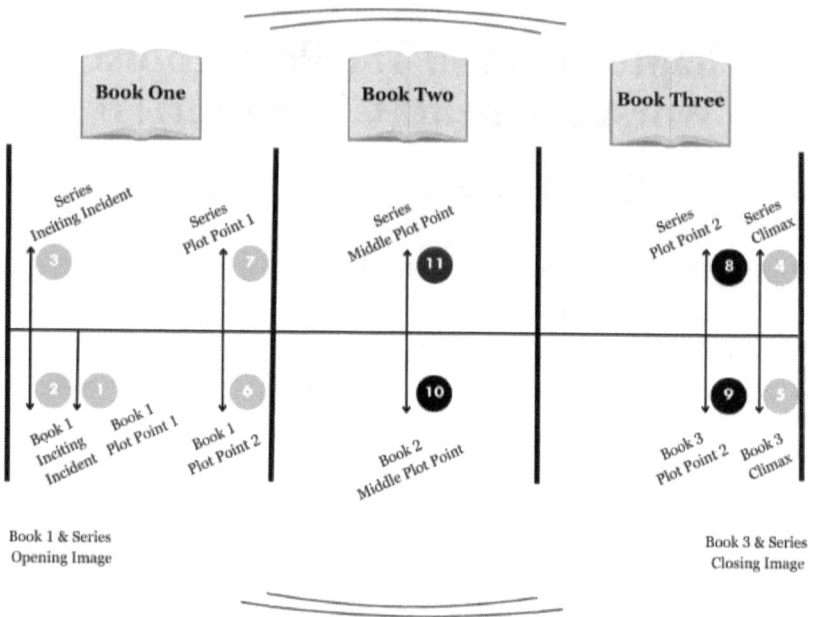

Here's a quick recap of the plot point 2 duties:

- Cause the protagonist to be at their lowest emotional point of the story so far in the series.
- Share the final piece of information the protagonist needs to address the series goal.
- Create a sense of urgency.
- Mirror the series plot point 1.

When deciding on the main event for plot point 2 for the final novel in the series, the main event must be the worst moment for the protagonist in the series. None of the other plot point 2 scenes can be as bad as this one.

Evolution Series Plot Point 2

For the Evolution series, we decided that as we outline, the series plot point 2 will be the same scene as our book three plot point 2.

So far for the Evolution series, we have the following assets we can make use of:

The series skeleton blurb: Jaz Cooper must **discover and eliminate the organization testing the ability on humans**; otherwise, Jaz and all the others who have the ability might be killed.

Book one skeleton blurb: Jaz Cooper must **find out who killed her husband, using her ability to see into a dog's mind**; otherwise, she might die.

Book three skeleton blurb: Jaz Cooper must **discover and eliminate the organization testing the ability on humans**; otherwise, Jaz and all the others who have the ability might be killed.

Plot Point 1 (Series): Jaz's actions cause someone close to her to die. That person is killed by the book one antagonist. The antagonist belongs to the testing organization. Although Jaz doesn't know it, this is where she accepts the story goal of destroying the group.

Climax (Series and Book Three): Jaz uses her ability to see into a dog's mind to eliminate the testing organization.

We know series plot point 1 and series plot point 2 will mirror each other.

Plot point 2 of the series must lead to the climax of the series, and it must give Jaz the final piece of information she needs to achieve the series goal.

This gives us a place to look for what must happen in the series plot point 2.

Let's start with the mirror. In series plot point 1, Jaz's action causes someone close to her to die. We could mirror that with Jaz saving the life of someone close to her. One choice is to have her save her daughter. However, this would not put her at her lowest moment. Another choice is for Jaz to kill book one's antagonist. In plot point 1, she thought her actions killed someone close to her, but it was really the antagonist who killed the person. The action of Jaz killing the antagonist is a mirror to the antagonist killing someone close to Jaz. This works much better than our first idea.

We must point out that the antagonist is a group antagonist. When Jaz kills one person, there will still be others who are part of the antagonist entity; otherwise, the story would be over.

The other action we require is Jaz learning the final piece of information she needs to reach the climax. Killing the antagonist shows her who is behind the organization, and she'll use that information to eliminate the testing organization.

You can play around with options until you find the one that you like best. When we come to creating the main event in plot point 2 for book two in the Evolution series, it must not be as bad as this main event.

This will work for us, so we decided the following is the **main event for the series and book three plot point 2**:

> *Jaz kills book one's antagonist and learns who is leading the testing organization.*

We've now mentioned book one's antagonist a few times. This shows us we'll need to add the character in book one. It's also hinting that this character will be someone close to Jaz, someone she doesn't suspect is her enemy.

The image below shows we've added "Jaz Kills Antagonist" to the series and book three plot point two scenes.

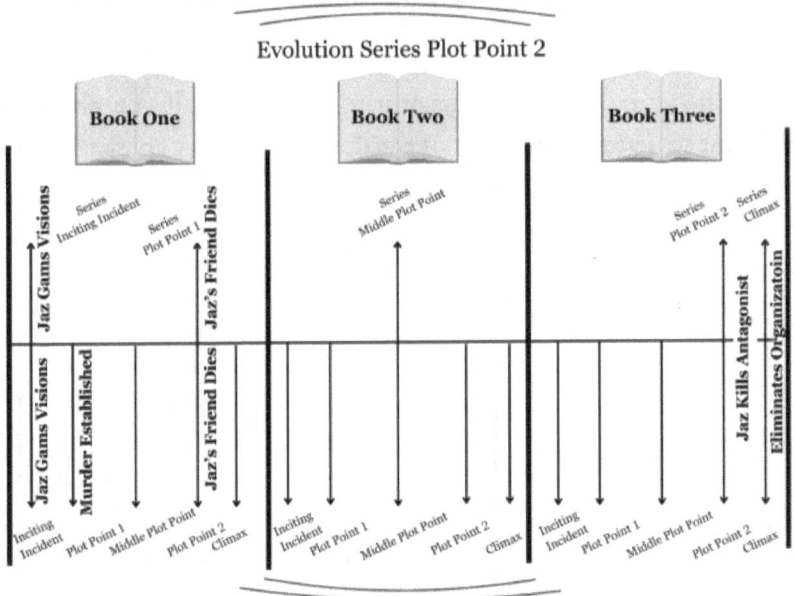

The Hunger Games Example

In the Hunger Games trilogy, plot point 1 of the series occurs at the end of book one, when Katniss chooses to defy the Capitol and eat poisonous berries instead of killing Peeta.

The series plot point 2 occurs at the end of book two, when Katniss wakes up in District 13 and learns Peeta has been captured by the Capitol and her home district has been bombed and no longer exists. Katniss learns two things here: one, that Peeta has been taken, and two, that her home is gone. These two pieces of information are what Katniss needs to decide she's going to kill President Snow.

Remember, one of the duties of plot point 2 is to give the protagonist the final piece of information they need to reach the climax.

The mirroring occurs between the series plot point 1 and plot point 2, because in the series plot point 1 Katniss is preparing for her and Peeta to die. In plot point 2, Katniss wants Peeta alive and back with her.

We're showing options for structuring your series. If you choose a different structure, keep track of the duties each story arc scene must perform and make sure they are addressed.

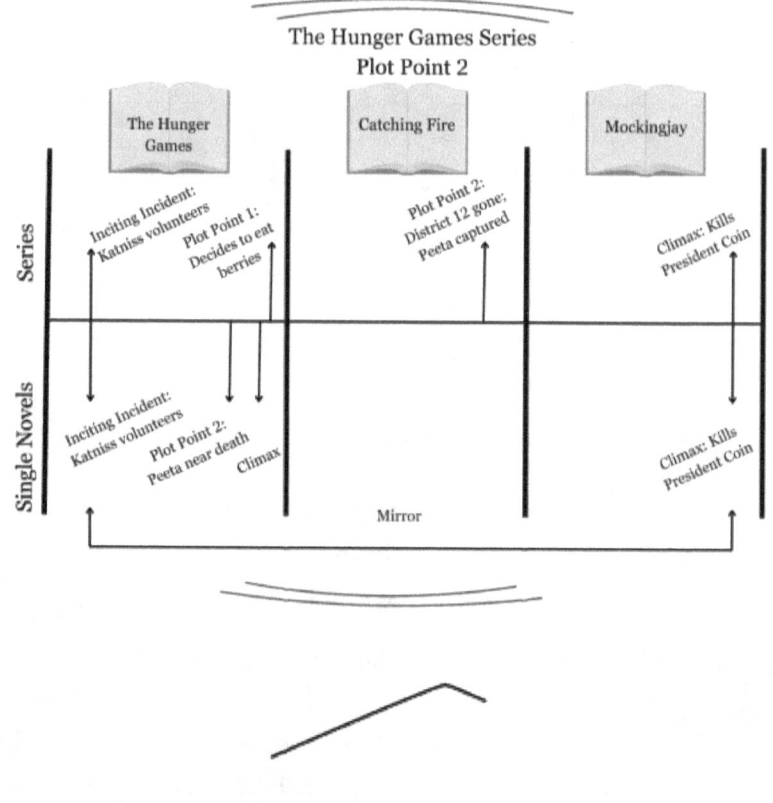

Your Fun Series Task

Go through the same process we just did for the Evolution series and update the series vault with the following:

- The main event for series plot point 2
- The main event for plot point 2 for the final novel in your series

Vault Heading	Evolution
Series Inciting Incident	Jaz saves a dog's life and gains the ability to see into the dog's mind.
Series Plot Point 1	Jaz's actions cause someone close to her to die. That person is killed by book one's antagonist. The antagonist belongs to the testing organization. Although Jaz doesn't know it, this is where she accepts the story goal of destroying the group.
Series Middle Plot Point	Jaz moves from reactive to proactive in relation to the series story goal.
Series Plot Point 2	**Jaz kills book one's antagonist and learns who is leading the testing organization.**
Climax	Jaz uses her ability to see into a dog's mind to eliminate the testing organization.

Where to Next?

Let's figure out what the series middle plot point is. Once you've done that, you've created the main events for the five story arc scenes in the closed series story arc. You'll have the framework you need to write your series and know it's structurally sound.

Chapter Thirteen: The Protagonist Gets Proactive (Closed Series)

In the middle plot point, the protagonist moves from reactive to proactive behavior. Let's remind ourselves of the middle plot point duties.

The middle plot point must do the following:

1. Be told from the protagonist's POV.
2. Be written in active form.
3. Show the protagonist leading the action by the end of the scene.
4. Show the protagonist proactively wanting to address the story goal.
5. Foreshadow the ending.

Point 5 above is the item we want. We know the main event in the climax of the series, and the main event in this scene should foreshadow that.

You've almost made it. You're on the final steps of creating the main events for your series story arc scenes. In this chapter, you'll complete steps 10 and 11 from the image below.

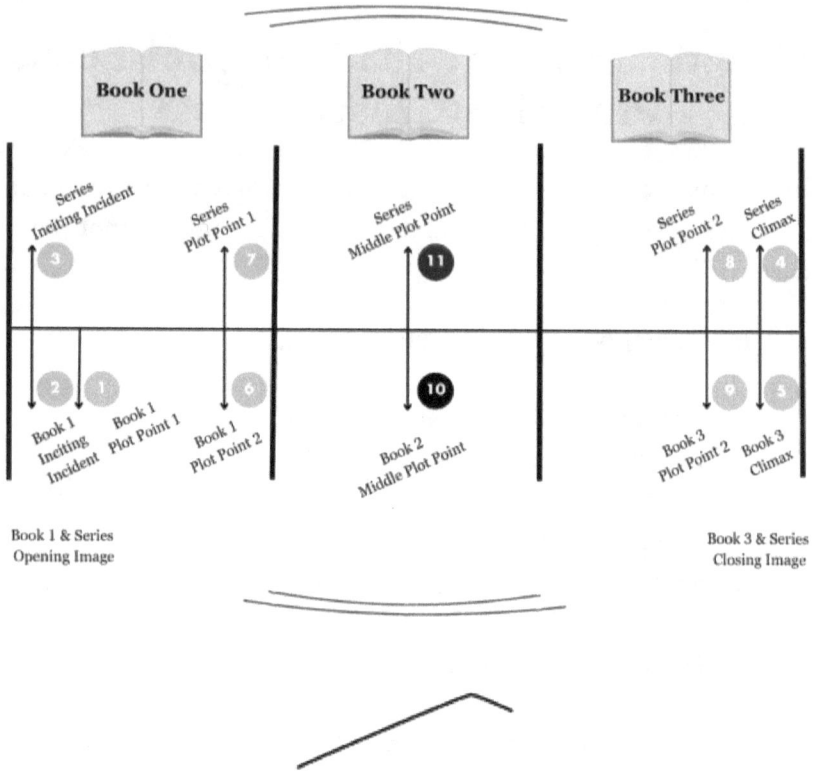

Evolution Series Middle Plot Point

For the Evolution series, we're going to have the middle plot point of book two be the same scene as the middle plot point of the series. This will make it easy to see the series story arc.

We'll open our series vault and refer to the series skeleton blurb, the book two skeleton blurb, and the series climax main event.

Series Skeleton Blurb:

*Jaz Cooper must **discover and eliminate the organization testing the ability on humans**; otherwise, Jaz and all the others who have the ability might be killed.*

Book Two Skeleton Blurb:

Jaz Cooper must keep others from discovering her daughter can see into a dog's mind; otherwise, her daughter might be killed.

Series Climax:

Jaz uses her ability to see into a dog's mind to eliminate the testing organization.

The middle plot point must be about Jaz keeping her daughter's ability secret, because that is in the skeleton blurb for book two.

The middle plot point must also be about shutting down the experimentation center, because that is the goal in the series skeleton blurb.

In addition, we want to foreshadow that Jaz is going to eliminate the testing organization.

For now we haven't outlined the story arc scenes for book two. What we want here is an event that will remind us of the double duty the middle plot point scene is going to perform.

We decided the following is the main event in the **middle plot point**:

Jaz does something that forces her to understand why she must keep her daughter's ability a secret. She also discovers something that leads her to the testing organization.

This is enough for us to move forward. When we outline book two in detail, we'll update the main event to be more specific. We'll add this to our series vault.

The Hunger Games Example

In *Catching Fire* (book two), Katniss understands the arena is structured like a clock. The other part of the middle plot point is that she figures out some of the tributes are working together to keep her alive.

The scene works beautifully as a middle plot point for both the series and book two.

The following is the series skeleton blurb we wrote:

Katniss Everdeen must become the leader of the rebellion and overturn the Capitol; otherwise, everyone she cares for will die.

The following is the skeleton blurb we wrote for *Catching Fire*:

Katniss Everdeen must find a way to keep Peeta alive; otherwise, she will have to live without him.

When Katniss understands the arena is structured like a clock, it means she can proactively fight to keep Peeta alive. This shows she's addressing the story goal for book two.

When she figures out some of the tributes are working together to keep her alive, it's moving her toward becoming the leader of the revolution. This foreshadows that others believe in her ability to save them and the district, and it foreshadows that Katniss will become the leader of the revolution and take down the Capitol.

The middle plot point for *Catching Fire* and for the Hunger Games series is the same scene.

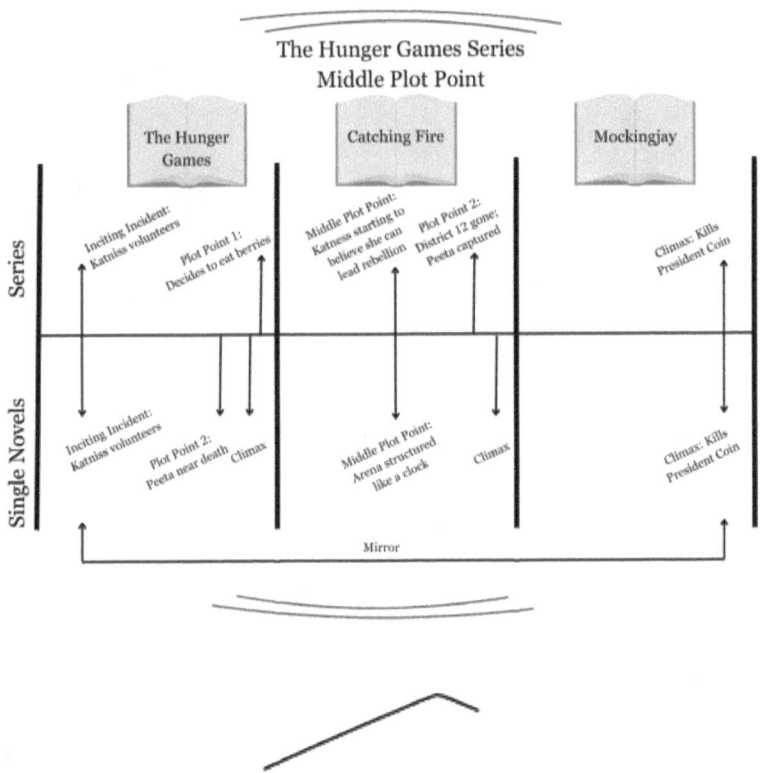

Your Fun Series Task

When you finish this task, you'll have the five story arc scenes outlined. Isn't that amazing?

1. Create the main event for the series middle plot point.
2. Create the main event for the book two middle plot point.
3. Add "Book Two Middle Plot Point" as a heading.
4. Add "Series Middle Plot Point" as a heading.
5. Add the main event to book two and the series middle plot point.

SECRETS TO WRITING A SERIES

Vault Heading	Evolution
Series Inciting Incident	Jaz saves a dog's life and gains the ability to see into the dog's mind.
Series Plot Point 1	Jaz's actions cause someone close to her to die. That person is killed by book one's antagonist. The antagonist belongs to the testing organization. Although Jaz doesn't know it, this is where she accepts the story goal of destroying the group.
Series Middle Plot Point	**Jaz does something that forces her to understand why she must keep her daughter's ability a secret.**
Series Plot Point 2	Jaz kills book one's antagonist and learns who is leading the testing organization.
Climax	Jaz uses her ability to see into a dog's mind to eliminate the testing organization.

Where to Next?

We've arrived at an exciting moment.

If you're writing a closed series, you've outlined the five story arc scenes for your series and some of the main events of the story arc scenes in the single novels in the series. That's a massive achievement. You now have the framework for your series.

But is that enough? We're going to show you the Series Structure Test for a closed series so you can objectively answer that question.

Chapter Fourteen: Closed Series Structure Test

We have arrived at your fifth artistic decision. Do you have a strong enough concept to support a series?

You've decided to write a closed series, created the skeleton blurbs you need, and outlined the five story arc scenes for the series. Now is the time to check whether the series is structurally sound. If you haven't created the skeleton blurb for each novel in the series itself and created the main event for the five story arc scenes in the series, we recommend doing that before testing the series structure.

For the series structure, ask yourself:

1. Does the climax scene in the final novel address the series story goal? Note: this goal cannot be addressed before the final novel. If it is, the series is not structurally sound.
2. Are the stakes higher in each consecutive novel? If they are not, go back and rewrite the skeleton blurbs so the stakes are raised with each novel.
3. Does each novel have a different climax scene? If the scenes are too similar, this is an indication the series is not strong enough yet. Rewrite the main event for the climax scene in each novel so they are all different.
4. Does the climax scene of the series (the last novel in the series) mirror one of the story arc scenes in one of the previous novels? If not, rewrite the main events.

The Hunger Games Series Skeleton Blurb

Let's test the Hunger Games series.

We created the following skeleton blurbs for the Hunger Games series to show you how to test your closed series.

The Hunger Games Series Skeleton Blurb

Katniss Everdeen must become the leader of the rebellion and overturn the Capitol; otherwise, everyone outside of the Capitol dies or is doomed to a life of misery.

The Hunger Games (book one) Skeleton Blurb

Katniss Everdeen must win the Hunger Games; otherwise, she dies.

Catching Fire (book two) Skeleton Blurb

Katniss Everdeen must find a way to keep Peeta alive; otherwise, Peeta dies and he can't protect her family.

Mockingjay (book three) Skeleton Blurb

Katniss Everdeen must become the leader of the rebellion and overturn the Capitol; otherwise, everyone outside of the Capitol dies or is doomed to a life of misery.

Is the Series Story Goal Addressed?

First, we'll check whether the climax scene in *Mockingjay* (book three) addresses the series story goal.

The following is the series goal from the skeleton blurb for the series: become the leader of the rebellion and overturn the Capitol.

In the climax scene, Katniss shoots President Coin and defeats the Capitol. During *Mockingjay* (book three), she becomes the leader of the rebellion. So yes, the series goal is addressed.

Are the Stakes Higher in Each Consecutive Novel?

The answer is yes, the stakes rise with every novel. In *The Hunger Games* (book one), only Katniss's life is at stake. In *Catching Fire* (book two), Peeta's and Katniss's families' lives are at stake. In *Mockingjay* (book three), everyone who is not part of the Capitol might die.

Is the Climax Scene Different in Each Book?

In the climax of *The Hunger Games* (book one), Katniss and Peeta win the Hunger Games. Katniss kills the final competitor. In the resolution, they threaten to commit suicide and decide to die instead of killing each other. The event is televised live, so the Capitol has no choice but to declare both winners.

In the climax of *Catching Fire* (book two), Katniss destroys the roof of the dome covering the Hunger Games arena. Katniss gets rescued and taken to District 13. Peeta gets taken by the Capitol, separating them.

In the climax of *Mockingjay* (book three), Katniss shoots President Coin with an arrow. This is the end of the Capitol.

The climax scenes are all different. In book one, Katniss achieves her goal of winning the Hunger Games. In book two, Katniss only partly achieves her goal, because she didn't keep Peeta safe. In book three, she achieves the goal of shutting down the Hunger Games.

Does the Climax Scene Mirror a Story Arc Scene from Book One?

In the series climax scene, Katniss kills President Coin. In the inciting incident of book one, Katniss takes her sister's place in the Hunger Games. She saved her sister's life. The mirror is to take a life versus save a life. In the final novel, Katniss beats the Capitol, but her sister dies. It is a bittersweet ending.

Evolution Series Structure Test

We know enough about the Evolution series to test whether the structure is strong enough to write the series.

Is the Series Story Goal Addressed?

Evolution Series Skeleton Blurb:

> *Jaz Cooper must **discover and eliminate the organization testing the ability on humans**; otherwise, Jaz and all the others who have the ability might be killed.*

The skeleton blurb for the third book in the Evolution series is the same as the skeleton blurb for the series. This means the climax scene in the final will address the series goal.

This is an enlightening moment. We've decided that Jaz will be successful in achieving the series goal. This reminds us of the main event in the climax scene of book three:

> *Jaz shuts down the experimentation center using her ability to see into a dog's mind.*

At this point, all we're interested in is the "what" for the scene. We're not ready to deal with how or why this happens.

The answer to "Does the climax scene in the final book address the series story goal?" is yes.

Are the Stakes Higher in Each Consecutive Novel?

Here we will refer to the skeleton blurbs for all three novels in the Evolution series.

Evolution Series (book one)

Jaz Cooper must find out who killed her husband, using her ability to see into a dog's mind; otherwise, she might die.

Evolution Series (book two)

Jaz Cooper must find out who is trying to take her daughter; otherwise, her daughter will be stolen by the testing organization and possibly be killed.

Evolution Series (book three)

*Jaz Cooper must **discover and eliminate the organization testing the ability on humans**; otherwise, Jaz and all the others who have the ability might be killed.*

Book One Stakes: Jaz might die.

Book Two Stakes: Jaz's daughter will be stolen by the testing organization and possibly be killed.

Book Three Stakes: Jaz and anyone with the dog-vision ability will be experimented on and possibly die.

The stakes start with Jaz's life. In the second novel the stakes are raised, because they now include her daughter. In the third and final novel, the stakes are even higher, because they include Jaz, her daughter, and anyone with the dog-vision ability.

So the answer to "Are the stakes higher in each consecutive novel?" is yes.

Is the Climax Scene Different in Each Book?

Without knowing what happens in the scene, you can answer this question. The climax scene must address the story goal.

Evolution Series (book one) Goal: find out who killed her husband, using her ability to see into a dog's mind.

Evolution Series (book two) Goal: find out who is trying to take her daughter.

Evolution Series (book three) Goal: discover and eliminate the organization testing the ability on humans;.

By having the goal be different for each book in the series, we know we can create climax scenes that are different from each other.

So the answer to "Does each novel have a different climax scene?" is yes.

Does the Climax Scene Mirror a Story Arc Scene from Book One?

We know the following is the main event in the inciting incident: Jaz saves a dog's life and gains the ability to see into the dog's mind.

We know the following is the main event for the climax scene in book three: Jaz shuts down the experimentation center using her ability to see into a dog's mind.

This shows us the mirror is going to be the dog-vision part of the scene. In the inciting incident, Jaz gains the ability to see into a dog's mind. In the climax she uses the ability to eliminate the experimentation center.

So the answer to "Does the Climax Scene Mirror a Story Arc Scene from Book One?" is yes.

We've answered all four questions with "yes" and are confident we have a strong enough concept to support a series. This is great news for us.

Your Fun Series Task

For a closed series, perform the Series Structure Test by answering these four questions:

1. Does the climax scene in the final novel address the series story goal?
2. Are the stakes higher in each consecutive novel?
3. Does each have a different climax scene?
4. Does the climax scene of the series (the last novel in the series) mirror one of the story arc scenes in one of the previous novels?

If you passed the test, congratulations.

If you didn't pass the test, go back to "Chapter Five: Meet Your Skeleton Blurbs" and go through the process again with the Series Structure Test in mind. Doing this work now will set you up for a structurally sound series.

Where to Next?

We're at another moment to celebrate. You've created the foundation for your series. That's super exciting.

When you're done celebrating, we'll start adding more depth to your series. At any time, you can start writing. This is up to you. You're the artist, and the process should be fun.

You know what your series is about. You even know what each novel is about. This puts you in a great place to look at the setup and resolution of each book in the context of the series.

You can either read the next section on open series, or you can skip to "Part Four: Add Depth to Your Series."

PART THREE: OUTLINE YOUR OPEN SERIES

Chapter Fifteen: Meet the Open Series Story Arc

In "Chapter Seven: Meet the Story Arc," we looked into how important a story arc is as a foundation for great stories. In this chapter, we'll cover an open series (open number of novels in the series), and the way the story arc works for an open series.

We're going to show you how to harness each novel's story arc to create unity across a series. There are structural connections you can create between each novel using the story arc scenes.

This method is not prescriptive. It is a form, not a formula, and you are in control of it. Also remember, even if you build these into your story, not every reader will notice them, as they will bring their own experiences to reading your novel. It will also open up new possibilities that will allow you to see how to strengthen your series unity.

In an open series, there are patterns to the story arc scenes across the series.

The open series story arc scenes must resonate through the series; otherwise, the series will not hold together. The great news is we have a simple process that you can follow as a beginner to writing a series, and you can use templates when you become more advanced.

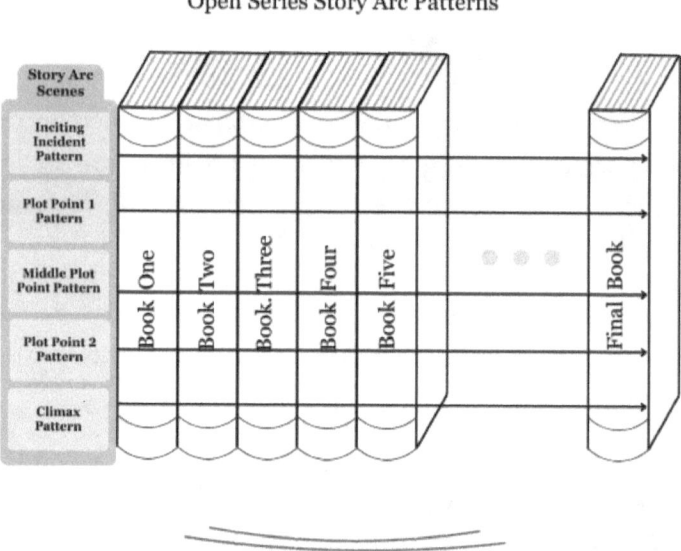

Open Series Story Arc Patterns

The Structure of the Story Arc Scenes

An open series does not have an overarching series story arc that has the series inciting incident in book one and the climax in the final book. But they do have the same tone and similar content, and they bring the reader back because the novels are similar but different.

Similarities in Story Arc Scenes

You've created your skeleton blurbs for your first three novels in your series and a generic skeleton blurb for the series. We are going to use these to create main events for each novel's story arc scenes.

Then you're going to work on creating the open series story arc unity. In case you didn't read "Chapter Eight: Meet the Closed Series Story Arc," we'll quickly recap a bit of theory for you.

The minimum number of scenes needed to create a story arc is five:

- Inciting incident
- Plot point 1
- Middle plot point
- Plot point 2
- Climax

All these scenes relate to how the protagonist addresses the story goal. This is critical for the open series.

In "Chapter Seven: Meet the Story Arc," we explained why there is no story if a story arc scene is missing. This applies to each novel in an open series. And if a story arc scene's open series unity is missing, then the reader may not understand why the novel was included in the series.

Open Series Single Novel Story Arc Examples

Creating a united series means creating story arc scenes that fulfill their roles in the novel and create a pattern throughout the series.

You'll create a main event for each story arc scene by using the duties a story arc must perform and combining that with patterns. You'll also add an event that makes the story arc scenes unique.

Strong story arc scenes fulfill the story arc duties, create a pattern across the series, and contain a unique storyline.

Where to Next?

We're going to delve into story arc patterns and show you how to make each novel's story arc scene have a pattern and still be unique. Once you see how this works, you'll never write without the patterns.

SECRETS TO WRITING A SERIES

Chapter Sixteen: Meet the Open Series Story Arc Patterns

We're going to bring all the open series theory together in this chapter and show you how to outline your first three novels. After you've set up the series unity and the series story arc patterns, you must check that each novel in the series is a unique story.

You've already decided what the uniting factor of your series will be. For an open series, you chose between character and setting. Refer to your series vault and make sure you're still happy with that decision.

Series unity is the high-level connection between the novels in the series. It's what makes the group of novels a series. To find patterns, it's helpful to outline the story arc scenes for the first three novels in the series.

To outline the first three novels in your series, you'll create the main events for each of these scenes. After you create the main events for three story arcs, you'll be able to find patterns in the story arc scenes. If you can't find any patterns, then you'll update the main events to create the patterns. These patterns will strengthen the series unity.

Without series unity, there is no series.

Readers are not looking for an identical story in every novel in an open series. They are looking for something similar but different.

There must be a balance between series unity, story arc patterns, and a unique story for each novel in the series.

Let's get started outlining the story arc scenes.

Open Series Story Arcs: Outline the Main Events

For an open series you've done the following:

- Decided you're writing an open series
- Decided whether the main series unity is character or setting
- Written a skeleton blurb for the first three novels
- Written the generic skeleton blurb for your series

We're going to outline the story arc scenes using the My Fairy Assassin series by creating the main events in each of the story arc scenes. That's three story arcs, and there are five story arc scenes in each novel, so we'll create fifteen main events. This covers the first three novels in the series.

You don't have to outline every scene in each novel to find the story arc patterns. The main events of the story arc scenes will highlight the main plot. In the next chapter, we'll use the main events to find story arc patterns.

In a closed series, the unity is found in the plot that spans the novels in the series.

SECRETS TO WRITING A SERIES

In an open series, the unity comes from character or settings and is found in patterns used in the story arc scenes across the novels in the series.

Just as in a closed series, you are looking at how to create a story arc. We'll create the main events for the story arc scenes:

1. Inciting incident
2. Plot point 1
3. Middle plot point
4. Plot point 2
5. Climax

We're going to establish the story arc pattern using the first three novels in your series. So when you write the fourth novel and the others that follow, that pattern will already be established, and the novels will be quicker to write.

Once established, this pattern can be changed—not all at once, but you can do it if you keep your series vault updated.

We'll look at two commercially successful series. The first is the Agatha Raisin series by M. C. Beaton, and this is a character-based series. The primary series unity is created by Agatha Raisin being the protagonist in every novel. There is a secondary unity created by setting. Agatha Raisin is an amateur sleuth, and each crime takes place in a small town in England.

The second series is the Bridgerton series by Julia Quinn. It's a setting-based series. The primary series unity is created by having every novel take place in Regency England. The unity exists because of the social constraints in place during that time period. There is a secondary unity using characters. Even though the protagonist changes in each novel, the character is always one of the Bridgerton siblings.

The series unity in the My Fairy Assassin series is character, because Liv Wright is the protagonist for each novel.

Agatha Raisin: A Character-Based Open Series

This section will show the story arc patterns for the first three novels in this series. Before we can check for patterns, we need to know what each novel is about. To do that, we need the skeleton blurbs.

Agatha Raisin Skeleton Blurbs

We wrote the skeleton blurbs for the first three books in the Agatha Raisin series.

Agatha Raisin and The Quiche of Death (book one): Agatha Raisin must find out who killed the judge at the local baking contest; otherwise, she might be killed.

Agatha Raisin and The Vicious Vet (book two): Agatha Raisin must find out who killed the local vet; otherwise, she might be killed.

Agatha Raisin and The Potted Gardener (book three): Agatha Raisin must find out who killed a woman romantically interested in her neighbor; otherwise, she might be killed.

By writing the skeleton blurbs for the three books, we were able to write the following generic series skeleton blurb:

Agatha Raisin must solve the murder that happened in her Cotswold village; otherwise, she might be killed.

This gives us our first pattern. For each novel, the reader expects that Agatha will solve a murder. By having Agatha Raisin solve the murder in each novel, the character unity is supported.

Agatha Raisin Story Arc Patterns

We are going to look at the main events in the story arc scenes and search for patterns. The main event we look at is the author-controlled main event. This is the reason the author has put this scene into the story.

In open series like Agatha Raisin, there is a quality of growth through the series. Things change. Agatha goes from being an amateur sleuth to a professional investigator.

Let's look at the story arc scenes for the first three novels and see if we can find a pattern.

Inciting Incident

The Quiche of Death (book one): Agatha eats a meal at the quiche-eating murder victim and murderer's house.

The Vicious Vet (book two): Agatha meets the new vet, who turns out to be the murder victim.

The Potted Gardener (book three): Agatha meets the village's new gardening fanatic, who turns out to be the murder victim.

The story arc pattern: the inciting incident is the main event that leads to the murder, and the event is always her meeting either the victim or the murderer.

Plot Point 1

The Quiche of Death (book one): Agatha learns the judge is dead from eating her quiche.

The Vicious Vet (book two): Agatha learns the vet has died the day after her date with him.

The Potted Gardener (book three): Agatha decides to beat the fanatic gardener and have the best garden in the village. Spoiler alert: this works because the fanatic gardener ends up being the murder victim, and Agatha is a suspect. The stakes are that she feels she is losing her position in the village.

The story arc pattern: Agatha is connected to each murder victim.

Middle Plot Point

The Quiche of Death (book one): Agatha is convinced the judge was murdered and it was not an accident.

The Vicious Vet (book two): The police ask Agatha not to investigate, and she ignores their request.

The Potted Gardener (book three): Agatha is interviewed about finding the body, and she wants to prove her innocence.

The story arc pattern does not come from finding the body in a particular story arc scene but comes from Agatha Raisin discussing the murder with the police. Each novel handles this scene differently.

Plot Point 2

The Quiche of Death (book one): Agatha discovers where the quiche was made. This is the quiche that killed the judge, the same quiche she entered into the competition.

The Vicious Vet (book two): Agatha discovers women were being blackmailed by the murder victim. This is also the man she dated.

The Potted Gardener (book three): Agatha discovers the murderer is the only one who speaks well of the victim. The victim was Agatha's main competition in the village for creating the best garden.

Each novel puts Agatha at her lowest point in the novel. This point is created by the story arc pattern. The story arc pattern is that Agatha discovers something that makes it look like she is the murderer.

Climax

The Quiche of Death (book one): Agatha confronts the murderer, and the murderer poisons and tries to kill Agatha in a house fire.

The Vicious Vet (book two): Agatha confronts the murderer, and the murderer tries to kill Agatha with the vet injections.

The Potted Gardener (book three): Agatha confronts the murderer, and the murderer kills his fish and himself.

The story arc pattern is Agatha confronting the murderer. The unique factor is how the murderer reacts to the confrontation. This creates climax scenes that are unique but similar.

The Bridgerton Series: A Setting-Based Open Series

The Bridgerton series' primary uniting factor is the setting. There is an underlying uniting factor using character, because a different Bridgerton family member is the protagonist in each novel.

Using tropes is a common story arc pattern for romance series, including historical romance novels. Not all open series novels must follow this, and we're using it to show the pattern that Julia Quinn follows in her historical romance novels.

The story arc patterns are where the main event for the story arc scene is the same from the higher-level viewpoint but different in the finer details.

Tropes Can Help Find the Factor

Using tropes helps the writer make each novel in the series be similar but still unique.

The Duke and I—Daphne's Story (book one) Trope: fake dating.

The Viscount Who Loved Me—Anthony's Story (book two) Trope: enemies to lovers.

An Offer from a Gentleman—Benedict's Story (book three): forbidden love.

The Willow Springs series by Laura Pavlov is another example of a series that uses tropes in the novel's title. By having the author put the trope in the book title, readers know quickly that this story is one that promises their favorite trope.

Frayed: A Small Town Sports Romance (Willow Springs Series, Book One)

Tangled: A Small Town, Brother's Best Friend Romance (Willow Springs Series, Book Two)

Charmed: A Small Town Enemies-to-Lovers Romance (Willow Springs Series, Book Three)

The Bridgerton Series Skeleton Blurbs

We wrote the skeleton blurbs for the first three books in the Bridgerton series. The blurbs help us create a generic series skeleton blurb so we can remind ourselves of the series unity.

The Duke and I—Daphne's Story (book one): Daphne must show Simon he's worthy of a full family life; otherwise, she won't find true love with Simon.

The Viscount Who Loved Me—Anthony's Story (book two): Anthony must overcome his fear of early death; otherwise, he won't find true love with Kate.

An Offer from a Gentleman—Benedict's Story (book three): Benedict must overcome the social judgement due to Sophie's birth; otherwise, he won't find true love with Sophie.

We used the three skeleton blurbs to write the generic series skeleton blurb:

A Bridgerton family member must overcome obstacles; otherwise, they won't find true love with love their interest.

The Bridgerton Series Story Arc Patterns

The main events for the story arc scenes in the first three novels show the story arc patterns.

Inciting Incident

The Duke and I—Daphne's Story (book one): Daphne meets Simon at a ball.

The Viscount Who Loved Me—Anthony's Story (book two): Anthony meets Kate at a ball.

An Offer from a Gentleman—Benedict's Story (book three): Benedict meets Sophie at a ball.

The story arc pattern in the inciting incident: the love interests meet for the first time at a ball. Quinn does this in an amazing way. There is something scandalizing about the way the characters meet. This is what keeps the scenes similar but different.

Plot Point 1

The Duke and I—Daphne's Story (book one): Simon offers Daphne a fake dating relationship to avoid other suitors.

The Viscount Who Loved Me—Anthony's Story (book two): Anthony kisses Kate to teach her a lesson, but they are still enemies.

An Offer from a Gentleman—Benedict's Story (book three): Benedict saves Sophie the housemaid from three brutes. She is a servant, and he is an aristocrat.

The story arc pattern is related to the romantic trope in the series. In each book there is a trope that the plot follows. Book one is fake dating. Book two is enemies to lovers. Book three is forbidden love. This story arc pattern comes from why the relationship won't work. This keeps these scenes similar but different.

Middle Plot Point

The Duke and I—Daphne's Story (book one): Daphne saves Simon from a duel.

The Viscount Who Loved Me—Anthony's Story (book two): Anthony saves Kate from a nightmare.

An Offer from a Gentleman—Benedict's Story (book three): Benedict saves Sophie from destitution by getting her a job in his mother's house.

This feeds into the story arc pattern that shows their love will save them—which, being a romance, shows love conquers all. This literal saving foreshadows how love will save them in the end.

Plot Point 2

The Duke and I—Daphne's Story (book one): Daphne is abandoned in her husband's ancestral home because he cannot commit to the relationship, so Daphne leaves for London.

The Viscount Who Loved Me—Anthony's Story (book two): Anthony leaves Kate because he realizes he loves her, and he thinks he is going to die young.

An Offer from a Gentleman—Benedict's Story (book three): Benedict leaves Sophie because he finds out she is illegitimate.

Between the middle plot point and plot point 2 in the first two books, the protagonist and the love interest get married. This does not happen in book three, meaning the marriage is not as important to the story as being able to be with someone they love. In the third book, they are not married until after the climax.

The story arc pattern occurs when each Bridgerton protagonist leaves their love interest because of a misunderstanding.

Climax

The Duke and I—Daphne's Story (book one): Daphne and Simon proclaim their love to each other after the Bridgerton brothers barge into their home.

The Viscount Who Loved Me—Anthony's Story (book two): Anthony and Kate proclaim their love to each other after a carriage crash.

An Offer from a Gentleman—Benedict's Story (book three): Benedict and Sophie proclaim their love to each other after Sophie is released from prison.

In each of the books, the Bridgerton protagonists say "I love you" for the first time. This keeps the scenes similar but different. The pattern of keeping scenes similar but different is a pattern in itself.

Chapter Seventeen: Create the Open Series Story Arc Patterns

My Fairy Assassin Story Arc Scenes

To create patterns across the My Fairy Assassin series, we'll outline three novels. When we have three novels outlined, we'll see the story arc patterns or we'll update the main events in the story arc scenes to create patterns. We'll use these patterns across any new novels we write in the series.

Let's remind ourselves of the skeleton blurbs for the My Fairy Assassin series and for book one. You have this information for your series in your series vault. Feel free to refer to it now and work along with us.

My Fairy Assassin Series Skeleton Blurb

Liv Wright must use the fairy time portal to save family members; otherwise, this world's worst person will end the world.

My Fairy Assassin Skeleton Blurb (book one)

Liv Wright must use the fairy time portal to save her fairy assassin sister; otherwise, a scientist will destroy the world.

My Fairy Assassin Series (book one) Story Arc Scenes

We'll start with plot point 1, as we can pull the main event directly from the skeleton blurb. We know plot point 1 is where Liv accepts the story goal of saving her sister. For Liv to use a time portal, the stakes must be dire, so we decided her sister is dying.

We decided the main event in plot point 1 is that Liv's sister is dying, and Liv must learn to time-travel to save her.

This leads us to the main event in the inciting incident. This is where Liv learns her sister is in trouble, but she doesn't understand she can help her.

We decided the main event in the inciting incident is that Liv discovers her sister is not dead yet but is stuck in a dying fairy world.

Plot point 2 will be the lowest point in the novel for Liv, and it will also mirror plot point 1.

We decided the main event in plot point 2 is that the time portal fails, and Liv cannot save her sister.

For the climax, we decided Liv is going to achieve the story goal. We decided the main event in the climax is that Liv saves her sister by reopening the time portal and injuring the scientist.

For the middle plot point, Liv must move from reactive to proactive. She needs to save her sister, and she needs a time portal.

We decided the main event in the middle plot point is that Liv time-travels to save her sister.

We'll look for structural unity across all the novels in the series, so knowing the story arc scenes for only book one is not enough to find this unity. We need the main events for the five story arc scenes in book two and book three. Once you know this for three books, you'll be able to create it for book four and so on.

Some of the story arc scenes will not have as much structural unity as others. And this is OK.

Once we start to see patterns, we'll update the series vault for each novel in the series. We'll also look for factors that make each novel unique.

My Fairy Assassin Series (book two) Story Arc Scenes

For book two in the My Fairy Assassin series, we know the skeleton blurb. We also know the main events for the story arc scenes in book one. To work along with us, refer to your series vault and review your book two skeleton blurb.

My Fairy Assassin (book two) Skeleton Blurb

> Liv Wright must use the fairy time portal to save her fairy saboteur mother; otherwise, a druid will destroy the world.

The first open series unity is about saving a family member. Each skeleton blurb shows us that Liv must save a family member. We'll be careful that the way she saves each member is different in each novel.

When we create the main events for the story arc scenes for series unity, we know we want similar plots, but we also know we want to have different outcomes. In book one of the My Fairy Assassin series, Liv defeated the antagonist (the scientist), but he did not get punished as she wished. This created a bittersweet ending. The challenge is to create a bittersweet ending in book two that happens differently than in book one.

We also know that My Fairy Assassin is a time-travel series. Liv will be traveling to a different time period in each novel. This is part of the series structure. Our first decision is what time period Liv will travel to.

This is purely an artistic decision based on the author's (in this case, Lucy's) interests.

The chosen time period was 77 CE.

We started by creating the main event for plot point 1. Here we got grounded by referring to the story goal. Liv's mother is a saboteur, and so we asked ourselves, What terrible action could she take? During the time period, the Romans were sacking Anglesey. Terrible actions happened there, so we're going to build on that.

We'll start with plot point 1. We know the book two skeleton blurb goal. Liv Wright must use the fairy time portal to save her fairy saboteur mother. From our research into the time period, we know that druids existed and dwelled among oak groves. This makes a strong match with the fairy theme. So plot point 1 is going to have something to do with Liv's mom, the druids, and sabotage.

We decided the following will be the main event for plot point 1 in book two:

Liv discovers her mother was caught sabotaging the Druid's oak grove, and Liv must time-travel to save her.

To help find the inciting incident for book two, let's go to the series vault and get our main event for the inciting incident of book one.

My Fairy Assassin Series (book one) Inciting Incident Main Event

Liv finds her sister is not dead but is stuck in a dying fairy world.

Here Liv discovers a family member is in danger. To create a story arc pattern, we can put another of Liv's family members in danger. This will give us character and plot unity.

In plot point 1, Liv's mother was caught sabotaging the druid's oak grove, so the inciting incident has to lead to this.

We decided that the following is the main event for the inciting incident in book two:

> *Liv discovers her mother was kidnapped by druids from Anglesey during 77 CE.*

In our process, we looked at the climax scene next. In book one of the My Fairy Assassin series, we made the ending bittersweet, so we want to do that again if we want to create a story arc pattern with the climax scenes.

We referred to our series vault and reviewed the main event for the climax in book one.

Climax: Liv saves her sister by reopening the time portal and injuring the scientist.

We see Liv save her sister. For a story arc pattern, we need Liv to at least try to save her mother. This gives us both plot and character unity. The plot unity comes from Liv trying to save a family member. The character unity comes from Liv, a family member, and the antagonist being in the scene. The antagonist was injured in the climax, so we can do the same or worse in book two.

We want to be careful that we make the climax scene different from the climax scene in book one and still have unity. To do this, we decided Liv doesn't save her mother, but she does kill the antagonist (the druid). This gives us our bittersweet ending and adds a twist to the climax.

We decided that the following is the main event in the climax for book two:

Liv doesn't save her mother but kills the druid.

In plot point 2, we know Liv will be at her lowest point in the novel and that she will receive the final piece of information she needs to achieve the story goal.

In book one, the following was plot point 2: The time portal fails, and Liv cannot save her sister.

This time we don't want the time portal to fail, but we can't allow Liv's mother to successfully use the portal. We don't know the "how" yet, but the time portal won't allow Liv's mother to pass. We can figure out the "how" later.

We decided that the following is the main event in plot point 2 for book two:

> *The time portal won't allow Liv's mother to time-travel, and Liv cannot save her mother.*

We have to create only the middle plot point for book two, and then we can move on to book three. Let's get the main event for the middle plot point in book one from our series vault.

The following is the main event for the middle plot point in book one: Liv time-travels to save her sister.

We see that Liv gets proactive and decides to time-travel to save a family member. The series unity can come from plot and character. The action can stay the same. The family members will change.

When we write this scene, we'll make sure that the way Liv time-travels is different in book two; otherwise, the reader will feel like they are reading book one again. There must be a balance between series unity and creating a unique story for each novel in the series. Remember the secret from the start of the chapter? It is so important we're going to repeat it here.

There must be a balance between series unity, story arc patterns, and creating a unique story for each novel in the series.

We decided that the following is the main event in the middle plot point for book two:

Liv time-travels to save her mother.

And just like that, we've outlined book two of the My Fairy Assassin series.

My Fairy Assassin Series (book two) Story Arc Scenes

Inciting Incident: Liv discovers her mother was kidnapped by druids from Anglesey during 77 CE.

Plot Point 1: Liv discovers her mother was caught sabotaging the druid's oak grove.

Middle Plot Point: Liv time-travels to save her mother.

Plot Point 2: The time portal won't allow Liv's mother to time-travel, and Liv cannot save her mother.

Climax: Liv doesn't save her mother but kills the druid.

As you read this outline, you can see that book one and book two have story unity by creating story arc patterns.

Now we are going to work on book three of the My Fairy Assassin series.

For book three in the series, we know the skeleton blurb. We also know the main events for the story arc scenes in book one and book two.

My Fairy Assassin Series (book three) Skeleton Blurb: Liv Wright must use the fairy time portal to save her fairy enforcer aunt; otherwise, an alchemist will destroy the world.

Let's remember that there were similarities with the main events for the story arc in book one and book two, but we also need to focus on different outcomes while still creating a story arc pattern.

In book one of the My Fairy Assassin series, Liv defeated the antagonist (the scientist), but he did not get punished as she wished. In book two, Liv doesn't save her mother but kills the druid and saves the world. Both are bittersweet. They both leave with Liv achieving part of the story goal. We'll try to create another bittersweet ending to book three.

The series unity is character because Liv Wright is the protagonist for each novel in the series.

The following are the story arc patterns for the first two novels:

Inciting Incident: Liv finds out a family member is in danger.

Plot Point 1: Liv accepts she is the one who has to save them.

Middle Plot Point: Liv time-travels.

Plot Point 2: The time portal breaks.

Climax: There is a bittersweet ending.

We will go into this in more detail when we have outlined the main events in three books. This process of finding the patterns gets easier when you have the first story outlined.

The following are the differences between the first two novels in the open series:

- Character: Liv must save a different family member.
- Plot: The climax changes in its bittersweet ending for each novel.
- Setting: The time period changes in each novel.

My Fairy Assassin Series (book three) Story Arc Scenes

In both book one and two of the My Fairy Assassin series, Liv time-travels. For book three, Liv will travel to a third time period. This is part of the series structure and unity.

Our first decision is the time period that Liv will travel to in book three.

This is another artistic decision based on the author's (Lucy's) interests.

The chosen time period is the 1840s.

Again, we started by outlining plot point 1 first. According to the skeleton blurb, Liv is trying to save her aunt. Liv's aunt is an enforcer, and so we asked ourselves. What could she be enforcing? During the time period, the world is experiencing a mini ice age. We're going to build on those events.

The method is the same as we used for book two. We created the main events for plot point 1, the inciting incident, plot point 2, the climax, and then the middle plot point.

We started with plot point 1. We know book three's skeleton blurb goal: Liv Wright must use the fairy time portal to save her fairy enforcer aunt.

What if the mini ice age was started on purpose? What kind of person unleashes a mini ice age, and why would they do that? It must be someone who is solely focused on their goal and believes the consequences are worth creating a disaster. How about an alchemist? Our alchemist won't worry about the consequences of achieving his goal.

Whenever there is an ice age, you can be sure that humanity blames the ice giants, which makes a strong match with the fairy theme. Plot point 1 is going to have something to do with Liv's aunt, ice giants, and enforcement. What would make a fairy enforcer need help?

We decided the following is the main event for plot point 1 in book three:

> Liv discovers her aunt is locked in an ice block in the Himalayas.

On to book three's inciting incident. Let's go to the series vault and get our main event for the inciting incident of book one and book two.

My Fairy Assassin Series (book one) Inciting Incident Main Event

> Liv finds her sister is not dead but is stuck in a dying fairy world.

My Fairy Assassin Series (book two) Inciting Incident Main Event

> *Liv discovers her mother was kidnapped by druids from Anglesey during 77 CE.*

The inciting incident in the first two novels shows Liv discovering a family member is in danger. To create unity, we need to put Liv's aunt in danger.

We know in plot point 1 that Liv's aunt was caught in an ice block in the Himalayas, so the inciting incident has to lead to this.

With this in mind, we decided the following is the main event for the inciting incident in book three:

> *Liv finds out her aunt has joined the ice giants in 1849.*

In our process, we look at the climax scene next. In book one and book two, we made the ending bittersweet, so we want to do that again, as we want to create series unity.

We referred to our series vault and reviewed the main event for the climax in book one: Liv saves her sister by reopening the time portal and injuring the scientist.

The main event for the book two climax scene: Liv doesn't save her mother but kills the druid.

In book three, we want Liv to be successful in saving her aunt, but perhaps the alchemist could get away and cause issues in future novels. Remember, the plot unity for the series comes from Liv trying to save a family member. The antagonist was injured in the climax in book one, and the druid is killed in book two, so we need to consider what happens to the alchemist in book three.

In an open series, the goal is to make each climax scene different from the previous climax scenes but still have series unity.

To do this, we decided Liv saves her aunt, but the antagonist and his ice giants get away. This gives us our bittersweet ending and potential for novels in the future.

We decided the following is the main event in the climax for book three:

> *Liv saves her aunt, but the alchemist and his ice giants escape.*

In plot point 2, we know Liv will be at her lowest point in the novel and that she will receive the final piece of information she needs to achieve the story goal.

In book one, the following is plot point 2: The time portal fails, and Liv cannot save her sister.

In book two, the following is plot point 2: The time portal won't allow Liv's mother to time-travel, and Liv cannot save her mother.

In book three, the weather plays an important role in creating conflict in the story. The ice age is a problem for Liv.

We decided the following is the main event in plot point 2 of book three:

> *The weather has frozen the time portal, so Liv cannot save her aunt.*

Let's get the main event for the middle plot point in book one and book two from our series vault.

The following is the main event for the middle plot point in book one: Liv time-travels to save her sister.

In both novels, we see that Liv gets proactive and decides to time-travel to save a family member. The series unity can come from plot and character. The action can stay the same. The family members will change.

When we write this scene, we'll make sure that the way Liv time-travels is different in book three.

We decided the following is the main event in the middle plot point for book two:

> *Liv time-travels to save her aunt.*

And just like that, we've outlined book three of the My Fairy Assassin series.

Book Three Skeleton Blurb: Liv Wright must use the fairy time portal to save her fairy enforcer aunt; otherwise, an alchemist will destroy the world.

Book Three Story Arc Scenes

Inciting Incident: Liv finds out her aunt has joined the ice giants in 1849.

Plot Point 1: Liv discovers her aunt is locked in an ice block in the Himalayas.

Middle Plot Point: Liv time-travels to save her aunt.

Plot Point 2: The weather has frozen the time portal, and Liv cannot save her aunt.

Climax: Liv saves her aunt, but the alchemist and his ice giants get away.

Your Fun Series Task

This is where you get to create the main events for the story arc scenes in the first three novels.

1. Create the main events for the story arc scenes in book one of your series.
2. Add those to your story vault.
3. Create the main events for the story arc scenes in book two of your series.
4. Add those to your story vault.
5. Create the main events for the story arc scenes in book three of your series.
6. Add those to your story vault.
7. Find the story arc patterns for the inciting incident, plot point 1, the middle plot point, plot point 2, and the climax.
8. Add the story arc patterns to your series vault.
9. Update the series vault with new patterns as they come to you.

My Fairy Assassin Series Vault:

SECRETS TO WRITING A SERIES

Vault Heading	My Fairy Assassin Book One
Inciting Incident	Liv discovers her sister is not dead yet but is stuck in a dying fairy world.
Plot Point 1	Liv's sister is dying, and Liv must learn to time travel to save her.
Middle Plot Point	Liv time travels to save sister.
Plot Point 2	The time portal fails, and Liv cannot save her sister.
Climax	Liv saves her sister by reopening the time portal and injuring the scientist.

Vault Heading	My Fairy Assassin Book Two
Inciting Incident	Liv discovers her mother was kidnapped by druids from Anglesey during 77 CE.
Plot Point 1	Liv discovers her mother was caught sabotaging the druid's oak grove.
Middle Plot Point	Liv time-travels to save her mother.
Plot Point 2	The time portal won't allow Liv's mother to time-travel, and Liv cannot save her mother.
Climax	Liv doesn't save her mother but kills the druid.

Vault Heading	My Fairy Assassin Book Three
Inciting Incident	Liv finds out her aunt has joined the ice giants in 1849.
Plot Point 1	Liv discovers her aunt is locked in an ice block in the Himalayas.
Middle Plot Point	Liv time-travels to save her aunt.
Plot Point 2	The weather has frozen the time portal, and Liv cannot save her aunt.
Climax	Liv saves her aunt, but the alchemist and his ice giants get away.

Vault Heading	My Fairy Assassin Story Arc Patterns
Inciting Incident	Liv finds out a family member is in danger
Plot Point 1	Liv accepts she is the one who has to save them.
Middle Plot Point	Liv time-travels.
Plot Point 2	The time portal breaks.
Climax	There is a bittersweet ending.

Where to Next?

Now it's time to test whether you have enough to support a series. The Series Structure Test gives you an objective way to determine whether you're ready to move forward with your series.

Chapter Eighteen: Open Series Structure Test

You've decided to write an open series. Just like a closed series, you'll want to make sure it's structurally sound.

1. Is there a setting or a character that unites all novels?
2. Is each novel a stand-alone story?
3. Does each novel address the open series story goal in an "answered for now" way?
4. Does each novel have different story arc scenes?

Let's use the Bridgerton series by Julia Quinn as an example.

The Bridgerton series is a Regency-set series based on the Bridgerton family.

We wrote the skeleton blurbs for the first three novels in the series.

The Duke and I (book one):

Daphne must show Simon he's worthy of a full family life; otherwise, she won't find true love with Simon.

The Viscount Who Loved Me (book two):

Anthony must overcome his fear of early death; otherwise, he won't find true love with Kate.

An Offer from a Gentleman (book three):

Benedict must overcome the social judgement due to Sophie's birth; otherwise, he won't find true love with Sophie.

This led us to writing a generic series skeleton blurb for the Bridgerton series:

> *A Bridgerton family member must overcome obstacles; otherwise,*
>
> *they won't find true love with love their interest.*

Each novel must show different obstacles and different reasons the love interests can't be together.

By writing a generic skeleton blurb that fits every novel in the series, we can see the series unity, but it's not enough to show us that the concept for the series is strong enough to support a series.

The unity for this series is the time period and the family. The family is large enough to create individual love stories around different family members. There are four brothers and four sisters in the Bridgerton family.

Let's answer our four questions from the open Series Structure Test.

1. Is there a setting or a character that unites all novels?
   Yes. The setting, along with the time period, is the primary uniting factor. The siblings in the Bridgerton family are the characters that create the secondary unity across the series.
2. Is each novel a stand-alone story?
   Yes. Each novel is a romance between a Bridgerton sibling and another character. That story goal is addressed by the end of each novel.
3. Does each novel address the open series story goal in an "answered for now" way?
   Yes. Each novel foreshadows that one by one the Bridgerton siblings will face obstacles when it comes time to find a spouse. The goal is "answered for now" in each book, because it is answered for one sibling and not all of

them.
4. Does each novel have different story arc scenes?
Yes. Each novel's story arc scenes contain an event unique to the protagonist for that novel. In each climax scene, love is declared but in a different manner.

It's no surprise that the Bridgerton series passes the Series Structure Test. Not only was it commercially successful as a series of novels, but it's also a commercially successful TV series.

My Fairy Assassin Series Structure Test

Let's review the Series Structure Test and determine whether the My Fairy Assassin series passes the open Series Structure Test. We must answer the following questions:

1. Is there a setting or a character that unites all novels?
2. Is each novel a stand-alone story?
3. Does each novel address the open series story goal in an "answered for now" way?
4. Does each novel have different story arc scenes?

We turned to our series vault for the information we needed to answer our questions.

Series Skeleton Blurb:

Book One Skeleton Blurb: Liv Wright must use the fairy time portal to save her fairy assassin sister; otherwise, a scientist will destroy the world.

Book Two Skeleton Blurb: Liv Wright must use the fairy time portal to save her fairy assassin mother; otherwise, a druid will destroy the world.

Book Three Skeleton Blurb: Liv Wright must use the fairy time portal to save her fairy assassin aunt; otherwise, an alchemist will destroy the world.

Let's look at the questions:

1. Is there a setting or characters that unite all novels?
   Liv Wright is the protagonist for every novel in the series. She is the character that unites the novels.
2. Is each novel a stand-alone story?
   Yes. Liv Wright addresses each novel's specific story goal in the climax scene.
3. Does each novel address the story goal in an "answered for now" way?
   Yes. In each novel, Liv either saves a family member or she doesn't.
4. Does each novel have different story arc scenes?
   Yes. Liv does not fully achieve the story goal in each novel. The method in which she saves a family member—or not—will be different in each novel.

This gives us confidence that we have enough of an idea to support a series. We know we will continue to make changes and update the skeleton blurbs as we outline. When that happens, we'll come back to this chapter and test whether the structure is strong.

Once we've outlined the first three novels in the series, we'll perform the Series Structure Test again.

Your Fun Series Task

For an open series, perform the Series Structure Test by answering these four questions:

1. Is there a setting or a character that unites all novels?
2. Is each novel a stand-alone story?
3. Does each novel address the open series story goal in an "answered for now" way?
4. Does each novel have different story arc scenes?

Where to Next?

You've passed the test! Well done. Now you get to add depth to your series.

PART FOUR: ADD DEPTH TO YOUR SERIES

Chapter Nineteen: The Setup of Each Novel in a Series

Now that you have created the framework for your series and passed the Series Structure Test, you can start building on that. With the framework in place, it should be easier to know what each novel needs for a setup and resolution.

We've come to the place in the journey where the process for a closed and open series joins together.

In a series the setup and resolution of each novel have more duties than in a stand-alone novel.

The setup is everything that comes before the inciting incident. The protagonist's ordinary world must be shown during the setup. Once the inciting incident happens, the ordinary world no longer exists.

For the main plot in each novel, you need at least the following scenes before the inciting incident for each novel in the series.

1. Opening image
2. Lead-up to the inciting incident

The resolution is everything that comes after the climax. For the main plot in each novel, you need at least the following scenes after the climax scene in each novel in the series.

1. Reaction to the climax
2. Resolution
3. Closing image

You can and probably will have more scenes than listed above. We're giving you a starting point. Each story is unique, so each story will have different needs for the setup and resolution.

This chapter will dive into the setup. The following chapter will cover the resolution.

Each novel in both a closed series and an open series builds on the previous novels. Book two and onward in the series brings a new challenge that doesn't exist in a stand-alone novel. Each novel in the series has an inciting incident. The new ordinary world lasts until the inciting incident in each novel.

*Each novel in a **closed series** must have an ordinary world that is different from the ordinary world in the previous novels.*

*Each novel in an **open series** must show the ordinary world, but in book two and onward the author must show that world quickly because the reader is already familiar with it.*

You have many choices on where to start each novel and what to include. Each series will be different, so how do you know what to include?

The story arc scenes and the skeleton blurbs come to the rescue. For a closed series, you know the story arc main events for the series. For an open series, you've listed the main events in the story arc scenes for multiple novels in your series. For both types of series, you can use this to determine where to start each novel and what to include.

The opening image is the first scene in a novel. The closing image is the last scene in a novel. The opening image must engage the reader quickly. The closing image in a single novel in a series must hook the reader so they want to read the next novel (unless it's the final novel).

In a single novel, the closing image should mirror the opening image. In a series, the closing image must work harder than in a stand-alone novel.

The Opening Image Versus the Ordinary World

There is a difference between opening images and the ordinary world.

The opening image happens on the first page of every novel. There is no flexibility in this. This is the first image the reader sees.

The ordinary world starts when the protagonist is introduced and ends at the inciting incident. This is because the inciting incident is what shakes up the protagonist's ordinary world. This could start at the same time as the opening image, but it doesn't have to.

If there is a prologue, it might show backstory and not the ordinary world. The Bridgerton series shows us a clear example of this. We'll get into that later in this chapter. Often the ordinary world starts in chapter one, but it doesn't have to.

The longer you wait to introduce the protagonist, the shorter time you have to show the ordinary world.

The opening image is always shown on the first page of a novel.

The ordinary world starts when the protagonist is introduced and ends at the inciting incident.

New Ordinary World

When you start a new novel in a series, you have decisions to make... again. You made decisions at the beginning of this process, and now we're going a level deeper. The answers to the following questions will help you determine what the opening image should be and what needs to be included in the ordinary world:

1. How much time has passed between novels?
2. What is the new ordinary world for the protagonist?
3. What information will be included in the backstory?
4. What information will be left out?

Did you notice that we said "new ordinary world" in the second point above? This is critical to the success of a series, especially for a closed series. By the end of a novel, the protagonist will either have succeeded or failed at achieving the story goal stated in the novel's skeleton blurb. Either way, their ordinary world will be different.

The start of the next novel in the series must show how the ordinary world is different. Some of this may have been shown in the previous novel after the climax scene. Now you have to show it in action to draw the reader into this novel too.

What to Include in a New Ordinary World

Focus on the main events that occur in the story arc scenes of previous novels. If they are not relevant, focus on what the reader needs to know about the characters or the settings that create the series unity.

The story arc scene contains events that have a profound effect on the protagonist, so the action in those scenes is most likely the information the readers need to know.

Closed Series Setup

The story arc scenes carry the spine of each novel in the series. Sharing the main events of previous novels in the series will help the reader remember what happened so they stay engaged in the current story. This is similar to streaming shows that offer an option to watch a recap. If the viewer hasn't watched the show in a while, they may need a reminder of what happened.

In a novel the reader is not given the choice, so they can't skip any repeated information. This means it's your job to choose only the events the reader needs to know to understand the novel they are reading.

Each novel in the series shows the new ordinary world of the protagonist. This means the inciting incident must show how it shakes up the new world. The protagonist will try to get a balance back to their life, and each inciting incident as the series progresses is going to make that harder.

If the ordinary world doesn't change from book one to book two, the series is going to drag. Just as in a stand-alone novel, if the inciting incident doesn't shake up the protagonist's ordinary world, the story will drag.

The Hunger Games Series Opening Images

We'll start with the opening images of the Hunger Games novels, because these show the reader the first part of the protagonist's ordinary world.

In *The Hunger Games* (book one), the opening image shows Katniss waking up to find that Prim is gone. Katniss is physically alone but emotionally connected to Prim.

In *Catching Fire* (book two), the opening image shows Katniss outside, alone and cold, dreading the day to come. She is physically alone but emotionally connected to Gale.

In *Mockingjay* (book three), the opening image shows Katniss staring at a missing bed that she used to share with Prim. She is physically alone but emotionally connected to Prim.

You most likely noticed the pattern of showing how Katniss is physically alone but connected emotionally to another character.

The Hunger Games Ordinary World

In *The Hunger Games* (book one), Katniss's ordinary world shows her trying to feed her family and avoid the Reaping. She feels trapped by her world. This lasts until she volunteers for the Reaping.

In *Catching Fire* (book two), Katniss's ordinary world shows she is wealthy and has an abundance of food for her family. This world lasts until the inciting incident, where President Snow reveals he knows about her defying the Capitol in the sequence with the poisonous berries. He threatens those she loves if she doesn't help calm the rebellion. She finds she's trapped in a worse way than in book one. She can feed her family but has lost her freedom.

In *Mockingjay* (book three), Katniss's ordinary world is now District 13. She lost her home in District 12. She is among strangers and feels alone against the Capitol. This world lasts until the inciting incident, where Katniss decides she is going to lead the rebellion and become the Mockingjay.

The Hunger Games trilogy gives us a clear example of how the protagonist's ordinary world is new in each novel. The inciting incident must lead to the main event in plot point 1. For *The Hunger Games* (book one), volunteering for the Hunger Games leads Katniss to plot point 1 of book one and to plot point 1 (poisonous berries) of the series.

In the main event in plot point 1 for the series, not plot point 1 for *The Hunger Games* (book one), Katniss doesn't know she accepts the series goal of taking down the Capitol when she decides to eat the poisonous berries. The reader might suspect it, as they know the series goal, but Katniss is unaware. By defying the Capitol, Katniss has kicked off the series of events that lead to her becoming the leader of the revolution. It's interesting to note that this is the end of act 1 and the beginning of act 2 for the series.

The inciting incident for both the Hunger Games series and *The Hunger Games* (book one) is the same scene. This is the scene at the end of chapter one, where Katniss volunteers to take her sister's place in the Hunger Games. Both the reader and the protagonist know the Reaping shook up the protagonist's ordinary life.

Let's see what else Suzanne Collins did.

1. How much time has passed between novels?
   The start of *Catching Fire* (book two) is one season after the first Hunger Games. The next games are about to begin. The start of *Mockingjay* (book three) is immediately after book two.
2. What is the new ordinary world for the protagonist?
   In *The Hunger Games* (book one), Katniss is poor and trying to feed her family. In *Catching Fire* (book two), Katniss's new ordinary world is as the winner of the Hunger Games, where she has wealth and an abundance of food. In *Mockingjay* (book three), Katniss is injured, she has lost District 12, and Peeta has been taken. Each new world is different for Katniss.
3. What information will be included in the backstory?
   In *Catching Fire* (book two), the reader is reminded of some of the key characters in *The Hunger Games* (book

one). They are also reminded that Katniss killed others in book one. We also learn how Katniss feels about Peeta and what that means for her in *Catching Fire* (book two). In *Mockingjay* (book three), the first chapter opens with backstory. This shows Katniss's home was destroyed in one of the previous books.

4. What information will be left out?
   In *Catching Fire* (book two), Suzanne Collins chose not to include how Katniss killed the others in *The Hunger Games* (book one). In *Mockingjay* (book three), Collins chose not to show how District 12 was destroyed or how Peeta was taken by the Capitol. She gives just enough information for the reader to understand these horrible events have happened, but not how.

The Divergent Series Opening Images

Let's cover the opening images of the Divergent novels, because these show the reader the first part of the protagonist's ordinary world.

In *Divergent* (book one), the opening image shows Tris with her mother.

In *Insurgent* (book two), the opening image shows Tris waking up on a moving train. She is with Tobias, and her first thought is the loss of Will (whom she shot in book one).

In *Allegiant* (book three), the opening image shows Tris with friends, locked in a jail cell.

Each opening image shows Tris in a worse place than in the previous novels. This raises the stakes in each novel.

The Divergent Series Ordinary World

In *Divergent* (book one), the ordinary world is Tris living with her parents in the Abnegation faction. This lasts until the inciting incident, where Tris takes a test that determines which faction she belongs to. She expects a clear result and that the test will show she is Abnegation. The test is inconclusive. This is the shakeup in her ordinary world. The setup is now over.

In *Insurgent* (book two), the ordinary world is Tris living without belonging to a faction among the Amity faction. This lasts until the inciting incident, where Tris learns that her birth faction, Abnegation, has a secret they are willing to die for. Her new ordinary life at Amity has just been shaken up.

In *Allegiant* (book three), the ordinary world is Tris living in jail, awaiting her sentence. This lasts until the inciting incident, where Tris sees a video revealing the purpose of divergents. This is the shakeup in Tris's ordinary world.

Each ordinary world is different from the previous ordinary world.

Veronica Roth made the following choices in the setup of *Insurgent* (book two) for her closed series. In plot point 2 of *Divergent* (book one), Tris kills her friend Will. She shoots him in self-defense. Early in books two and three, the reader learns this. The event is part of Tris's motivations and is crucial for the reader to understand why Tris behaves the way she does.

Let's see what decisions Roth made for the first two novels in her series.

1. No time passed between *Divergent* (book one) and *Insurgent* (book two).

2. In Tris's new ordinary world in *Insurgent* (book two), she has just left the Dauntless faction. She started *Divergent* (book one) in the Abnegation faction and chose Dauntless for her future. Her new ordinary world in *Insurgent* (book two) is life without a faction.
3. For backstory *Insurgent* (book two), Roth includes that Tris shot Will and Peter. She does not include the "how" or "why" of this. She's including the main event of *Divergent* (book one) plot point 2 in the backstory. This is similar to you creating a main event for each scene as you outline your series.
4. Roth leaves out details that will make the reader curious.
   a. She doesn't say who Marcus and Peter are in the opening scene.
   b. She includes that Tris has a shoulder injury but not that Tris was shot.

Open Series Setup

An open series has different challenges from the ones we found in a closed series. The main events in the story arc scenes may or may not be related to the current novel's story. Here it's important to look for events that are related to the series as a whole.

Character-Based Series

We're going to analyze the Stephanie Plum series by Janet Evanovich and the Agatha Raisin series by M. C. Beaton. Both are an open series about an amateur sleuth. The series unity comes from the characters.

The Stephanie Plum Series Opening Images

The Stephanie Plum series shows us an example of a series where the opening of every story is Stephanie getting assigned a new suspect to chase down and bring back.

One for the Money (book one): The opening image is written in backstory and shows Stephanie being warned off Joe Morelli by her mother.

Two for the Dough (book two): The opening image shows Stephanie alone in the dark with Ranger. He is the third part of the love triangle between Stephanie, Joe, and Ranger.

Three to Get Deadly (book three): The opening image shows Stephanie refusing a case. She is in the bail bond office with her cousin Vincent Plum.

You can see the pattern being set up. The first novel introduces the reader to Stephanie very quickly. The next two novels show the reader what the case will be for the story.

The Stephanie Plum Ordinary World

The Stephanie Plum series is unique because Stephanie's ordinary world doesn't change from novel to novel.

One for the Money (book one): The ordinary world shows Stephanie has a history with Joe Morelli going back to their teenage years, and then quickly gets to Stephanie losing her job. This is the setup for Stephanie to become a bounty hunter, where her first job is to hunt down Joe.

Two for the Dough (book two): In Stephanie's new ordinary world, she has the experience of one case. This novel opens with Ranger in action, watching for a criminal.

Three to Get Deadly (book three): Stephanie is on to her third case. The story world remains similar to the previous novels. It opens with Stephanie refusing a case while she's in a bail bond office.

This shows how Evanovich is creating the love triangle that will last for over thirty novels. She's foreshadowing which of the two men will have a major role in the novel.

Janet Evanovich made the following decisions with her Stephanie Plum open series.

1. How much time has passed between novels?
   No time has passed between novels. Evanovich chose to have each novel take place in the same historical time. This means things such as technology, fashion, and cars don't change from book to book. It's also the reason Stephanie Plum doesn't change much.
2. What is the new ordinary world for the protagonist?
   Stephanie's ordinary world doesn't change. She stays in the same time period, and she stays in the same job. This is what creates the series unity. We love this example because it shows how all story theory is only a guideline. The Stephanie Plum series was commercially successful even though it didn't create a new ordinary world in each novel.

This came down to an artistic choice.
3. What information was included in the backstory?
   There is very little backstory in any of the novel openings. Evanovich establishes the location. For backstory she established what Stephanie does for a job, what she looks like, and the backstory of others in the opening scene. One paragraph says that she works for Vincent Plum, and she makes money when people don't show up to court and she catches them. One paragraph describes who Ranger is. This is the backstory Evanovich chose to include, and it is all written in short paragraphs and mixed with action.
4. What information is left out?
   Janet Evanovich leaves out the information about the state of the love triangle. Near the end of each book, Morelli hints at things going further, but this is not addressed in the opening scene, so the reader will read on to find out how the backstory from the previous stories has developed.

Agatha Raisin Series Opening Images

M. C. Beaton makes a different decision about the timing of each novel than Janet Evanovich did for the Stephanie Plum series. Time moves forward in the Agatha Raisin series. This means technology, fashion, and cars must change from novel to novel. Agatha must also change. She grows from being an amateur sleuth to a detective. Choosing how you deal with time is important to how you'll write your series.

Agatha Raisin is a cozy mystery series, and the setup to each novel is about transporting the reader into the world of the Cotswolds. In each of the first three novels in the series, Agatha Raisin is coming to the village. In the first novel she is coming for the first time, and in the next two novels she is coming back from a holiday. Each time she describes what she sees.

The Quiche of Death (book one): The opening image shows Agatha Raisin sitting at her desk in London, England, about to begin her retirement.

The Vicious Vet (book two): The opening image shows Agatha arriving at Heathrow, London, airport. She's embarrassed about her behavior of chasing her neighbor romantically. She is returning from a holiday.

The Potted Gardener (book three): The opening image shows Agatha in her car, driving toward the village of Carsley. She is returning from a holiday.

Agatha Raisin Series Ordinary World

The Agatha Raisin series' ordinary world has similarities and differences in each novel.

The Quiche of Death (book one): The ordinary world is shown from Agatha's perspective, and she is leaving her life, her job, and everyone she knows. She is retiring to a "quiet" Cotswold village. And she is desperate to fit in.

The Vicious Vet (book two): The ordinary world is shown from Agatha's perspective. arriving at London's Heathrow Airport. She wants to know if she has been missed.

The Potted Gardener (book three): The ordinary world shows Agatha in her car, driving toward the village of Carsley. She is returning from a holiday.

M. C. Beaton created a pattern. Agatha is traveling to the Cotswold village in each story and paying attention to her surroundings. This is cunning, really, as the POV character notices changes and mentally comments on them.

As we mentioned, M. C. Beaton made different choices for her series than Janet Evanovich did for the Stephanie Plum series. Both series are character based. Both have a female protagonist who becomes an amateur sleuth.

The ordinary world is one place they differ. We'll use our four questions to illustrate the differences:

1. How much time has passed between novels?
   Agatha takes a break between novels and usually is just returning from a vacation. Time has passed.
2. What is the new ordinary world for the protagonist?
   For Agatha, she gains experience from the previous crime she solved. She becomes more part of the village. People warm up to her.
3. What information will be included in the backstory?
   These include Agatha Raisin's reasons she is nervous returning to the village, her village relationships with other characters, and what the village seems like after being away.
4. What information will be left out?
   The finer details of how the last crime was solved. There are hints of dealings with the police and previous cases, but the details aren't shown.

Setting-Based Series

The Bridgerton Series Opening Images

We wrote earlier that the series unity in the Bridgerton open series comes from the setting unity. The societal constraints mean that in every story, the reader comes back to find out how each character navigates these constraints.

The opening image of each novel is told in a prologue, and in that prologue we learn the impact the historical period has had on one of the love interests and something about their backstory.

The Duke and I (book one) shows Simon Basset's backstory as a child and his relationship with his father. This destructive relationship is the motivation for his behavior. Simon is Daphne Bridgerton's love interest, and it is his background that will impede Daphne from finding the path to their true love. The opening image is written from Simon's POV.

In *The Viscount Who Loved Me* (book two), the POV character for the prologue is Anthony Bridgerton. Anthony's loss of his father is the obstacle to his love for Kate.

In *An Offer from a Gentleman* (book three), the POV character for the prologue is Benedict Bridgerton's love interest, Sophie Beckett. The circumstances of her birth are the obstacle for them.

Readers may need a refresher on the world's rules, politics, and geography, especially in genres like fantasy or science fiction, and your series vault is going to help you.

The Bridgerton Series Ordinary World

The ordinary world is similar but different in each novel in the Bridgerton series.

The Duke and I (book one): The ordinary world is shown from Daphne Bridgerton's perspective. She is single and has had very few marriage proposals. In her ordinary world, there is intense pressure to get married, and she is holding out so she can marry someone she could be content with.

The Viscount Who Loved Me (book two): The ordinary world is shown from Kate Sheffield's POV. Kate is already twenty-one. She is unmarried. She has a sister everyone adores and wants to marry. She is ignored by all gentlemen suitors and is not interested in getting married.

An Offer from a Gentleman (book three): The ordinary world is shown from Sophie Beckett's POV. In her ordinary world, Sophie is living with a family that is not her own, and she is treated like a servant. She has no prospect of getting married or being included in London society.

A pattern is emerging here. The ordinary world shows the different obstacles women faced in the time period. Each woman's trouble is different, and this makes the novels unique within the series.

Julia Quinn answered our four questions in a way that created patterns in her series and strengthened the series unity.

1. How much time has passed between novels?
   Each novel starts in the next debutante season. This creates series unity by having the love story revolve around finding a spouse.
2. What is the new ordinary world for your protagonist?
   Each new ordinary world is based on the difficulties the female love interest experiences in trying to find a husband. Each new ordinary world is based on that character's backstory.
3. What information will you include in the backstory?
   This is a major technique used by Quinn. She bases the

character's difficulties on societal constraints. She also includes backstory via *Lady Whistledown's Society Papers* on why the love interest is not suitable. The backstory is used to create conflict and obstacles.
4. What information will you leave out?
   Each new novel shared only the minimum amount about the previous novels. The reader doesn't need to know the details, but a mention of the love affair might entice them to go back and read a previous novel in the series.

Where to Next?

We haven't given you a fun series task for this chapter, because it will be easier to create the opening and closing images together instead of trying to create all the opening images now. If you know the opening images now, please add them to your series vault and see if they stay the same after you work on the closing images.

We've covered how to open each novel and what to include in the setup. In the spirit of mirroring information, we're going to move to the end of novels and look at the resolution and closing images in a series.

Chapter Twenty: The Resolution of Each Novel in a Series

The resolution is everything that comes after the climax. For the main plot in each novel, you need at least the following scenes after the climax scene in each novel in the series:

1. Reaction to the climax
2. Resolution
3. Closing image

The closing image scene must flow into the first scene of the next novel in the series. This is called a series hook. Series hooks are questions that will keep the reader coming back to the series. These are similar to an exit hook that gets a reader to turn the page to the next scene, except now you're asking the reader to buy your next book.

The stakes are large, and a fine balance is needed between making the reader feel satisfied with the single novel and making them want to read the next novel. Let's cover the exit hook first. You can place an exit hook in any of the three scenes listed above.

If the exit hook is too large, the reader will be frustrated. For example, leaving a reader uncertain whether a major character is dead or alive could be too much. Leaving the reader without knowing whether the protagonist achieved the story goal for that novel is definitely too much. The reader will feel cheated. It can make them feel the author is forcing them to buy the next novel. And readers don't like to be forced.

The main story goal of a novel must be addressed in the climax scene of that novel. If it's not, the climax scene has not fulfilled its duties.

Now make sure the closing image doesn't reopen the main story goal for that novel. It can, however, open the series story goal.

In the resolution scene, if a reader has a question related to the skeleton blurb for the novel they are reading, it's the wrong question. If a question is related to the skeleton blurb for the next novel in the series, it's the right question.

In a closed series, finding the exit hook for book one and the entry hook for book two go together. Finding the exit hook for book two and the entry hook for book three also go together. If you can relate the exit hook of one novel in the series to the entry hook of the next novel in the series, the flow of the story across the novels will be strong.

The final novel in the series doesn't have an exit hook. All subplots are closed. The series skeleton blurb is addressed, and the reader is left satisfied.

Closing Image Examples

A closing image is the final image the reader is left with at the end of a single novel. It's shown in the final paragraph or two of the final scene.

The Hunger Games Series Closing Images (Closed Series)

The closing images in the Hunger Games trilogy show how Katniss is or is not alone.

The Hunger Games (book one) closes with Katniss holding hands with Peeta. They are together physically but alone emotionally.

Catching Fire (book two) closes with Katniss together with Gale, where she must face an awful truth. Prim is still alive, but District 12 has been destroyed. This is worse than the closing image in book one. They are together physically but alone emotionally. Using the closing image to mention Prim reminds the reader that Katniss's primary goal in the inciting incident was to save Prim. This is a strong way to foreshadow Prim's fate.

Mockingjay (book three) closes with Peeta and Katniss declaring love. The series closed with Katniss being physically and emotionally connected to another human.

Divergent Series Closing Images (Closed Series)

There is an interesting pattern in the closing images of each novel in the Divergent series. The first two novels end with Tris trying to figure out who she is, and the last novel ends with Tobias knowing who he is.

Divergent (book one) closes with Tris knowing she's factionless and has to figure out who she is.

Insurgent (book two) closes with Tris learning the purpose of the divergent (which is what she is). She must figure out what to do with the information.

Allegiant (book three) closes with Tobias mourning Tris's death but knowing who he is and that he is not broken.

Let's take a look at the final scene of *Divergent* (book one). Remember, this is a closed series, so there is a series story arc.

Just as a reminder, here is the series skeleton blurb and the book one skeleton blurb:

Series Skeleton Blurb

Tris must accept that she is divergent; otherwise, the people of Chicago will remain part of an experiment.

***Divergent* (book one) Skeleton Blurb**

Tris must successfully join the Dauntless; otherwise, she will live her life as factionless.

The final scene (closing image) is two paragraphs long. Tris is the POV character.

This is where the POV goal comes in. This POV goal is what the POV character is trying to achieve in the final scene. They might succeed, or they might fail, but either way, the result should raise new questions or create new challenges related to the series goal.

In essence, the ending of a novel in a series serves two purposes. It wraps up the story of that novel, but it also propels the overall series narrative forward, building anticipation for the next installment.

Think about the goals as facets of time. The novel's story goal was the past goal. It has been addressed in this novel. The present POV goal is what is happening in the closing image scene. And the series goal is the goal for the future. It's what the protagonist must still address.

In *Divergent* (book one), Tris started the story as a selfless member of the Abnegation faction. Then she chose the Dauntless faction, where she must be brave.

The middle of the final scene shows Tris thinking she has lost everything.

The climax of the final scene shows Tris learning she is not just selfless or brave. She is something else.

At the end of the final scene (the closing image), Tris's goal is to figure out what to do next.

The exit hook for the reader to keep reading is that we don't know what Tris is going to become or how she will survive without belonging to a faction.

Tris fails to achieve her book one goal of becoming a successful member of the Dauntless. In plot point 1, she chose the Dauntless as her new faction for life. At the end of this book, she can never go back to the Dauntless faction. The question is: What will she do next? The reader must read *Insurgent* (book two) to find out.

Opening and Closing Images Examples

Let's pull all the opening and closing images together so we can see how the single novels in our series examples flow.

The Hunger Games Opening and Closing Images

The Hunger Games **(book one)**

Opening Image: Katniss wakes up and Prim is gone. Katniss is physically alone but emotionally connected to Prim.

Closing Image: Katniss holding hands with Peeta. They are physically together but emotionally alone.

Catching Fire **(book two)**

Opening Image: Katniss is outside, alone, and cold, dreading the day to come. She is physically alone but emotionally connected to Gale.

Closing Image: Katniss is alone with Gale and must face an awful truth, worse than the truth of the closing image in book one. They are physically together but emotionally alone.

Mockingjay **(book three)**

Opening Image: Katniss is staring at a missing bed that she used to share with Prim. She is physically alone but emotionally connected to Prim.

Closing Image: Peeta and Katniss declare love. There is no more dread. They are physically and emotionally connected.

Divergent Series Opening and Closing Images

Divergent **(book one)**

Opening Image: Tris is with her mother, living in her home faction.

Closing Image: Tris knows she's factionless and has to figure out who she is.

Insurgent (book two)

Opening Image: Tris wakes up on a moving train. She is with Tobias, and her first thought is the loss of Will (whom she shot in book one).

Closing Image: Tris learns the purpose of the divergent (which is what she is). She must figure out what to do with the information.

Allegiant (book three)

Opening Image: Tris and her friends are locked in a jail cell.

Closing Image: Tobias is mourning Tris's death but knows who he is and that he is not broken.

Stephanie Plum Opening and Closing Images

One for the Money (book one)

Opening Image: This image is written in backstory from Stephanie's POV and shows Stephanie being warned off Joe Morelli by her mother.

Closing Image: This image has Stephanie and Joe Morelli sharing a pizza. Joe apologizes for his past behavior, but Stephanie is not in the mood to forgive him. Joe says he gives good pizza. The image leaves the reader wanting to know what happens after the last word.

Two for the Dough (book two)

Opening Image: Stephanie is alone in the dark with Ranger. He is the third part of the love triangle between Stephanie, Joe, and Ranger.

Closing Image: Stephanie half apologizes to Morelli for abandoning him, although she had left him with a gun. Morelli infuriates her, and she storms off, saying it is war. Morelli's last words for the book are: "I give good war." This leaves the reader wanting to know what happens after the last word.

Three to Get Deadly (book three)

Opening Image: Stephanie refuses a case. She is in the bail bond office with her cousin Vincent Plum.

Closing Image: Stephanie and Joe are discussing whether Joe will invite her to his house for a BBQ. The last image in the book is Joe kissing her neck, reminding her of their past flings—which were mentioned in the first chapter of book one—and she says Joe has sent a jolt of fire to her "doodah." This leaves the reader wanting to know what happens after the last word.

The sexual tension in all three books' closing images is strong. And this anticipation was built in from the first chapter of the first book. Janet Evanovich ties the unity back to the opening scene of book one using the closing images in the first three books. This is like an in-joke between the reader and the author. They feel they know the books, and the writer is delivering on their series promise each time.

Agatha Raisin Opening and Closing Images

The Quiche of Death (book one)

Opening Image: Agatha Raisin is sitting at her desk in London, England, about to begin her retirement.

Closing Image: Agatha and Bill, the policeman, chat that James is single. Agatha Raisin hammers in a post that renames her cottage "Raisin's Cottage," showing she wants to stay. This sets up the story for the next book, as the reader knows that Agatha will be chasing after James now.

The Vicious Vet (book two)

Opening Image: Agatha is arriving at London's Heathrow Airport. She's embarrassed about her behavior of chasing her neighbor romantically. She is returning from a holiday.

Closing Image: Freda, a village friend and former love rival for James, and Agatha stumble back drunk from the pub. Agatha sticks her finger up at James. She and Freda sing My Way. The reader will want to know how Agatha will deal with her embarrassment of being rude to James.

The Potted Gardener (book three)

Opening Image: Agatha is in her car driving toward the village of Carsley. She is returning from a holiday.

Closing Image (Epilogue): This is the first epilogue in the Agatha Raisin open series. This shows that you can still have unity, and patterns, and change things. Agatha has to pay back her debt to Pedmans and work in London for six months. Her last thought is that her village—Carsley—could wait. The reader is now wondering whether Agatha will go back to the village.

In each of the closing images, the reader wonders how Agatha will deal with the latest pickle she has gotten herself into. The entry into book four is slightly different from the previous books. She is coming back from her stint in London instead of from a holiday, but the effect will be the same. She is coming home to Carsley, wanting to know what has changed.

The Bridgerton Series Opening and Closing Images

Julia Quinn opens every novel in the Bridgerton series with a prologue. She closes every novel in the series with an epilogue. There is symmetry and consistency in this.

Just as a reminder, we are analyzing the first publication of the series, where only one epilogue was included in the single novels.

The Duke and I (book one)

Opening Image (Prologue): This shows Simon Basset's backstory as a child and his relationship with his father. This bad relationship is the motivation for his behavior. The POV character for book one's prologue is Daphne's love interest, Simon, and it is his background that will impede Daphne from finding the path to their true love.

Closing Image (Epilogue): The final image in the epilogue is the start of the next installment of *Lady Whistledown's Society Papers*. This is the hook to the next book. The first half of the epilogue shows how Daphne and Simon's life together has turned out.

The Viscount Who Loved Me (book two)

Opening Image (Prologue): The POV character for the prologue is Anthony Bridgerton. It is Anthony's loss of his father that is the obstacle to his love for Kate.

Closing Image (Epilogue): The final image in the epilogue is the start of the next installment of *Lady Whistledown's Society Papers*. This is the hook to the next book. The epilogue comes after the resolution and shows how Anthony and Kate's life together has turned out—what their happy-ever-after looks like.

An Offer from a Gentleman (**book three**)

Opening Image (Prologue): The POV character for the prologue is Benedict's love interest, Sophie Beckett. The circumstances of her birth will be the obstacle for them.

Closing Image (Epilogue): The final image in the epilogue is Lady Whistledown not wanting to carry on writing her gossip paper. This is the hook to the next book. The epilogue comes after the resolution and shows how Benedict and Sophie's life together has turned out—what their happy-ever-after looks like.

The opening and closing images show us a pattern. Each novel opens with why one of the love interests is alone. Each novel closes with showing how they are no longer alone and what their new ordinary world looks like. It's the perfect way to frame a novel.

Evolution Series Opening and Closing Images

We set up the first novel in the Evolution series for the opening and closing images to be complementary of each other in action and opposite at an emotional level.

The opening scene is at Jaz's husband's funeral, and she stays disconnected emotionally from everyone at the funeral. In the closing image, Jaz takes her family to her husband's grave. This is complementary in action because a funeral site and grave site complement each other. It's opposite at the emotional level because Jaz connects with the people at the ceremony. This gives the closing image extra power. We're going to attempt the same symmetry with the opening image of book one and the closing image of book three in the Evolution series.

For the action plot in book one, the scene locations in the opening and closing images are similar: a funeral and a grave.

For the emotion, they are opposites. At the opening, Jaz is raw and can't connect with others. At the closing, she accepts her husband's death and connects with her family. We will foreshadow that this connection won't last long. Book two is going to ruin this connection for Jaz.

From our work outlining book one, we know the main event in the first scene is that Jaz abandons her family and bolts from her husband's funeral.

The opening image happens at the beginning of the scene. We're going to show Jaz arriving at her husband's funeral.

We know the skeleton blurb for each novel and the series skeleton blurb.

We're going to turn to our series vault for the Evolution series.

The following is the series skeleton blurb:

*Jaz Cooper must **keep her ability to see into a dog's mind a secret**; otherwise, she and those with the ability will be experimented on and possibly die.*

Book One Skeleton Blurb:

> *Jaz Cooper must **find out who killed her husband, using her ability to see into a dog's mind**; otherwise, she might die.*

Book Two Skeleton Blurb:

> *Jaz Cooper must **keep others from discovering her daughter can see into a dog's mind**; otherwise, **her daughter might be killed**.*

Book Three Skeleton Blurb:

> *Jaz Cooper must **discover and eliminate the organization testing the ability on humans**; otherwise, Jaz and all the others who have the ability might be killed.*

The final scene of book one shows Jaz with her family getting the closure she needs surrounding her husband's death. That's strong enough for a single novel but not for the series. The story goal for book two is to keep others from discovering her daughter can see into a dog's mind.

From this we decided the main event for the closing image of book one must show Jaz realizing her daughter has the same talent. It has to be a strong enough hint that the reader picks up on it, too, and understands this is dangerous for Jaz's daughter.

Here is the updated main event for the closing image of book one:

> *Together with her family, Jaz visits her husband's grave. Jaz sees her daughter react to a dog's vision.*

The closing image we want to leave the reader with is Jaz seeing her daughter react to a dog's vision. That's a strong hook into the next novel.

This leads us right to the opening image of book two. Jaz's ordinary world now consists of both her and her daughter having the ability to see into a dog's mind.

We decided the following is the main event in the opening image for book two:

Jaz tests her daughter's abilities to see into a dog's mind.

The opening image of book two will show Jaz alone with her daughter and a dog. We'll need a little hint of why she is alone and what she intends to do. This can come in a short passage of backstory reliving the final image of book one.

To test the first scene and not just the opening image, we'll answer each of the four questions we stated earlier:

1. How much time has passed between novels?
   We decided the opening scene of book two will happen the day after book one ends. Jaz must wait until she's alone with her daughter.
2. What is the new ordinary world for the protagnosist?

Jaz's new ordinary world is having her daughter with the same ability she has.

1. What information is included in the backstory?
   We're going to include how Jaz gained the ability to see into a dog's mind and the main event from book one's climax: Using a dog's vision, Jaz discovers who murdered her husband.
2. What information will you leave out?
   We won't include the other story arc scene main events.

Answering these four questions shows us we have a plan for the opening image and for the first scene of book two.

We may come back and change this later. As we continue our outline, sometimes new ideas pop up, and we have to update the outline. As you write your series, you may find this happens too. The key is to keep the series vault updated as you go so you can see where a change impacts other parts of the story.

The opening and closing images of book two should mirror each other. The closing image of book two will contain an exit hook to book three.

To mirror the opening scene, we can show Jaz's daughter's ability to have grown or learned throughout book two. Because Jaz's daughter is a child, she can't control what she does, and she can't understand the threat if someone finds out what she can do. This led us to decide that having the ability grow throughout book two will add more tension to the story.

This also gave us an idea for a subplot: Jaz's daughter's journey. We'll see if that works when we've finished outlining the series.

The following are the story stakes if Jaz doesn't achieve the story goal for book three: Jaz and all the others who have the ability might be killed.

We need to hint that others in the story are going to have the ability to see into a dog's mind. The hook in the closing image can hint at this.

We decided the following is the main event in the final scene for book two:

Jaz's daughter shows an increase in her ability to see into a dog's mind, and one of Jaz's friends notices the ability.

By having a friend of Jaz notice the ability in Jaz's daughter, we foreshadow that there will be more at stake in book three.

The closing image will be Jaz realizing her friend has understood her daughter has the ability to see into a dog's mind. Notice how this is an extension of the final image in book one.

We can now think about the opening image in book three. This is going to mirror the closing image in book three, so we'll get to that shortly.

First, let's discover the main event in the first scene in book three. We know a character other than Jaz got a glimpse of what Jaz's daughter can do at the end of book two.

We decided the following is the opening image for book three:

Jaz decides to trust her friend and share that she and her daughter can see into a dog's mind.

To test this, we'll answer each of the four questions we stated earlier:

1. How much time has passed between books?
   We decided the opening scene of book three will happen the day after book two ends. This is consistent with the time between book one and book two.
2. What is the new ordinary world for your protagonist?
   Jaz's new ordinary world is having someone else know her daughter has the same ability as she does. This adds risk to Jaz's life.
3. What information will you include in the backstory?
   We're not sure, because we haven't outlined the story arc

SECRETS TO WRITING A SERIES

scenes for book two yet. We'll decide this later.
4. What information will you leave out?
We won't include the other story arc scene main events.

For the closing image in book three, we need the following:

- Opening image in book one
- Closing image in book one
- Opening image in book three

The following is the main event for the opening image for book one: Jaz abandons her family and bolts from her husband's funeral.

The following is the main event for the closing image for book one: Together with her family, Jaz visits her husband's grave. Jaz sees her daughter react to a dog's vision.

The following is the main event in the opening image for book two: Jaz tests her daughter's abilities to see into a dog's mind.

The following is the main event in the closing image for book two: Jaz's daughter shows an increase in her ability to see into a dog's mind, and one of Jaz's friends notices the ability.

The following is the opening image for book three: Jaz decides to trust her friend and share that she and her daughter can see into a dog's mind.

Series Skeleton Blurb and Book Three Skeleton Blurb:

> *Jaz Cooper must **discover and eliminate the organization testing the ability on humans**; otherwise, Jaz and all the others who have the ability might be killed.*

The closing image will show how Jaz comes to terms with the climax scene and hint at where her life will go. At this point, we think the closing image needs Jaz, her daughter, and her friend.

We decided the following is the main event in the final scene of book three and for the series:

Jaz and her friend create a secret community for those with the ability.

The final image will be Jaz surrounded by people and dogs who are all part of the secret community. These are people she wants to be with. This mirrors the opening image of book one where Jaz is surrounded by people she doesn't want to be with.

My Fairy Assassin Series Opening and Closing Images

Here we will determine the opening and closing images for the first three novels in the My Fairy Assassin series.

We know the skeleton blurb for each novel and the generic series skeleton blurb.

Generic Series Skeleton Blurb

> *Liv Wright must use the fairy time portal to save family members; otherwise, this world's worst person will end the world.*

Book One Skeleton Blurb

Liv Wright must use the fairy time portal to save her fairy assassin sister; otherwise, a scientist will destroy the world.

Book Two Skeleton Blurb

Liv Wright must use the fairy time portal to save her fairy saboteur mother; otherwise, a druid will destroy the world.

Book Three Skeleton Blurb

Liv Wright must use the fairy time portal to save her fairy enforcer aunt; otherwise, an alchemist will destroy the world.

As this is an open series, this needs to be strong enough for a single novel and foreshadow the next novel.

To deepen the character unity, we are also going to use setting unity in the My Fairy Assassin series to help us find the opening image. The opening images will use setting to create an emotional impact and to show whom Liv will try to save in each novel.

We decided Liv will be in a room full of the memories of the family member she will time-travel to save.

In book one, Liv is in her sister's room, and the story is about finding her sister. This is a little foreshadowing through the use of setting.

The opening image for book two will be Liv in the Fairy Great Library. This is where Liv's mother was last seen. Liv will time-travel to save her mother.

From this, we decided the closing image for book one must show Liv discovering who last saw her mother in the Fairy Great Library. It has to be a strong enough hint that the reader picks up on it and understands that Liv will be going on another adventure.

Here is the main event for the closing image of book one:

Liv, her sister, and a fairy celebrate. Liv discovers her mother was last seen in the Fairy Great Library.

This leads us right to the opening image of book two. Liv's ordinary world now is that Liv is looking for clues in the library that nobody will go near.

We decided the following is the main event in the opening image for book two:

Liv finds fairy magic in the library while looking for a clue about her mother.

To test this, we'll answer each of the four questions we stated earlier.

1. How much time has passed between novels?
   We decided that a week has passed since the end of book one and the beginning of book two. When the world has changed, the time portal needs to rest for two weeks. The different worlds are like layers of blankets, and when one comes to the top, and the time portal must check that the world is still stable.
2. What is the new ordinary world for your protagonist?
   Liv's new ordinary world is that Liv has a magical binding to a time-traveling fairy, and she changed the course of the world in the climax of book one, so the environmental Armageddon did not happen. But the world is still not perfect. Liv spends time getting to know her new ordinary world. It seems very much like the world the reader is in, except for a couple of oddities that will allow the reader to know that Liv is in a parallel universe.
3. What information will you include in the backstory?

SECRETS TO WRITING A SERIES

> The backstory will show Liv walking through the fairy's entrance, which she had to navigate in plot point 1 of book one.
> 4. What information will you leave out?
> We won't introduce the fairy, or the sister, in this scene. This scene is for the reader and Liv to get to know each other.

Answering these four questions shows us we have a plan for the opening image of book two.

The closing image of book two should have structural similarities to the closing image of book one and contain an exit hook to book three.

To mirror the closing scene, we can show Liv, her sister, and the fairy together, getting bad news. Liv was not successful in saving her mother in book two, but she did save the world. This led us to decide that having the bittersweet ending of not being fully successful would add depth to future novels. This constant looking for her mother could start a subplot that Liv is looking for her mother in other novels while trying to achieve the story goal of each novel.

If Liv doesn't achieve the story goal in every novel, the story stakes for the series become the following:

> *This world's worst person will end the world.*

We need the readers to understand the worlds that Liv time-travels to are all parallel universes, and the reader will want to come back and find out what is different about each world. The main event in the closing image can hint at this.

To help us find the closing image for book two, we need to refer to the book three skeleton blurb. Liv Wright must use the fairy time portal to save her fairy enforcer aunt; otherwise, a druid will destroy the world.

We decided the following is the main event in the closing image for book two:

Liv, her sister, and a fairy are together when the king orders Liv and the fairy to save Liv's aunt.

Liv will find out over the course of the open series that her family and the fairy world have always been entwined, and that there are people who want to harm the fairy world. Sometimes the fairies must protect their world using humans, and Liv's aunt is the person the fairies use. This way, in each novel, we can look at which family member might make sense to add to the story. We can add aunts, uncles, her father, and grandparents. This is similar to the Bridgerton series, which follows the love story of a new family member in each novel.

For each opening image, it is important to choose a place where Liv would feel connected to her family member. In book one, this was her sister's room. In book two, the connection with her mother was in the Fairy Great Library. So we asked ourselves, Where would the enforcer aunt have been found?

The aunt is an enforcer, and how we see an enforcer is someone who is used as a guard. In book one, Liv's aunt could have been in control of the guards protecting the door to the fairy world, which was plot point 1 of book one.

Remember we are looking for series patterns so that the reader will feel the unity with the story.

From this exercise, we realized that each of the settings must be included in previous novels so the next novel's story goal can be mentioned.

Let's discover the opening image in book three. We know a character other than Liv will be there.

We decided the following is the opening image for book three:

> *Liv is hanging out with a guard when some humans ram the fairy world and drop fairy magic.*

We will test this to see how we'll answer each of the four questions.

1. How much time has passed between novels?
   We decided the opening scene of book three will happen two weeks after book two ends. This sets up the series unity with time between book one and book two. Again, the time portal needs to make sure the new world has been realigned in a correct manner. Liv finds the delay intolerable, and it also means that a future book could present a situation in which the time portal is not given enough time to make sure the world is stable.
2. What is the new ordinary world for your protagonist?
   Liv's new ordinary world is that her mother is still missing, but Liv thinks she can find her aunt, who will be able to help Liv find her mother.
3. What information will you include in the backstory?
   That fairies are real.
4. What information will you leave out?
   We won't meet the fairy in the first scene. Liv needs to have a scene to shine. Fairies cast a long shadow, and if a fairy is in this scene, the new-to-the-series reader might not have time to connect with Liv. We decided she will be alone.

For the closing image in book three, we need the following:

Book One Opening Image Main Event

> *Liv is tidying up her sister's room and finds fairy magic.*

Book One Closing Image Main Event

> *Liv, her sister, and a fairy celebrate. Liv discovers her mother was last seen in the Great Fairy Library.*

Book Two Opening Image Main Event

> *Liv finds fairy magic in the Great Fairy Library while looking for a clue about her mother.*

Book Two Closing Image Main Event

> *Liv, her sister, and a fairy are together when the king orders Liv and the fairy to save Liv's aunt.*

Book Three Opening Image Main Event

> *Liv is hanging out with a guard when some humans ram the fairy world and drop fairy magic.*

We need to start looking at the series unity patterns. And we would like this to be a successful mission for Liv so she saves her aunt.

The closing image will show Liv with her sister and a fairy.

We decided the following is the closing image for book three:

> *Liv, her sister, and a fairy celebrate with her aunt when the king informs them Liv's father is in danger.*

As you can see, we are using everything from this novel to help focus on the opening and closing image of the first three novels. And the beauty of this process is that anytime we wish to create another novel, we can get the opening and closing images to fit the series patterns. How wonderful is that?

Your Fun Series Task

You're starting to add depth to the novels within your series.

For a closed series:

1. Create the main event in the opening image for each novel in your series.
2. Add the main events to your series vault.
3. Create a one-sentence description of the new ordinary world for the second novel in your series through to the last novel in your series.
4. Add the new ordinary worlds to your series vault.
5. Decide how much time has passed between the end of one novel and the next.
6. Add the time passed to your series vault.
7. Create the main event for the closing image for each novel in your series.
8. Add the main events to your series vault.

For an open series:

1. Create the main event in the opening image for the first three novels in your series.

2. Add these main events to your series vault.
3. Create the main event in the opening image for the first three novels in your series.
4. Create the main event in the closing image for the first three novels in your series.
5. Add these main events to your series vault.
6. Decide how much time has passed between the end of one novel and the next novel.
7. Add the time passed to your series vault.
8. Create the main event for the closing image for the first three novels in your series.
9. Add the main events to your series vault.

SECRETS TO WRITING A SERIES

Outlined Scenes: Book One

Vault Heading	Evolution	My Fairy Assassin
Opening Image	Jaz abandons her family and bolts from her husband's funeral.	Liv is tidying up her sister's room and finds fairy magic.
Inciting Incident	Jaz saves a dog's life and gains the ability to see into the dog's mind.	Liv discovers her sister is not dead yet but is stuck in a dying fairy world.
Reaction to the Inciting Incident	Jaz has her first dog vision. Jaz hides her first dog vision from another person.	Not applicable.
Plot Point 1	Jaz uses a dog vision and finally believes her husband was murdered.	Liv's sister is dying, and Liv must learn to time travel to save her.
Middle Plot Point	Not applicable.	Liv time travels to save sister.
Plot Point 2	Jaz's actions cause someone close to her to die.	The time portal fails, and Liv cannot save her sister.
Climax	Not applicable.	Liv saves her sister by reopening the time portal and injuring the scientist.
Closing Image	Together with her family, Jaz visits her husband's grave. Jaz sees her daughter react to a dog's vision.	Liv, her sister, and a fairy celebrate. Liv discovers her mother was last seen in the Fairy Library.

Outlined Scenes: Book Two

Vault Heading	Evolution	My Fairy Assassin
Time Passed	One day.	Two weeks.
New Ordinary World	Jaz's daughter has the same ability as she does.	Liv is in a parallel world
Opening Image	Jaz tests her daughter's abilities to see into a dog's mind.	Liv finds fairy magic in the Library whilst looking for a clue about her mother.
Backstory	Using a dog's vision, Jaz discovered who murdered her husband. Jaz caused someone close to her to die.	Liv knows how to time travel.
Inciting Incident	Jaz discovers her daughter is in danger.	Liv finds out her mother was kidnapped by druids from Anglesey during 77 CE.
Plot Point 1	To be determined.	Liv discovers her mother was caught sabotaging the Druid's oak grove, and Liv must time travel to save her.
Middle Plot Point	Jaz does something that forces her to understand why she must keep her daughter's ability a secret. She also discovers something that leads her to the testing organization.	Liv time travels to save her mother.

Outlined Scenes: Book Two
Continued

Vault Heading	Evolution	My Fairy Assassin
Plot Point 2	To be determined.	The time portal won't allow Liv's mother to time travel, and Liv cannot save her mother.
Climax	To be determined.	Liv doesn't save her mother but kills the druid.
Closing Image	Jaz's daughter shows an increase in her ability to see into a dog's mind and one of Jaz's friends notices the ability.	Liv, her sister, and a fairy are together when the king orders Liv and the fairy to save Liv's aunt.

Outlined Scenes: Book Three

Vault Heading	Evolution	My Fairy Assassin
Time Passed	One day.	Two weeks.
New Ordinary World	Someone else knows Jaz's daughter has the same ability as she does. This adds risk to Jaz's life.	Liv's mother is still missing, but Liv thinks she can find her aunt who will be able to help Liv find her mother.
Opening Image	Jaz tests her daughter's abilities to see into a dog's mind.	Liv is hanging out with a guard when some humans decide to ram the Fairy world and drop some fairy magic.
Backstory	To be determined.	The time portal doesn't always work as expected.
Inciting Incident	Jaz discovers her daughter is in danger.	Liv finds out her aunt has joined the Ice giants in 1849.
Plot Point 1	To be determined.	Liv discovers her aunt is locked in an ice block in the Himalayas.
Middle Plot Point	To be determined.	Liv time travels to save her aunt.

Outlined Scenes: Book Three Continued

Vault Heading	Evolution	My Fairy Assassin
Plot Point 2	Series and Book Three Plot Point 2: Jaz kills book one's antagonist and learns who is leading the testing organization.	The weather has frozen the time portal, and Liv cannot save her aunt.
Climax	Series and Book Three Climax: Jaz uses her ability to see into a dog's mind to eliminate the testing organization.	Liv saves her aunt, but the alchemist and his Ice Giants get away.
Closing Image	Jaz and her friend create a secret community for those with the ability.	Liv, her sister, and a fairy celebrate with her aunt, when the king informs them Liv's father is in danger.

Where to Next?

We hope you noticed the framework of your series in your series vault. Seeing the opening image, the five story arc scenes, and the closing image together gives you a picture of your series in a concise manner. This will keep you focused during the entire process of writing the series.

You've done a lot of work on your series, and we're going to help you do even more. We'll dive into the protagonist and POV character strategies and help you decide how you're going to handle each of these for your series.

Chapter Twenty-One: Protagonist versus POV Characters

In this chapter we'll define what protagonist and POV characters are, show you the difference between the two, and then work together to create a protagonist and POV character strategy.

At the end of this chapter, we'll help you choose the tense for your series. You'll plan for the past or present or a combination of the two.

Definition of a Protagonist

The protagonist is the story's main character or main character entity who drives the story forward by pursuing the story goal stated in the skeleton blurb. The protagonist is the character who has the most to gain or lose depending on whether they achieve the story goal. They are not always the character who changes the most, but they can be.

In the Hunger Games closed series, Katniss Everdeen is the protagonist in every novel.

In the Jason Bourne closed series, Jason Bourne is the protagonist in every novel.

In the Divergent closed series, Tris is the protagonist for books one and two in the series. Tris and Tobias are a combined protagonist for book three.

In the Game of Thrones closed series, the protagonist entity is a group protagonist in every novel made up of the humans who are fighting the White Walkers.

In the Stephanie Plum open series, Stephanie Plum is the protagonist in every novel.

In the Jack Reacher open series, Jack Reacher is the protagonist in every novel.

In the Bridgerton open series, the protagonist is a different Bridgerton sibling in every novel.

In the Chestnut Springs open series, the protagonist is different in every novel.

Definition of a POV Character

A POV character is the character telling the story at any given time. This may or may not be the protagonist.

The protagonist can be both the protagonist and a POV character.

Writing from multiple POVs can create tension, because it creates a knowledge gap where the reader knows more than the character knows, and each character is acting on incomplete information. This is an artistic choice, and here are some examples of choices authors make.

In the Hunger Games closed series, Katniss Everdeen is the protagonist and POV character for every scene in all three novels.

In the Jason Bourne series, Jason Bourne is the protagonist in every novel, but there are many other characters who have the POV for scenes throughout the series.

In the Divergent closed series, Tris is the protagonist and POV character for every scene in books one and two. Tris and Tobias are a combined protagonist for book three. They each are the POV characters for scenes throughout book three.

In the Game of Thrones closed series, the protagonist is a group protagonist made up of the humans who are fighting the White Walkers. There are nine POV characters in the first novel in the series. They are all part of the group protagonist.

In the Stephanie Plum open series, Stephanie Plum is the protagonist and POV character in every novel.

In the Jack Reacher open series, Jack Reacher is the protagonist in every novel in the series. Lee Child writes the novels from multiple POVs.

In the Bridgerton open series, the protagonist is different for each novel. In each of the novels, the protagonist is a Bridgerton family member. A Bridgerton family member and their future partner are the POV characters for their respective novels.

In the Chestnut Springs open series, just as in the Bridgerton series, the protagonist is different for each novel in the series. The POV strategy in each novel is to alternate between the two love interests.

Protagonist Strategy

A protagonist strategy means you're deciding whether you're writing with a single, combined, or group protagonist.

When you wrote your series skeleton blurb, you may have added your protagonist strategy to your series vault. If you didn't do it then, try to create that now. It will be hard to start writing your series if you don't know what the protagonist strategy is, so the sooner you can decide this, the faster you can get to writing.

Once you have a protagonist strategy, it's time to test that strategy and see whether it works for the series you want to write.

Choosing Protagonist Strategy Is Important

The Hunger Games trilogy provides us with a great example. Katniss Everdeen is the protagonist for the entire series.

We wrote the skeleton blurb as follows:

Katniss Everdeen must become the leader of the rebellion and overturn the Capitol; otherwise, everyone she cares for will die or be doomed to a life of misery.

Her primary goal in the series is to overturn the Capitol. The subplot is the romance between Katniss and Peeta.

Peeta's primary goal is to marry Katniss.

Now imagine if Peeta were the protagonist. The skeleton blurb for the series could be the following:

Peeta must help Katniss to survive the Hunger Games; otherwise, he can't marry her.

The story would be a love story with the subplot of the Hunger Games.

Neither is right or wrong. Our point here is to illustrate the importance of choosing a protagonist that fits the story you want to tell.

If the Hunger Games series were written with Katniss and Peeta as a combined protagonist, then they both have to have the same story goal. This means Peeta's goal wouldn't be to marry Katniss; it would be to survive the Hunger Games. Again, this means it would be a different story.

To understand whether the protagonist strategy is the one that works best for your series, you need to test your strategy.

Creating the Protagonist Strategy for Your Series

When you write a stand-alone novel, you decide whether you're going to have a single protagonist, a combined protagonist, or a group protagonist.

The next decision you make is whether that novel will be told from a single POV or multiple POVs.

Single Protagonist—Single Point of View

If you have one protagonist for the entire series and write each scene for every novel in the series from that character's POV, then your strategy is straightforward.

This means every novel in the series has the same protagonist, and every scene in each of the novels will be told from that character's POV.

When you write with a single protagonist and a single POV, the reader knows everything the protagonist knows. The reader cannot know anything else. This means the series will not contain any knowledge gaps where the reader knows something the protagonist doesn't.

The Hunger Games by Suzanne Collins is this type of novel.

Single Protagonist—Multiple Points of View

In this case, all the novels in the series have the same protagonist.

The story becomes more complex to write because you'll choose which POV character tells each scene.

Once you choose a POV strategy for the first novel in the series, it's important to stay consistent. The reader bought your second novel because they liked the first novel. This includes how you structured the novel. If you start with multiple POVs, stay with multiple POVs.

The reverse is not true. You can start with a single POV and expand later novels to be multiple POVs. The Divergent series does this. Books one and two are written from Tris's POV. Book three is written from both Tris's and Tobias's POVs.

This worked because the reader grew to love Tobias and wanted more from him. He became Tris's partner, and they are as one, and this makes story sense.

If Veronica Roth had written book one from both Tris's and Tobias's POVs, and then taken one away, there's a good chance the reader wouldn't have enjoyed books two and three as much. Something would have been missing.

The Jason Bourne series is an example where the protagonist is a single protagonist, Jason Bourne, but the story is written from multiple POVs.

Writing from multiple POVs gives you the opportunity to create knowledge gaps where the reader knows more than the characters do. This can add tension to the story. If the reader knows there is a bomb in a car, and the character is about to drive the car without knowing the bomb is there, this creates a knowledge gap and tension.

Varying Protagonist Types

Here again we get more complex. If you recall, there are three protagonist entities:

- Single protagonist
- Combined protagonist
- Group protagonist

The Divergent series gives us a single protagonist in books one and two, and a combined protagonist in the third novel.

If a novel is written from a single POV, then the novel must have a single protagonist. The opposite is not true. If a novel is written from multiple POVs, then it can have a single protagonist, and it can also be a \ protagonist, or even a group protagonist.

If you choose to write every scene from one character's POV, you are usually choosing that character as the protagonist. The exception is if there is a narrator and a protagonist. You can find this strategy in *The Great Gatsby* by F. Scott Fitzgerald.

If a series has a combined protagonist, the reader will expect to have POV scenes from both characters who make up the combined protagonist. If there is only one POV character, the reader will assume that character is the protagonist. A novel with multiple POVs does not mean the protagonist is a combined protagonist.

If a novel is written with a group protagonist, there must be multiple POVs. If there is only one POV character, the reader will assume that character is the protagonist. A novel with multiple POVs does not mean the protagonist is a group protagonist.

Without a protagonist strategy, it will be difficult to choose a POV strategy.

Perhaps you know your story needs to be told from one character's POV. This means you are writing a single protagonist story.

Do you have two characters with the same goal experiencing the **same** adventure? Then you have a combined protagonist.

Do you have multiple characters with the same story goal, but they are experiencing **different** adventures? Then you have a group protagonist.

There are series where each novel in the series has a single protagonist, and that protagonist changes on a per-novel basis. The Bridgerton series is this type of series.

Keep in mind that when you change protagonists in a series, you're asking the reader to connect with the new protagonist. They must be ready to accept the time it takes to connect to the character.

Definition of a POV Strategy

Writing from a character's POV means the story or scene is filtered through one character's perspective. This means the reader is experiencing a scene through that character. They see, hear, feel, smell, and taste what that character does.

For your series, you'll need a POV strategy. At this point in our process, we are outlining the main plot of the series. This is an important point, because you may change the POV strategy when you add a subplot.

A POV strategy is how you're going to handle writing from a character's perspective. You have two choices:

1. There is one POV character, meaning every scene will be written from one character's perspective.
2. There will be more than one POV character, meaning for each scene you must choose whose perspective the scene will be written from.

When you choose to write your series in a single POV, you're deciding the reader will know everything the protagonist knows. This connects the reader to the protagonist and their journey.

When you choose to write your series from multiple POVs, you're deciding the reader will know things the protagonist doesn't. This creates knowledge gaps, and knowledge gaps create tension.

With the Evolution series, we are starting with a single protagonist and a single POV for the main plot. When we add a subplot, we may decide that we need another character to have the POV for that storyline. Subplots are a great place to use POV characters who are not the protagonist. We don't know this yet, and as we discover our story through this process, we can decide that.

With the My Fairy Assassin series, the POV will always be in Liv Wright's POV. This gives the space for us to create a mildly unreliable narrator. Being only in her perspective, the reader only gets her views on the world or worlds she visits, so her bias is something we can play with. We don't necessarily have to go down this route, but seeing the story from one perspective would also make the complicated time-traveling plot easier to follow. Again, this is our plan, and a plan can change.

For now think about your main plot and decide on a POV strategy for that plotline.

Multiple Point-of-View Guidelines

There are no strict rules about how many POV characters there can be, but we can provide you with some guidelines.

The more POV characters there are, the less time the reader has to connect with the characters. The goal is to have as few POV characters as possible and still have a strong story.

SECRETS TO WRITING A SERIES

We recommend the protagonist is the POV character for more than half the scenes. If they aren't, then you might have chosen the wrong protagonist.

We recommend that the protagonist is the POV character for all the story arc scenes in the series—the inciting incident, plot point 1, the middle plot point, plot point 2, and the climax. The exception to this is the romance genre. In this case, either love interest can have the POV for the story arc scenes.

There is a strong case that the protagonist is the POV character for the opening and closing scenes too. That will be up to you to decide.

Choosing a POV strategy is an important decision. Consistency across the series will improve the overall story. Once you choose a POV strategy for your series, stick to it. Readers are following your series because they like the way you tell a story.

In the Hunger Games closed series, the POV character for every scene is Katniss Everdeen.

In the Divergent closed series, Tris is the POV character for every scene in *Divergent* (book one) and *Insurgent* (book two). Tris and Tobias alternate POVs in *Allegiant* (book three).

In *Game of Thrones* (book one), the POV characters include Catelyn Stark, Ned Stark, Jon Snow, Tyrion Lannister, Bran Stark, Sansa Stark, Arya Stark, Daenerys Targaryen, and Will. That's a total of nine POV characters. If you want to read scenes where the author has full control over POV, this is a great series to study.

In the Stephanie Plum open series, Stephanie Plum is the POV character for every novel in the series.

In the Bridgerton open series, the protagonist is different for each novel in the series. The POV characters also change for each novel in the series.

In the Evolution closed series, the protagonist is Jaz Cooper for each novel in the series, and she is the POV character for each scene in the main plotline.

In the My Fairy Assassin open series, the protagonist is Liv Wright for each novel in the series, and she is the POV character for every scene.

Narrative Strategy

Now that you have created the series protagonist strategy and POV strategy, you can decide what narrative strategy works for your series. There are many good books on narrative strategy, so we're not going to cover this in detail.

There are three main narrative choices. These are the first person, the second person, and the third person.

First Person: "Don't tell me what to do," I said.

Second Person: "Don't tell me what to do," you said.

Third Person: "Don't tell me what to do," she said.

Just like POV, you can write scenes within the same novel all in first, second, or third person. You can write one character's scenes in first person and another's in third person. For a series, it's important to make a choice and be consistent.

Tense Strategy: Past or Present Tense

This is your final decision before you start writing your series. As with all the other decisions, don't get stuck here. Make a choice and move on. After you've written a bit of your first draft, you may decide you want to change this, and that's OK. By consciously deciding now, you'll be more aware as you write your scenes that this is a choice. This means you're more likely to notice it and decide early if it needs changing.

For now, all you need to do is decide if you're writing your series in past or present tense.

Usually people make these decisions based on genre expectations or the type of novels they like to read. There is no right or wrong answer, but there are guidelines.

Once you've decided how you're going to use person and tense, be consistent across the series. For example, if one character is always written in first-person present tense, and all the others are third-person past tense, use this strategy for the entire series.

You don't have to write every scene in the same person or the same tense. Sometimes a flashback is written in a different tense or from a different person.

A series written in the first-person present tense can present an issue for the writer if they want to kill off the protagonist in the final novel of a series.

The Divergent series had to be written in present tense because Tris is the protagonist in the first two novels, and she dies in the climax scene of the final novel. She can't have been telling the story from her POV in past tense, because she isn't alive at the end.

When writing in present tense, you will lose credibility with a reader if you give too many hints of what's to come in the future. A protagonist telling their story in present tense can't reveal what hasn't happened yet. Writing in past tense allows you to do that.

In the present tense, you can't move through time in the story (except for using a flashback that is in the character's mind). Since present tense implies the story is taking place as it's being read, jumping forward in time will jar the reader from the story. All actions have to happen in sequence.

In the Evolution closed series, the story will be written in the past tense.

In the My Fairy Assassin open series, the story will be written in the present tense.

Your Fun Series Task

We hope you're excited. After this chapter, you're going to start writing your series. That's a big moment, so you might want to take a break and celebrate.

Decide on the protagonist strategy for your series. We're at an early stage of structuring the series, so you can always change this later as you discover more about your story.

1. Update your series vault with the protagonist type:
    a. Single
    b. Combined
    c. Group

Update your series vault with the following:

1. POV Strategy
2. Narrative Strategy
3. Tense

As usual, our series vaults for Evolution and My Fairy Assassin are below.

Vault Heading	Evolution	My Fairy Assassin
Protagonist Type	Single	Single
POV Strategy	Single (Jaz Cooper)	Single (Liv Wright)
Narrative Strategy	First Person	First Person
Tense	Past	Present

Where to Next?

Backstory in a series has different duties from backstory in a stand-alone novel. Next, you'll add backstory to some of your scenes to create the first level of depth.

Chapter Twenty-Two: Backstory

Why did we include backstory in the chapter on how to add depth to your series? We have another secret.

Writing backstory for a stand-alone novel and writing backstory for each novel in a series are different.

In a stand-alone novel, you, the author, decide what the reader learns about a character's past. The reader will never read the notes you kept on a character's past, so you choose what they get to know.

In a series, for book two onward, you and the reader know the same backstory, if the reader has read book one. This is why backstory must be included in a discussion on writing each novel in a series.

The key to success with backstory is to include only what the reader needs to know. But how do you choose? There is a lot written about effective backstory for stand-alone novels, so let's focus on a series starting with book two.

The goal is to include enough backstory that the reader understands the story if they haven't read the previous novels, but not so much that it bores the reader if they have.

Backstory in a series is most effective when it's drawn from turning points in the previous novels. The turning points can be at the scene, story, or series level.

Key turning points in previous novels happened in the five story arc scenes. This is the first place to look for backstory that could be included in subsequent novels.

When you include backstory, check whether it's related to the series skeleton blurb or the skeleton blurb for the novel it's included in. If it's not, this is when you ask yourself whether the backstory is really needed.

Divergent Closed Series Backstory Example

In the first scene of *Insurgent* (book two), Tris refers to a hard drive in her pocket. She doesn't say what is on it, but the reader knows from reading *Divergent* (book one). This makes the reader feel like they are part of the author's inner circle. They know something others don't.

In *Divergent* (book one), plot point 2 happens over a series of scenes. Tobias, Tris's boyfriend, gets captured. Tris kills her friend Will, and Tris's mom dies. That's three big events in Tris's life.

Insurgent (book two) opens with Tris seeing (in her mind) Will dying. Roth used backstory from *Divergent* (book one) plot point 2 to create a hook into *Insurgent* (book two). Opening with backstory about Tris's lowest point in *Divergent* (book one) works as a brilliant entry hook. This proves that when backstory is used well, it can add tension, increase character depth, and get the reader hooked on the scene.

Tris killing Will and her mom dying are also both shown as backstory early in *Allegiant* (book three). This reminds the reader of key events that are important to events in the third novel.

The Bridgerton Open Series Backstory Example

In *The Duke and I* (book one) of the Bridgerton series, Viscount Anthony Bridgerton nearly has a duel with Simon over a slight to his sister's honor. This happens in the middle plot point. This is so important that *Viscount* is in the title of book two.

In *The Viscount Who Loved Me* (book two), Viscount Anthony Bridgerton appears in chapter one. He discusses women's honor and mentions his near miss in a duel, defending one of his sisters. He does not name Daphne, but everyone who has read book one feels they are in on the story. This collusion draws the reader in, promising book two in the series is going to be just as brilliant as the one before it.

In the inciting incident in *An Offer from a Gentleman* (book three), Benedict and Sophie meet at the masquerade ball, where they discuss Lady Whistledown's insight into Benedict's older brother's wedding, and that Lady Whistledown did not know the full story. This is genius. If the reader has read book two, this makes the reader feel more knowledgeable than one of the characters. If they have not read book two, they will want to go back and read it.

Evolution Series Backstory

We're going to have a look at what backstory we want to include in book two and book three of the Evolution series.

We need the main events for the story arc scenes from *Evolution* (book one) to help us choose the backstory.

The following are three of the story arc scenes we created for *Evolution* (book one):

Inciting Incident: Jaz saves a dog's life and gains the ability to see into the dog's mind.

Plot Point 1: Jaz uses a dog's vision and finally believes her husband was murdered.

Plot Point 2: Jaz's actions cause someone close to her to die.

We also want to include the main event in the closing image of *Evolution* (book one) because it has an important revelation.

Closing Image: Together with her family, Jaz visits her husband's grave. **Jaz sees her daughter react to a dog's vision.**

Early in book two of the Evolution series, we are going to show Jaz's revelation about her daughter in the opening image as backstory. The reader must know this in order to understand the opening image of book two, where Jaz tests her daughter's ability to see into a dog's mind.

In *Evolution* (book one), Jaz believes her husband was murdered. We're going to include this as backstory before the inciting incident in book two. We don't know what the inciting incident is yet, only that it will be the moment Jaz discovers her daughter is in danger. The knowledge that her husband was murdered in book one will motivate her to take the threat against her daughter seriously. The reader will also believe the threat.

For now, let's add the main event for the inciting incident in book two.

Jaz discovers her daughter is in danger.

We'll add that to the series vault.

In plot point 2 of *Evolution* (book one) Jaz causes someone close to her to die. This will alter how she behaves. She'll know the risks are life threatening. We want to use this revelation to show her motivation for her actions in book two. We also think this should be added before the inciting incident of book two.

This doesn't mean we won't include other backstory. Once we write book one, we may find other backstory that we need to include in book two. We've given ourselves a starting point.

We'll follow a similar process for book three.

My Fairy Assassin Backstory

In *My Fairy Assassin* (book one), the world's ecosystem has collapsed. This means life as Liv knows it on Earth is ending, all because a scientist invented something that caused an ecological disaster. Liv alters history, and the world is saved.

This backstory means the reader understands the harsh decisions that humanity has taken. This backstory means the reader also knows how critical Liv's time travel is.

When she returns to the new world, it is "saved." And yet there is something wrong, and that starts the next novel. The previous story creates a new world that needs to be saved.

To find the backstory we need for book two of the My Fairy Assassin series, we need to review the following main events from book one. We pulled these from our story vault.

Inciting Incident: Liv discovers her sister is not dead yet but is stuck in a dying fairy world.

Plot Point 1: Liv's sister is dying, and Liv must learn to time-travel to save her.

Middle Plot Point: Liv time-travels to save her sister.

Plot Point 2: The time portal fails, and Liv cannot save her sister.

Climax: Liv saves her sister by reopening the time portal and injuring the scientist.

When we read these, we are drawn to plot point 1. Liv must learn to time-travel. This skill is critical to Liv in each story, so we decided it must be included somewhere in the setup of each novel in the series.

We reviewed the main events for the story arc scene in book two, and plot point 2 contained the backstory we needed.

Plot Point 2: The time portal won't allow Liv's mother to time-travel, and Liv cannot save her mother.

This is where Liv learns the time portal doesn't always behave as expected. It's the reason she failed to save her mother. We'll add this backstory to the opening of book three to show how hard it will be for Liv to save her aunt. She can't take the use of the time portal for granted.

You can use the method we just did to find the relevant backstory.

Your Fun Series Task

SECRETS TO WRITING A SERIES

Start selecting the backstory you want to include in novels two and forward in your series. You'll do this for each new book you write, and you'll have your series vault for reference to make this easy.

1. Review the main events for the story arc scenes in book one.
2. Choose the backstory you want to include in book two.
3. Add that backstory to your series vault.

Do this for each book where you've created the main events for the story arc scenes for the previous book in the series.

Outlined Scenes: Book Two

Vault Heading	Evolution	My Fairy Assassin
Time Passed	One day.	Two weeks.
New Ordinary World	Jaz's daughter has the same ability as she does.	Liv is in a parallel world
Opening Image	Jaz tests her daughter's abilities to see into a dog's mind.	Liv finds fairy magic in the Library whilst looking for a clue about her mother.
Backstory	Using a dog's vision, Jaz discovered who murdered her husband. Jaz caused someone close to her to die.	Liv knows how to time travel.
Inciting Incident	Jaz discovers her daughter is in danger.	Liv finds out her mother was kidnapped by druids from Anglesey during 77 CE.
Plot Point 1	To be determined.	Liv discovers her mother was caught sabotaging the Druid's oak grove, and Liv must time travel to save her.
Middle Plot Point	Jaz does something that forces her to understand why she must keep her daughter's ability a secret. She also discovers something that leads her to the testing organization.	Liv time travels to save her mother.

Outlined Scenes: Book Three

Vault Heading	Evolution	My Fairy Assassin
Time Passed	One day.	Two weeks.
New Ordinary World	Someone else knows Jaz's daughter has the same ability as she does. This adds risk to Jaz's life.	Liv's mother is still missing, but Liv thinks she can find her aunt who will be able to help Liv find her mother.
Opening Image	Jaz tests her daughter's abilities to see into a dog's mind.	Liv is hanging out with a guard when some humans decide to ram the Fairy world and drop some fairy magic.
Backstory	To be determined.	The time portal doesn't always work as expected.
Inciting Incident	Jaz discovers her daughter is in danger.	Liv finds out her aunt has joined the Ice giants in 1849.
Plot Point 1	To be determined.	Liv discovers her aunt is locked in an ice block in the Himalayas.
Middle Plot Point	To be determined.	Liv time travels to save her aunt.

Where to Next?

With the main plot under control, we are in a great place to look at subplots. A subplot is a storyline that supports the main external plot. You need subplots to add depth and tension to your story. You have the knowledge to create well-structured subplots that support your main plot, so let's get going.

Chapter Twenty-Three: Subplots

A subplot is a storyline that supports the main external plot. It will have a beginning, a middle, and an end just like the main plot, but it shouldn't take up as much page time.

Subplots are designed to make it harder or easier for the protagonist to achieve the story goal. To make it harder, the subplot gets in the way of the main external story goal, which is a good thing, because it causes conflict in the story. To make it easier, the subplot supports the protagonist in their quest to achieve the story goal. This is also good because it adds depth to the story.

There are many reasons to have a subplot, and conflict is an important one. Some subplots show how the past can influence the future. Some subplots echo the main plot. Some show what will happen if the protagonist is not successful. Some show how a helper character supports the protagonist. You've got endless possibilities to choose from.

Subplots can be written from the protagonist's POV or from a secondary character's POV.

Each novel can close a subplot or carry it on throughout the series. The love triangle in the Stephanie Plum series is a great example of a subplot being carried on through the series without addressing the subplot goal of Stephanie choosing either Joe or Ranger as her one true love.

Subplots must relate to the main series plot; otherwise, they are distracting and probably don't belong in the story.

Subplot Guidelines and Duties

Just as story arc scenes have duties, so do subplots. There must be a purpose for adding a subplot to your main plot.

Subplots can do the following:

- Be in a closed or an open series.
- Make it harder or easier for the protagonist to achieve the external story goal.
- Add depth to the protagonist.
- Speed up or slow down pacing.
- Be specific to a novel within the series (or they can span the series).

Likewise, subplots *must* do the following:

- Be related to the series goal or the single novel goal.
- Raise the stakes for the protagonist.
- Be less important than the main plot described in the series skeleton blurb or a single novel skeleton blurb.

Subplot Decisions

1. What genre will your subplot be?
2. How many subplots will you include?
3. Will they span the series or only be part of some of the single novels?
4. Whose POV will they be written from?

To create the foundation for subplots, follow the same process we covered in this book and interweave the subplots into the main plot. You'll start with a subplot skeleton blurb and go from there.

Story Arcs for the Hunger Games Romance Subplot

In this section, we're going to show you the Hunger Games series' romance subplot story arc scenes and where the scenes are placed in the series.

The Series Inciting Incident and Series Subplots for the Hunger Games

The inciting incident for the main action plotline is Katniss volunteering for the Hunger Games. The same scene is the inciting incident for the romance subplot, as it's where Peeta is chosen at the Reaping, and Katniss meets him on the stage. This scene is also the inciting incident for the family tragedy subplot, as this is where Katniss takes her first action to risk her own life to save her sister.

To recap, the inciting incident in the Hunger Games trilogy is the same scene for all the following:

1. The Hunger Games series
2. Book one of the Hunger Games trilogy
3. The romance subplot (Katniss and Peeta)
4. The family tragedy subplot (Prim's death)

That's a powerful scene.

Book One Plot Point 2 and Romance Subplot Plot Point 1

To find the subplot, we turned to plot point 2 of book one. In plot point 2 of book one, Katniss seeks out Peeta, finds him seriously injured, and needs to nurse him back to health. She must risk her life to get some medicine, and she succeeds. She embraces the romantic story they've been faking for the audience watching the games.

This makes a great plot point 1 for the romance subplot. Katniss discovers she might have feelings for Peeta. Before this she's been pretending to love him. Here we see how a plot point from the main plot is linked to a subplot plot point. This isn't always the case.

Series Middle Plot Point and Romance Subplot Middle Plot Point

In book two, Katniss proactively decides to protect Peeta. Her goal is to die saving him. You can see how the story of the romance subplot is following the same duties as the main plot story arc scenes.

Book Three Middle Plot Point and the Romance Subplot Plot Point 2

The lowest point for Katniss in the romance subplot occurs in the middle plot point of *Mockingjay* (book three). Peeta, who had been captured by the Capitol, is used as a weapon against Katniss and the rebellion. During an interview broadcasted to all the districts, he pleads for a cease-fire and looks visibly tortured and gaunt. Later he is rescued, but it's revealed that the Capitol has "hijacked" him, using a method of torture to brainwash him into fearing and hating

Katniss. This is the first time she believes she's lost Peeta to the Capitol.

The Series Climax and Romance Subplot

The climax for the romance subplot is subtle. It occurs when Gale understands his role in Katniss's life was to protect her family, and he failed. He was the one who created the bomb that killed her sister, Prim. That means Peeta wins Katniss's love. Notice how this links the main action plot and the family tragedy subplot. This scene happens after the main plot climax. It also doesn't outshine the main climax scene.

The family tragedy subplot was closed before the series climax when Prim is killed, and the romance subplot was closed after the series climax. It's important to note both subplots are closed in a way that fits the story and links the subplots to the main plot.

The image below shows this series plot and the romance subplot together.

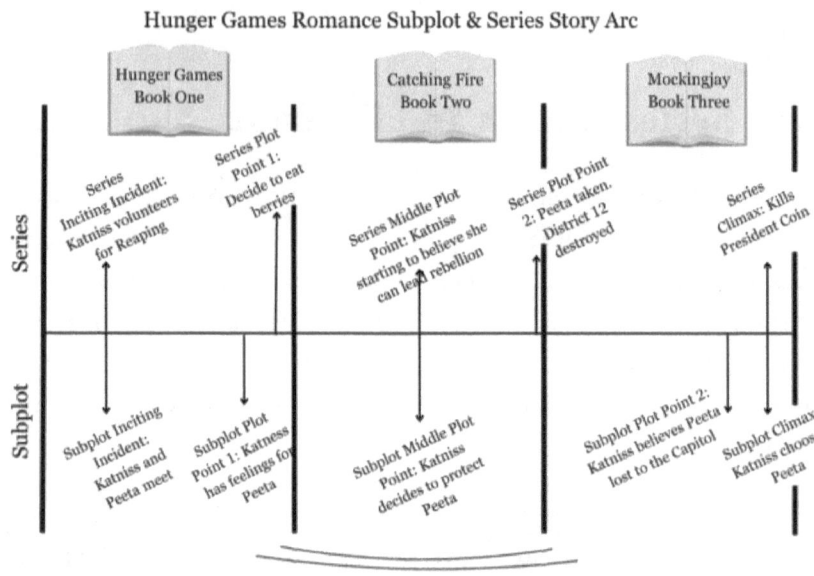

Evolution Subplot

We referred to our series vault, the series goal, and the series closing image of the Evolution series to generate ideas for the first subplot. This subplot needs to relate to Jaz's series goal of shutting down the experimentation center using her ability to see into a dog's mind.

The main event in the series' closing image is that Jaz and her friend create a secret community for those with the ability to see into a dog's mind.

This gives us the goal for the subplot. The goal is to create a secret community for those with the ability to see into a dog's mind. This shows us the subplot is either adventure or thriller. It also gives us the opportunity to write a subplot that supports part of the series goal: using the ability to see into a dog's mind.

It also gives us the main characters for the subplot. They will be Jaz and her friend. Jaz remains the protagonist throughout the series.

The Evolution series blurb

Jaz Cooper must discover and eliminate the organization testing the ability on humans; otherwise, Jaz and all the others who have the ability might be killed.

The Evolution series is a paranormal mystery. The mystery means there must be a crime, and maybe even a murder, in each novel in the series. We've labeled it paranormal because of the ability to see into dogs' minds. The series blurb has both those aspects.

For the subplot, the main event in the series climax includes both Jaz and a friend. This shows us that we need a subplot that includes this friend throughout the series. To find this friend, we'll look at the story arc scenes from book one.

Book One and Series Inciting Incident: Jaz saves a dog's life and gains the ability to see into the dog's mind.

Jaz is alone in the inciting incident, so we need a scene where her friend is introduced. We're going to add a main event in the "reaction to the inciting incident scene." The friend will be introduced in that scene, and this kicks off the subplot. This scene will be the subplot inciting incident.

We know the climax scene for the subplot because it is the closing image of the series. We've just created the framework for our subplot. That is an exciting moment. We literally did that as we were writing this chapter. We'll add this to our series vault.

The main plot is about finding and destroying the organization that killed Jaz's husband. The subplot is related to the ability to see into a dog's mind. This ability will put Jaz's life in danger. This makes it harder for Jaz to achieve her series goal, and that's what we want.

We also see an opportunity to add tension using knowledge gaps. Now that we know there will be a secondary character that stays with Jaz from the reaction to the inciting incident in book one to the closing image of book three, we have an opportunity to add a second POV character.

Earlier in this book, we decided the Evolution series was going to be written from a single POV. We've just changed that decision, and we're going to add a second POV character. That POV character will drive the subplot. This means we have to update our series vault with a new POV strategy.

Here's the kicker. When we updated our series vault, the next item in the vault is the narrative strategy. Our original plan was to write the series in the first person. With a second POV character, we must decide whether this still works. We could write two characters in the first-person tense. This might be jarring to the reader. We could write Jaz from first person and the second character in third person. This might also be jarring to the reader. From this, we come to the conclusion that the best decision is to write both characters in the third person.

So back to the series vault we go. We'll update the vault to show we're now going to write the series in third person.

This shows how valuable the series vault is and how important it is to keep it up to date.

Let's give our subplot a series subplot skeleton blurb:

Jaz and her friend must create a secret community for those with the ability to see into a dog's mind; otherwise, these people will always be hunted as a danger to society.

From the main event in the closing image, we know that Jaz and her friend are going to succeed at achieving their goal. They will form the community. This leads us right back to plot point 1 of the subplot. Jaz and her friend will accept the story goal.

The following is the main event for plot point 1 in the series subplot:

Jaz and her friend accept the series subplot goal and decide to create a community for those with the ability to see into a dog's mind.

And now we'll go back through the process we covered for the main plot and build out our subplot.

This image shows what the Evolution series subplot looks like when mapped onto the Evolution series story arc. We added the subplot's middle plot point in the image; however, we didn't discover what that event was for that scene until we named the series and the three novels in the series.

The image gives us a clear view of the structure. As we write the series, we know we'll figure out where plot point 1 and plot point 2 for the subplots should be located. We think the subplot plot point 1 will be in book one, but we're not sure yet where.

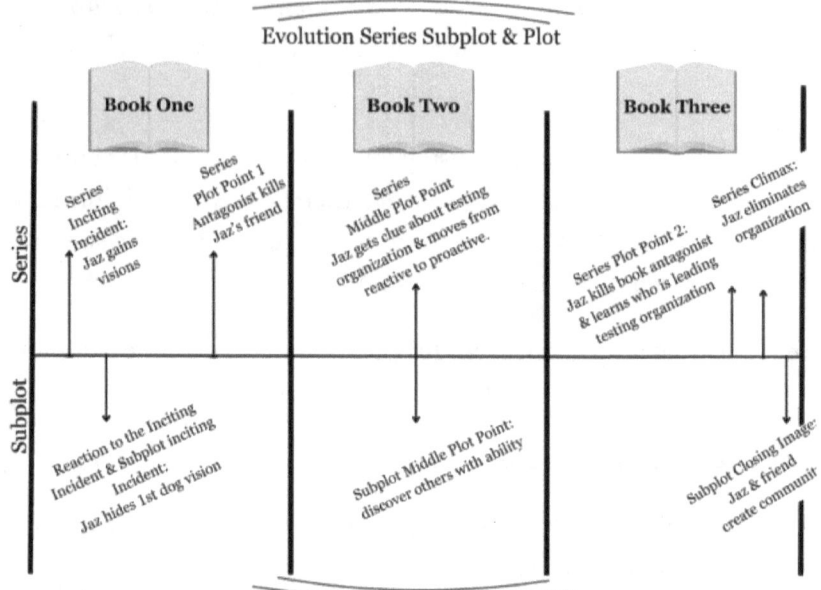

My Fairy Assassin Subplot

In each novel of the My Fairy Assassin open series, Liv Wright must use the time portal to go back in time to help a family member and defeat an antagonist.

To find a subplot, we'll explore another side of the young adult genre. A fledgling relationship is often part of this genre, so let's see if that works.

For motivation, we're going to look at the example from the Stephanie Plum series. She is the single protagonist written in a single POV. Throughout the series she manages to always have love interests. This shows us that one of the subplots falls in the romance genre.

One of the love interests appears in the key scenes. This gives us an idea for the My Fairy Assassin series. We can use romance as our subgenre. A fairy is going to be Liv's main love interest, so we'll create a subplot around a romance between Liv and the fairy.

We decided the following is the **series subplot skeleton blurb**:

Liv Wright must overcome her and the fairy's obstacles; otherwise, she will not be able to find true love.

We'll introduce the fairy in *My Fairy Assassin* (book one) and show the love interests meeting for the first time. In the romance genre this is often referred to as the meet-cute. This can be used for series unity by having the fairy enter each story in the inciting incident scene.

We also want to place the fairy in plot point 1, the middle plot point, plot point 2, and the climax. This is an artistic choice. The subplot characters don't have to be in all the story arc scenes.

The young adult genre demands true love and an obstacle to that love. Here we had an aha moment. We know from our series vault that the time portal doesn't always behave as expected, and we need a reason for this. We're going to expand on that and have decided the time portal can't handle true love, because love is a magic that can alter the time portal magic. Now this sounds interesting to us.

We're going to use the story arc scene duties for a romance novel to create the main events for each of our subplot story arc scenes. These will be generic for now.

My Fairy Assassin (**book one**)

Subplot Inciting Incident: Liv meets the fairy.

Subplot Plot Point 1: Liv chooses the fairy.

Subplot Middle Plot Point: Liv and the fairy share a connection.

Subplot Plot Point 2: Liv and the fairy have a falling out.

Subplot Climax: Liv gets a little closer to the fairy because of a romantic gesture.

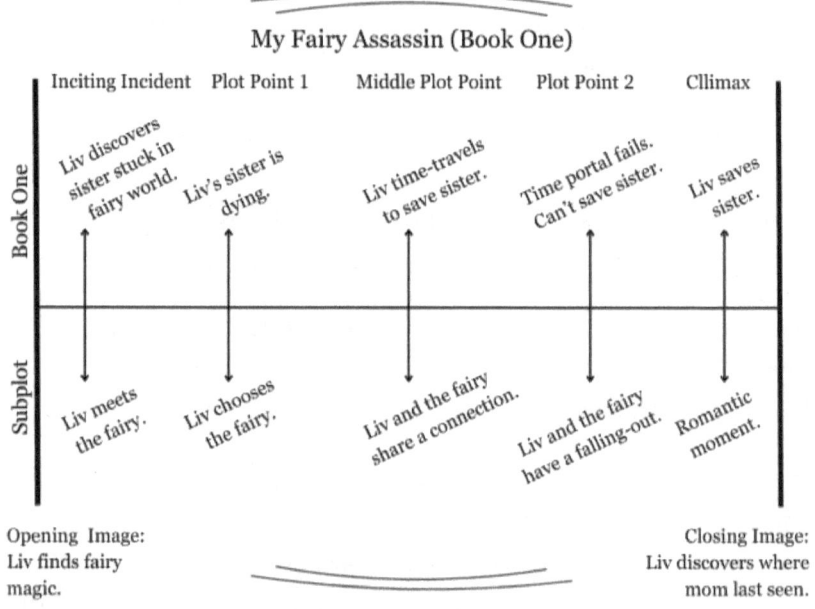

We can use this structure for each novel in the series. As we outline each novel, we'll make sure each of the subplot story arc scenes is different from the others. Perhaps we'll have Liv and the fairy be separated at the end of each novel, and they meet in a new way in the next novel in the series.

We'll get to these decisions as we write the novels. It's exciting that there is still so much room for creativity in the process.

Your Fun Series Task

If you read through how we created the first subplot for the Evolution series, you'll know how important it is to go through the process. We made a major change to our story structure because of a discovery we made.

For a closed series:

1. Review the scenes you've created the main events for. These are all listed in your series vault.
2. From the main event you choose, create the subplot goal.
3. From the goal, create the subplot stakes.
4. Choose the character who will drive the subplot.
5. Create a subplot skeleton goal.
6. Add the subplot skeleton blurb to your series vault.
7. Choose a scene that can be the subplot inciting incident.
8. Create the main event for the subplot inciting incident.
9. Add that main event to your series vault.
10. Decide whether the subplot goal will be achieved.
11. Create the main event for the subplot climax scene.
12. Add that main event to your series vault.
13. Depending on the event, choose where these events will be placed within your main plot.
14. Add that placement to your story vault.
15. Add any other changes to your series vault that you made because of going through the process of creating a subplot outline.

This will give you enough to start writing the subplot.

For the first novel in your open series, choose a subplot for the first novel in the series:

1. Decide on the subplot genre.
2. Write your subplot skeleton blurb.
3. Add the subplot skeleton blurb to your series vault.
4. List the main events expected in the five story arc scenes for that genre.
5. Create a main event for each of the five subplot story arc scenes.
6. Add the subplot main events to your series vault.

Vault Heading	Evolution	My Fairy Assassin
Protagonist Type	Single	Single
POV Strategy	~~Single (Jaz Cooper)~~ Two Characters	Single (Liv Wright)
Narrative Strategy	~~First Person~~ Third Person	First Person
Tense	Past	Present

Subplot: Evolution and My Fairy Assassin Series

Vault Heading	Evolution	My Fairy Assassin
Subplot Skeleton Blurb	Jaz and her friend must create a secret community for those with the ability to see into a dog's mind; otherwise, these people will always be hunted as a danger to society.	Liv Wright must overcome her and the fairy's obstacles; otherwise, she will not be able to find true love.
Subplot Inciting Incident	This comes from the reaction to the inciting incident in book one. Jaz has her first dog vision. Jaz hides her first dog vision from another person.	Liv meets the fairy.
Subplot Plot Point 1	Jaz and her friend decide to create a community for those with the ability to see into a dog's mind.	Liv admits to herself she likes the fairy.

Subplot: Evolution and My Fairy Assassin Series Con't

Vault Heading	Evolution	My Fairy Assassin
Subplot Middle Plot Point	Jaz and her friend discover others with the ability to see into a dog's mind are willing to help protect her daughter.	Liv chooses the fairy.
Subplot Plot Point 2	Jaz kills book one's antagonist and learns who is leading the testing organization.	Liv and the fairy have a falling-out.
Subplot Climax	This comes from the closing image in book three. Jaz and her friend create a secret community for those with the ability.	In each novel, there must be a romantic gesture where Liv gets a little closer to the fairy.

Vault Heading	Evolution
Book One Inciting Incident	Jaz saves a dog's life and gains the ability to see into the dog's mind.
Book One Reaction to Inciting Incident	**Jaz has her first dog vision. Jaz hides her first dog vision from another person.**
Book One Plot Point 1	Jaz uses a dog vision and finally believes her husband was murdered.
Book One Plot Point 2	Jaz's actions cause someone close to her to die.
Book Three Climax	Jaz uses her ability to see into a dog's mind to eliminate the testing organization.

Where to Next?

You've done so much, and we're almost to the end. In the next chapter we're going to help you name your series and the novels within the series. The goal at this point is to create names to help you stay focused. You can change the name anytime until you publish the novels.

Chapter Twenty-Four: Novel and Series Titles

The Importance of Naming a Series

There is a power to naming a series, because you're claiming the whole series is about this name. Naming shows your authorship of the series, and as in all parts of writing a series, you need a strategy.

Let's lay out some basics for the series name. A reader wants to recommend a novel they love, and if they hesitate because the name was unclear, unmemorable, or embarrassing to repeat, then that is a series name that has not done its job.

For a series name to work, it must be clear, memorable, and not embarrassing.

Novel and series names are brand names. And as such we recommend that you test the names to see if they are ready to publish.

We need a process to test for clear, memorable, and not embarrassing names. Let's look at what to consider.

Series Naming Clarity

The old saying "Don't judge a book by its cover" is around because people do. They judge the artwork, and they judge the title.

To have a clear title, the series name must hint at what the series is about.

How can we incorporate this into the process of creating a series name?

First, consider how a reader figures out what the series is about just from reading the title. Think of the title as an entry hook into the series or novel. You won't be surprised that title ideas can come from the characters, plot, or setting. There are also other places to find titles.

Here are five places you can look to for inspiration:

1. **First Novel**: *A Court of Thorns and Roses* is the first name in Sarah J Maas's series, and it also names the series. This is the same for the Hunger Games series by Suzanne Collins.
2. **Character**: *Harry Potter and* ... All the novels in the Harry Potter closed series start with his name. This is also a great idea with mysteries and thrillers that are a character-based open series.
3. **Plot Device:** The Millennium series by Stieg Larsson. *Millennium* is the name of the magazine that the main characters are linked through.
4. **Setting:** Elsie Silver names her sassy, sexy romance small-town series the Chestnut Springs series. It is a setting-based open romance series, so using the setting to name the series is a great branding move.
5. **Series Goal:** The Lord of the Rings series is about who will possess the ring.

Naming Guidelines

A series name should be memorable. After all, you want your readers to remember the name so they let other readers know about your series.

If the list above didn't give you an idea for a memorable name, you can try naming each novel in three words or fewer. Then turn these into a series name.

Naming a novel is like naming a scene. When editing a novel, we recommend you name each scene in three words or fewer. This shows you the scene is focused and you know what the scene is about.

If you can name each novel in three words or fewer, you'll know each novel is focused. For now you'll use these as working titles. As you'll see with the Evolution series, these are most likely not the titles we'll use in the published editions of the novels. The titles show us what each novel is trying to achieve.

The series and individual skeleton blurbs should give you a hint for naming your novels.

Our guess is Janet Evanovich came up with her series strategy and series blurbs before she named any of her novels. Each novel title starts with a number.

One for the Money

Two for the Dough

Three to Get Deadly

And so on...

Name Each Book in Evolution

Based on the skeleton blurbs, we're going to call the series Evolution.

Book One Skeleton Blurb: Jaz Cooper must find out who killed her husband, using her ability to see into a dog's mind; otherwise, she might die.

In book one, Jaz **discovers** she has the ability to see into a dog's mind.

Book Two Skeleton Blurb: Jaz Cooper must keep others from discovering her daughter can see into a dog's mind; otherwise, her daughter might be killed.

In book two, Jaz will do anything to **protect** her daughter.

Book Three Skeleton Blurb: Jaz Cooper must discover and **eliminate** the organization testing the ability on humans; otherwise, Jaz and all the others who have the ability might be killed.

In book three, Jaz must eliminate (meaning destroy) the testing organization.

These three skeleton blurbs led us to the following working titles:

Book One: *Discover*

Book Two: *Protect*

Book Three: *Destroy*

These are working titles that remind us of the theme for each novel. You can also use Book One, Book Two, and Book Three.

We can now think about themes for each novel based on the names.

Book One: How will a person deal with a new ability? (*Discover*)

Book Two: What will a person sacrifice for someone they love? (*Protect*)

Book Three: What will a person do to protect those they love? (*Destroy*)

You don't have to have a theme for each novel. This was something that came to us as we were naming each novel, so we thought it might trigger the same creativity in you. This is a fluid process, and you have to go where your muse takes you.

The following is the series skeleton blurb: Jaz Cooper must keep her ability to see into a dog's mind a secret; otherwise, she and those with the ability will be experimented on and possibly die.

This shows the evolution of humans and dogs. They evolve in the way they can communicate. Hence the series title: Evolution.

Naming the novels gave us an idea for the middle plot point for book two. Book two is about Jaz protecting her daughter.

The following is the middle plot point for the series and for book three: Jaz does something that forces her to understand why she must keep her daughter's ability a secret. She also discovers something that leads her to the testing organization.

We can now see how to enhance this with the subplot's middle plot point. This is going to happen in the same scene as the series' middle plot point. Jaz and her friend must move from reactive to proactive if they are going to achieve the subplot goal of creating a secret community for those with the ability to see into a dog's mind. At the series and book two middle plot point, Jaz realizes there are others who can help protect her daughter.

We've decided the middle plot point for the subplot is as follows:

> *Jaz and her friend discover others with the ability to see into a dog's mind are willing to help protect her daughter.*

This is the moment they decide to proactively build a community of people with the dog-vision ability. We think that makes a strong middle plot point for the series, for the subplot, and for book two. We'll add this to the Evolution series vault.

Name Three Books in My Fairy Assassin

Looking at the skeleton blurbs, we are going to call the series Liv Wright.

Book One Skeleton Blurb: Liv Wright must use the fairy time portal to save her fairy assassin sister; otherwise, a scientist will destroy the world.

In book one, Liv discovers she can time-travel, and when she does, she saves her sister and the world.

Book Two Skeleton Blurb: Liv Wright must use the fairy time portal to save her fairy saboteur mother; otherwise, a druid will destroy the world.

In book two, Liv discovers her mother is in danger, so she time-travels and saves the world, but not her mother.

Book Three Skeleton Blurb: Liv Wright must use the fairy time portal to save her fairy enforcer aunt; otherwise, an alchemist will destroy the world.

In book three, Liv time-travels to save her aunt and the world.

Based on the character Liv is trying to save, the three skeleton blurbs led us to the following working titles.

Book One: *My Fairy Assassin*

Book Two: *My Fairy Saboteur*

Book Three: *My Fairy Enforcer*

These are working titles that point to the family members that Liv must time-travel to save. Focusing on Liv and her family members in the title means that the family member will be part of the story goal when we write the novel.

Book One: Who is the fairy assassin? Liv's sister.

Book Two: Who is the fairy saboteur? Liv's mother.

Book Three: Who is the fairy enforcer? Liv's aunt.

This creates the question of who Liv is trying to save in each story.

Seeing the series unity through the series skeleton blurb, we can see how we can add more novels to this open series.

Your Fun Series Task

You'll continue to grow your series vault as you work through this book. Now it's time to do the following:

1. Name each novel in the series for a closed series. Name the first three novels if your series is an open series.
2. Name your series.
3. Add the above information to your series vault.

Evolution and My Fairy Assassin Vault: Titles

Vault Heading	Evolution	My Fairy Assassin
Series Type	Closed	Open
# of Novels	3	Undecided
Uniting Factor	Plot	Character
Protagonist Type	Single	Single
Protagonist Name	Jaz Cooper	Liv Wright
Series Name	Evolution	Liv Wright
Book One Title	Discover	My Fairy Assassin
Book Two Title	Protect	My Fairy Saboteur
Book Three Title	Destroy	My Fairy Enforcer
POV Strategy	Two Characters	Single POV
Narrative Strategy	Third-this changes from first to third	First
Tense	Past	Present

Where to Next?

We are at another drumroll moment. It's finally time to start writing your series. We did this, too, and in the next chapter we've included a draft version of the inciting incident for the Evolution and My Fairy Assassin series. You can choose any scene to write. That's the fun of being an artist.

Chapter Twenty-Five: Write Your Series

If you've done your fun series tasks throughout the novel, you're in the perfect place to start writing.

The series vault is an important asset, so don't forget to refer to it and update it while you're writing. With it, you'll see the series taking life right in front of you.

You'll write your novel one scene at a time. This doesn't mean you have to write those scenes in order. You can write them in any order you want.

For a closed series, outline book one and then choose from the list below.

Options for Writing

1. Start with book one and write the story arc scenes for that novel.
2. Write the inciting incident in book one and the climax in the final novel in the series.
3. Write the opening images and go forward scene by scene until you've written a novel. Then move on to the second novel.
4. Write scenes in the order they come to you.

For an open series, outline book one, and then choose from the list below.

Options for Writing

1. Start with book one and write the story arc scenes for that novel.

2. Write the inciting incident and climax scene in book one of the series.
3. Write the opening images and go forward scene by scene until you've written a novel. Then move on to the second novel.
4. Write scenes in the order they come to you.

You're the artist, and the order you write in is just one more artistic choice you have.

How to Write a Scene

You already know the main events for your story arc scenes, and when you know the main event, you won't be staring at a blank page. It gives you the premise for that scene. After a scene is written, it will have the following:

1. A scene entry hook
2. A POV character
3. A POV goal
4. The scene middle
5. The scene climax
6. A scene exit hook

The list above is the structure of a strong scene. Once you're sure you have the main structure covered, you can add more depth to each scene.

If you choose a story arc scene to write first, you already know the POV character is the protagonist.

If you don't choose one of the story arc scenes, then choose the POV character by deciding which character will cause the most tension.

This could be the character who has the most to lose if they don't achieve the scene POV goal.

Start with the Main Plot

If you write the main plot first, it will be much easier to add in a subplot and interweave the subplot into the main plot in a way that causes the most tension.

We recommend writing at least the five story arc scenes before moving on to outlining and writing subplots. By writing these scenes first, you'll learn what your main plot needs from the subplot.

Perhaps you find it easier to write the main plot and the subplot at the same time. If that's you, go for it.

Evolution Inciting Incident (Draft)

For the Evolution series, the first scene Kristina wanted to write was the inciting incident. The following is a draft version. Keep in mind this is the first scene written in the series, and it will most likely change by the time the full series is written. This scene has not gone through a copy edit or a story edit yet (since the story isn't written).

> The coffee maker beeped, telling me the coffee was brewed. Ignoring the tempting aroma, I pressed my face deep into Bandit's bed. I could almost feel his breath on my face, the lick of his tongue on my cheek, the thump of his tail against my leg. Almost.

A dog's howl roared through the storm's bluster. I held my breath and listened. The wind rattled the trees near the house.

I waited.

Another howl was followed by the sound of slapping water. I scrambled to the window but couldn't see anything. I stepped onto my porch, a mere thirty feet from the frozen lake, and concentrated on the sound. Hard snow bit into my eyes, forcing me to squint.

A bark. More slapping water.

The moon broke through the clouds, streaming light onto the lake.

Paws grasped at the edge of a hole in the ice. Water splashed.

Without thinking, I ran toward the dog. My slippers got stuck in the snow and ripped from my feet. The cold burned my bare skin. I reached the lake's icy surface and kept running. I didn't care about my safety, only the dog's.

Katie's Great Dane, Daisy, battled the edge of the ice. She must have run onto the frozen lake from next door. Her rump slid underwater, and her front claws strained against the snow. Her nostrils flared in exertion.

A few yards onto the lake's surface, my heels slid across black ice, and I tumbled backward. My tailbone slammed onto the hard surface, and my elbow cracked. I rolled onto my side, then onto my stomach. I slithered forward over the partly frozen lake, closer but not close enough to grab Daisy's paws.

Daisy slipped backward into the water. Her head dropped below the surface.

I reached for her front legs.

She burst through the surface, snorting water and scraping her paws over the edge of the ice. She barked. Her nails clawed at the ice but couldn't grip the surface. Fear in her eyes? Pleading?

I crawled forward on my stomach, ignoring my throbbing elbow. I should have grabbed a rope. A hundred-pound panicking dog would not be easy to hoist out of the water. Sleet soaked my back and neck. My pajama bottoms clung to my legs.

I grabbed one paw. Daisy's nails dug into my arm, and I let go. I didn't mean to, but the pain was too much. The dog had power in her limbs. I had to get closer. I'd have to leverage her out of the water.

Her rump remained below the surface, but her head stayed above water. For now.

Another howl. Anyone listening would think I was torturing the dog. I inched closer. The darkness below welcomed me. I could slide past her into the water. Moments would pass, the pain would end, and I would be with Nick and Bandit. But Daisy would drown too. How selfish.

Crack.

The sound jarred me into action. One big shove with my feet and my arms slid underneath her pits and around her shoulders. She dug her claws into the back of my neck. A warm liquid trickled across my skin. She'd cut me, but I didn't let go.

Adrenaline pounded my temples. My skin prickled. Daisy's terror bled into me, so strong that I gasped.

Daisy dug her claws deep into my neck and shoulders, gaining traction. She hefted herself out of the water, tumbled over my head, across my back, and away from the hole.

I knew I should get off the ice, but I couldn't move. I lay on my back, panting. The black water called me. All I had to do was roll over and slide in.

Daisy closed her jaws around my arm and pulled. She dragged me a few feet from the hole of death.

She hovered over me. Her huge front paws pranced near my shoulder. She licked my face and neck with her cold tongue.

I wrapped my arms around her gigantic frame and cried.

The ice cracked again.

Daisy nuzzled her wet snout into my cheek. She pawed my shoulder and whined.

Another crack.

Daisy wasn't leaving without me, and if I kept her there much longer, we might both disappear into the frothing darkness.

This scene is 707 words long. This is a bit short for an inciting incident, but we're not going to worry about that now. What we want at this point is to write a draft of the main plot in the Evolution series.

Don't focus on the word count per scene until you have a full draft of one novel written.

We know that prior to this scene we'll write at least an "opening image" scene and a "lead-up to the inciting incident" scene, so we'll have Jaz's ordinary world established.

Let's look at the series skeleton blurb and the book one skeleton blurb.

Series Skeleton Blurb

Jaz Cooper must discover and eliminate the organization testing the ability on humans; otherwise, Jaz and all the others who have the ability might be killed.

Evolution (book one) Skeleton Blurb

Jaz Cooper must find out who killed her husband, using her ability to see into a dog's mind; otherwise, she might die.

You'll have noticed that what both skeleton blurbs have in common is Jaz's ability to see into a dog's mind. In the inciting incident, Jaz doesn't know that she is about to gain this ability, but the reader does. The reader learned this from reading the final story blurb used to sell the series. This is great news.

Why?

Because it creates a knowledge gap. The reader knows something Jaz doesn't, and this adds to the tension in the scene. The scene does double duty. Jaz's ordinary world is changed because she realizes she is suicidal. She doesn't know yet that the event has given her the ability to see into a dog's mind. This knowledge will come in the "reaction to the inciting incident" scene. Boom! We've just discovered what the main event in the next scene will be. As we're writing this, we took a moment and added this to the series vault for Evolution. You'll get these moments too. When they happen, update your series vault.

Evolution (book one) Reaction to the Inciting Incident Main Event:

Jaz has her first dog vision.

You may remember that for Evolution, we decided the inciting incident is the same scene for both the series and book one.

This means the main event for book one must disrupt Jaz's world and cause her to react in the context of our **book one story goal** (find out who killed her husband, using her ability to see into a dog's mind).

It also means the main event in this scene must disrupt Jaz's world and cause her to react in the context of our **series story goal** (keep her ability to see into a dog's mind a secret). This gives us the second event in the reaction to the inciting incident:

> *Jaz hides her first dog vision.*

We'll add this to our series vault. This shows us that if she's hiding the dog vision, then another character must be in the scene with her. We just don't know how yet. We'll update the event to be as follows:

> *Jaz hides her first dog vision from another person.*

We'll go back to our series vault and add this change.

We're going to delve a little deeper here so we can ensure we've covered the story elements that help us write a better scene. We're doing this to practice. Once these story elements come naturally, then it's time to write the draft without pausing to check these elements. You can do that later when you perform a story edit.

1. A scene entry hook
2. The POV character
3. The POV goal
4. The scene middle
5. The scene climax
6. A scene exit hook

The entry hook: *A dog's howl roared through the storm's bluster.*

This is the first sentence in paragraph two. The hook: Why is the dog howling? We're happy with that.

The POV character: Jaz Cooper.

This meets the criteria that a story arc scene is written from the protagonist's POV.

The POV goal: *I held my breath and listened.*

This appears in the second paragraph. This shows us that Jaz's goal is to find out why the dog is howling in a storm. The goal is in line with the entry hook.

Scene middle: *Crack. The sound jarred me into action.*

Right before this, Jaz still wants to die. This is the moment the scene turns, and she decides she's going to save the dog. That works for a scene middle, because she moves from reactive to proactive.

Scene climax: Jaz pulls the dog from the ice, but she remains by the hole. This works because Jaz has addressed her scene goal that developed throughout the scene, and she's saved the dog. She hasn't saved herself yet.

Exit hook: *Daisy wasn't leaving without me, and if I kept her there much longer, we might both disappear into the frothing darkness.*

Here the reader doesn't know whether Jaz will succumb and roll into the water, or whether she'll leave with Daisy.

And that's it. We're happy with the scene for now.

The scene has met the criteria for a well-structured scene.

We are looking at this from a high-level perspective so we can move on to the next scene. Don't get stuck here perfecting this scene. Get the main event written and move on to the rest of your story. The goal is to get a draft written, and then you can go back and write the subplots. After that you'll perform a story edit.

My Fairy Assassin Inciting Incident (Draft)

For *My Fairy Assassin*, the first scene Lucy wanted to write was the inciting incident. The following is a draft version. Keep in mind this is the first scene written in the series, and it will most likely change by the time the full series is written. This scene has not gone through a copy edit or a story edit yet (since the story isn't written).

> Everyone is running toward the Front Gates with gardening forks, with spades, with piping. The corridor is warm and suffocating. Even though I stand in the long, high metal artery of a corridor, still I cannot catch my breath. What happens if I am caught? I stand in the shadows. Another person runs past with a part of the air ducting.
>
> Why are they armed?
>
> Will they notice me in the corridor?
>
> I groan as a medic with a blue face mask marches up to me and stands in front of me, looming. I can't tell who it is.
>
> "Oye, you are needed." His voice is urgent and genuine. Here is yet another person barking orders, thinking this noise will stop the world from spinning out of control. The medic puts his hand under my arm. "I've been told to fetch you."
>
> My back pushes against the rough, rusty wall. There is no give to the Eco-Ark, probably good news for keeping the broken environment outside, but not such good news when I want to hide.

How does Richard know I got out? "No, I don't want to be fetched."

He is wearing the scrubs that all the medics do, and a blue mask, and a hat. I assume it is a he. I recognize every single voice in my Eco-Ark. Perhaps he is from Eco-Ark 7.

I pull away from him. Everyone is always trying to tell me what to do. He probably doesn't know I am Richard's stepdaughter.

"No," I whisper. This is a futile act of defiance. However, sometimes even the smallest *no* feels like a victory.

The clatter of feet on the corridor dissolves my words. He hooks his hand under my elbow, again. He is gentler than I expect, but I am always being yanked, pulled, pushed—but not this time.

He shakes his head in irritation. His long blond hair falls about his face.

He should tie his hair back. Medics always do that. Is he even a medic?

"The Mercy Heroes are arriving back any minute, and we must get to the w—" The medic sighs.

I stand in front of him.

He lets go of his grasp and says, "Eco-Ark 7 has collapsed."

We both run.

I guess we are needed after all.

He stops me.

We are just outside the woodland enclave.

Right, he is a medic. We are going to need willow bark and meadowsweet. We are going to need garlic for sure.

Behind me is the last hope, our ark of nature, and once we figure out how to save the environment, we can use it to re-green the world. That is what we wanted to do with Eco-Ark 7.

Eco-Ark 7 was our closest neighbor, and the only other Eco-Ark left.

I stagger back and lean against the iron door to the woodland enclave. This door is the sturdiest door in the Eco-Ark.

It has to be.

It houses our most precious treasure: two hundred acres of deciduous forest, with ancient trees and young saplings alike, all entombed in the fragile steel and concrete. In the infirmary, when someone is hooked up, we monitor their vitals. The woodland enclave is monitored, the last of our trees, hooked up, locked up "safe" here in the Eco-Ark. It is the last of the natural world.

I will be safe from my stepfather in there.

None of us are safe, though.

Eco-Ark 7 can't have collapsed. Our Mercy Missionaries are always able to patch up Eco-Ark 7.

There is normally chaos when a Mercy Mission comes back. We count in the missionaries. We have medicine at the ready, and our arms are full of food, flowers, and mostly hugs.

"You are needed to—" The medic stops me, looking at everyone else.

"What's happening?" I shout. I wish I had not shouted. The woodland enclave doors hiss open, and I hear Richard's voice first. I loop my arm into the medic's and lean on his shoulder to hide myself.

"We have run out of medication to save the Eco-Ark 7 survivors." My stepfather has meadowsweet in his hands, and it looks like he ripped it from the ground. So wasteful, so my stepfather, not to leave the roots to let them regrow.

"What are you doing here, Liv?" Richard shakes the meadowsweet at me. The sweet floral smell does not calm me like it usually does. "Get to the Front Gates, and only let in Mercy Missionaries."

My stepfather's voice breaks.

"The gates are locked to everyone who does not belong—it will be the same as the Big Lock-In."

My mouth opens and closes.

I have no words.

Richard rubs his chin.

He must be remembering the Big Lock-In.

Obviously I don't remember the day of the Big Lock-In because, back then, I was only a day old, but Mum said it broke everyone, and before that day my stepfather had not been all bad.

Richard shakes his head. "The banging—"

I stop listening to him. I am not going to watch this, listen to this. My stepfather is a coward. Would he really abandon everyone from the other Eco-Ark?

I need to help everyone.

How?

He looks crumbled; then he rolls his shoulders down. This is his fight stance. Nobody openly crosses Richard.

The returning heroes, the Mercy Mission that Misty was meant to be on, is coming back. Could I convince them to let in the others?

But my stepfather would be there.

My eye throbs, and the pain will not go away. Surely there was some way that I could save the last of the survivors. The last of our humanity. I was not going to be like my stepfather.

The sirens of the Front Gates wail. This flimsy shell, the giant Front Gates, more rusty metal, covered with our red flaky paint made from all the shells we collect from the woodland enclave.

There isn't a way. I let out a sigh.

"Liv, be prepared to fight for your life." Richard grabs me by the back of my collar.

I cannot breathe. Panicking is futile—he would pull my collar tighter. Trying to relax, I look around. Through the glass double doors, I can make out the silhouette of the trees. *Think about them, think about the oaks.* Calm returns.

Richard yanks me, and we march towards the Front Gates.

Richard ignores the medic, but the medic does not ignore him. The medic holds me by the crook of my elbow. Muttering to himself.

The medic somehow lifts me a little so my stepfather's hold doesn't cut off my air.

The Front Gates are only a minute walk from the woodland enclave. There are more people heading towards them. The weapons are primed now.

Misty would have found a way, wouldn't she? I can almost hear her voice, steady and calm, navigating the chaos. But she's not here, and it's just me.

The doors rumble, about to open. The smell of burnt toast comes from outside. The smell of burning, of heat, smothers everything.

My stepfather lets go of my collar and pushes past me to the front of the crowd.

Everyone is here. Just like everyone normally is at a return of a Mercy Mission, but this time everyone is bearing arms instead of welcoming with open arms. The energy in the room is tight.

Nobody dares to defy Richard.

"The Mercy Missionaries have to enter first." My stepfather's command booms above the melee, reverberating off the rusted, creaking metal walls. "Then we lock the doors."

The energy in the room calms. We are in the eye of the storm now.

Silence.

I glance at the medic. Is he scared or confused? Hard to tell. I don't even know if any of us understand what my stepfather is proposing.

"We have to save the woodland enclave." Richard's cold, analytical mind is at work. He storms towards me.

The medic trips him.

My stepfather stumbles into the back of the crowd.

The medic yanks my hand, pulling me away from the Front Gates, the opposite way to the crowd, and back towards the door of the woodland enclave.

He makes strange hand signs, leaving a trail of forget-me-not blue light behind.

It's mesmerizing. The blue lights fall onto the washed out concrete floor as we near the woodland enclave. Nobody is here. We got here so quickly, but how?

Fear can make you compliant, even desperate.

The footsteps echo from behind me. My stepfather has caught up.

We dart into the woodland enclave just as I hear Richard shout.

"Wait!" My stepfather's command rings out too late, and the closing door seals him away from me.

As the door shuts, the medic springs into action. With a swift movement, he reaches for the electronic door panel and slams his fist against it. The screen flickers and dies, denying everyone else entry to the woodland enclave. No going back now.

Richard pounds on the door, each thud a hammer strike against my racing heart.

"Liv, you cannot lock us out of the woodland enclave. You will kill us all." Richard's voice is distant. "After I stop Eco-Ark 7 from getting in, I am going to destroy you."

I step away from the door. Richard's shadow is no longer the other side of the glass door. He must have left to deal with the Mercy Mission. How will he live with himself?

I can feel the world spinning.

When Richard comes back, he will kill me.

SECRETS TO WRITING A SERIES

I will not spend my last thirty minutes worrying about dying. Having lived on a dead planet my whole life, I guess I'm finally OK with dying.

I let out a breath.

Now, when I know I am going to die, I finally have no fear of Richard. I turn my back to the door and smile.

I feel free.

"I was told to fetch you. And fetch you I did; otherwise the fetches would fetch you, and you would rather they didn't." The medic's voice is a balm, like the night cream. "Look, your sister is not dead. She is stuck in my world."

The medic removes his mask. Blue lights flicker around him, and I cannot believe the face on this medic.

He is beautiful.

He grins at me.

I laugh.

And then he pulls his long blond hair behind his ears.

I gasp.

This scene is over sixteen hundred words long, so it's a good length for an inciting incident.

The following is the skeleton blurb for *My Fairy Assassin*:

> Liv Wright must use the fairy time portal to save her fairy assassin sister; otherwise, a scientist will destroy the world.

The entry hook: *Everyone is running towards the Front Gates, with gardening forks, with spades, with piping.*

This is the opening line of the scene, and it makes the reader ask, Why are people armed and running?

The POV character: Liv Wright.

This meets the criteria that a story arc scene is written from the protagonist's POV.

The POV goal: *No way am I going to see him.*

Liv does not want to be fetched by the medic. This happens early in the scene and shows the reader there is conflict coming. The medic wants Liv to do something she doesn't want to do.

Scene middle: *"The Mercy Missionaries have to enter first." Richard's command booms above the melee, reverberating off the rusted, creaking metal walls. The energy in the room calms. We are in the eye of the storm now. "Then we lock the doors."*

The scene middle ratchets up the tension. Richard intends to lock everyone out of the Eco-Ark. It's also a turning point for Liv, because she can't believe what Richard wants to do.

Scene climax: *"Liv, you cannot lock us out of the woodland enclave. You will kill us all." Richard's voice is distant. "After I stop Eco-Ark 7 from getting in, I am going to destroy you."*

Liv has defied her stepfather and will have to deal with the consequences. Her life has just had a major disruption, and this is exactly what an inciting incident should do.

Exit hook: *And then he pulls his long blond hair behind his ears. I gasp.*

This leaves the reader with the question, Why does Liv gasp at the medic's ears? The exit hook is placed after the climax in the final two sentences of the scene. The reader must read on to find out.

And that's it. We're happy with the scene for now.

As with the scene from the Evolution series, we are looking at this from a high-level perspective, so we can move on to the next scene. Remember not to get stuck here perfecting this scene. Get the main event written and move on. You have a series to write. Keep an eye on the goal: get a draft written, and then you can go back and write the subplots. Then you'll perform a story edit.

Your Fun Series Task

Choose the scene you most want to write and use the story elements to write the scene.

Where to Next?

We're going to give you some tips on how to make the most out of your series vault as you continue through your journey of writing your series.

Chapter Twenty-Six: The Series Vault

A series vault is an evolving document that's instrumental in maintaining consistency and coherence across the novels in a series. As we've shown, it's beneficial to begin the series vault as you're planning the first novel and documenting essential series-related information. This initial groundwork lays a foundation that can be expanded upon as the series progresses.

As you write, you'll likely develop new characters, settings, and subplots that weren't part of the initial plan. It's essential to update the series vault with these elements as they emerge. This will avoid inconsistencies later.

Once you've finished writing a novel in the series, it's an excellent time to review the series vault and add or update information that emerged during the writing process. This is a thorough check to ensure that everything is accurately represented and ready for reference while you're writing the next novel.

A series vault is not a "set and forget" document. It requires ongoing attention and should be considered a living document that evolves with the series. By treating it as an integral part of the creative process, writers can harness its full potential to enhance the coherence and depth of a series.

Before Starting a New Novel in the Series

Beginning a new novel in a series offers both opportunities and challenges. By consulting the series vault, you can immerse yourself in the existing narrative and reacquaint yourself with the nuances of the world you've created. It's a time to assess what's been achieved, fill in any gaps, and contemplate how the series will progress. This stage is a blend of reflection and forward thinking, bridging the gap between what has been written and what lies ahead.

During the Editing Phase

Editing is a rigorous process of refining the story. Changes made here can affect the series trajectory, and the series vault must reflect those changes. Keeping the document in sync with the manuscript ensures that the series maintains internal logic and continuity, making this a crucial step in the series-development process.

When Collaborating with Others

Collaborations introduce new voices and perspectives into the creative process. The series vault becomes a shared language that ensures everyone involved understands the vision and parameters of the series. It acts as a guide and a touchstone, facilitating clear communication and maintaining a consistent direction, even as multiple creative minds contribute to the project.

Series Vaults

Vault Heading	Evolution	My Fairy Assassin
Series Type	Closed	Open
# of Novels	3	Undecided
Uniting Factor	Plot	Character
Protagonist Type	Single	Single
Protagonist Name	Jaz Cooper	Liv Wright
Series Name	Evolution	Liv Wright
Book One Title	Discover	My Fairy Assassin
Book Two Title	Protect	My Fairy Saboteur
Book Three Title	Destroy	My Fairy Enforcer
POV Strategy	Two Characters	Single POV
Narrative Strategy	Third-this changes from first to third	First
Tense	Past	Present

Skeleton Blurbs

Vault Heading	Evolution	My Fairy Assassin
Series/ Generic Skeleton Blurb	Jaz Cooper must discover and eliminate the organization testing the ability on humans; otherwise, Jaz and all the others who have the ability might be killed.	Liv Wright must use the fairy time portal to save her family member; otherwise, the world will be destroyed.
Book One Skeleton Blurb	Jaz Cooper must find out who killed her husband using her ability to see into a dog's mind; otherwise, she might die.	Liv Wright must use the fairy time portal to save her fairy assassin sister; otherwise, a scientist will destroy the world.
Book Two Skeleton Blurb	Jaz Cooper must keep others from discovering her daughter can see into a dog's mind; otherwise, her daughter might be killed.	Liv Wright must use the fairy time portal to save her fairy saboteur mother; otherwise, a druid will destroy the world.
Book Three Skeleton Blurb	Jaz Cooper must discover and eliminate the organization testing the ability on humans; otherwise. Jaz and all the others who have the ability might be killed.	Liv Wright must use the fairy time portal to save her fairy enforcer aunt; otherwise, an alchemist will destroy the world.

Evolution Series and My Fairy Assassin Series Story Arc

Vault Heading	Evolution	My Fairy Assassin
Series Inciting Incident	Disrupts Jaz's world and causes her to react in the context of the single novel story goal and the series goal.	Liv finds out a family member is in danger.
Series Plot Point 1	Jaz accepts the series story goal.	Liv accepts she is the one who has to save them.
Series Middle Plot Point	Jaz moves from reactive to proactive in relation to the series goal.	Liv time travels.
Series Plot Point 2	Jaz is at her lowest point in the final novel and in the series. She also discovers the final piece of information she needs to reach the climax of the series.	The time portal breaks.
Series Climax	Jaz achieves the series story goal and the final novel's story goal.	A variation of bittersweet endings.

Outlined Scenes: Book One

Vault Heading	Evolution	My Fairy Assassin
Opening Image	Jaz abandons her family and bolts from her husband's funeral.	Liv is tidying up her sister's room and finds fairy magic.
Inciting Incident	Jaz saves a dog's life and gains the ability to see into the dog's mind.	Liv discovers her sister is not dead yet but is stuck in a dying fairy world.
Reaction to the Inciting Incident	Jaz has her first dog vision. Jaz hides her first dog vision from another person.	To be determined.
Plot Point 1	Jaz uses a dog vision and finally believes her husband was murdered.	Liv's sister is dying, and Liv must learn to time-travel to save her.
Middle Plot Point	To be determined.	Liv time travels to save sister.

Outlined Scenes: Book One Continued

Vault Heading	Evolution	My Fairy Assassin
Plot Point 2	Jaz's actions cause someone close to die.	The time portal fails, and Liv cannot save her sister.
Climax	To be determined.	Liv saves her sister by reopening the time portal and injuring the scientist.
Closing Image	Together with her family, Jaz visits her husband's grave. Jaz sees her daughter react to a dog's vision.	Liv, her sister, and a fairy celebrate. Liv discovers her mother was last seen in the Fairy Library.

Outlined Scenes: Book Two

Vault Heading	Evolution	My Fairy Assassin
Time Passed	One day.	Two weeks.
New Ordinary World	Jaz's daughter has the same ability as she does.	Liv is in a parallel world
Opening Image	Jaz tests her daughter's ability to see into a dog's mind.	Liv finds fairy magic while looking for clues about her mother.
Backstory	Using a dog's vision, Jaz discovered who murdered her husband. Jaz caused someone to die.	Liv knows how to time travel.
Inciting Incident	Jaz discovers her daughter is in danger.	Liv finds out her mother was kidnapped by druids from Anglesey during 77 CE.

Outlined Scenes: Book Two Continued

Vault Heading	Evolution	My Fairy Assassin
Plot Point 1	To be determined.	Liv discovers her mother was caught sabotaging the druid's oak grove, and Liv must time travel to save her.
Middle Plot Point	Jaz does something that forces her to understand why she must keep her daughter's ability a secret. She discovers something leading her to the testing organization.	Liv time travels to save her mother.
Plot Point 2	Series and Book Three Plot Point 2: Jaz kills book one's antagonist and learns who is leading the testing organization.	The weather has frozen the time portal, and Liv cannot save her aunt.

Outlined Scenes: Book Two Continued

Vault Heading	Evolution	My Fairy Assassin
Climax	To be determined.	Liv doesn't save her mother but kills the druid.
Closing Image	Jaz's daughter shows an increase in her ability to see into a dog's mind and one of Jaz's friends notices the ability.	Liv, her sister, and a fairy are together when the king orders Liv and the fairy to save Liv's aunt.

Outlined Scenes: Book Three

Vault Heading	Evolution	My Fairy Assassin
Time Passed	One day.	Two weeks.
New Ordinary World	Someone else knows Jaz's daughter has the same ability as she does. This adds risk to Jaz's life.	Liv's mother is still missing, but Liv thinks she can find her aunt who will be able to help Liv find her mother.
Opening Image	Jaz tests her daughter's abilities to see into a dog's mind.	Liv is hanging out with a guard when some humans decide to ram the Fairy world and drop some fairy magic.
Backstory	To be determined.	The time portal doesn't always work as expected.
Inciting Incident	Jaz discovers her daughter is in danger.	Liv finds out her aunt has joined the Ice giants in 1849.

Outlined Scenes: Book Three Continued

Vault Heading	Evolution	My Fairy Assassin
Plot Point 1	To be determined.	Liv discovers her aunt is locked in an ice block in the Himalayas.
Middle Plot Point	To be determined.	Liv time travels to save her aunt.
Plot Point 2	Series and Book Three Plot Point 2: Jaz kills book one's antagonist and learns who is leading the testing organization.	The weather has frozen the time portal, and Liv cannot save her aunt.
Climax	Series and Book Three Climax: Jaz uses her ability to see into a dog's mind to eliminate the testing organization.	Liv saves her aunt, but the alchemist and his Ice Giants get away.
Closing Image	Jaz and a friend create a secret community for those with ability.	Liv & family celebrate. King informs them Liv's father is in danger.

Subplot: Evolution and My Fairy Assassin Series

Vault Heading	Evolution	My Fairy Assassin
Subplot Skeleton Blurb	Jaz and her friend must create a secret community for those with the ability to see into a dog's mind; otherwise, these people will always be hunted as a danger to society.	Liv Wright must overcome her and the fairy's obstacles; otherwise, she will not be able to find true love.
Subplot Inciting Incident	This comes from the reaction to the inciting incident in book one. Jaz has her first dog vision. Jaz hides her first dog vision from another person.	Liv meets the fairy.
Subplot Plot Point 1	Jaz and her friend decide to create a community for those with the ability to see into a dog's mind.	Liv admits to herself she likes the fairy.

Subplot: Evolution and My Fairy Assassin Series Con't

Vault Heading	Evolution	My Fairy Assassin
Subplot Middle Plot Point	Jaz and her friend discover others with the ability to see into a dog's mind are willing to help protect her daughter.	Liv chooses the fairy.
Subplot Plot Point 2	Jaz kills book one's antagonist and learns who is leading the testing organization.	Liv and the fairy have a falling-out.
Subplot Climax	This comes from the closing image in book three. Jaz and her friend create a secret community for those with the ability.	In each novel, there must be a romantic gesture where Liv gets a little closer to the fairy.

SECRETS TO WRITING A SERIES

Subplot: Evolution and My Fairy Assassin Series Con't

Vault Heading	Evolution	My Fairy Assassin
Subplot Middle Plot Point	Jaz and her friend discover others with the ability to see into a dog's mind are willing to help protect her daughter.	Liv chooses the fairy.
Subplot Plot Point 2	Jaz kills book one's antagonist and learns who is leading the testing organization.	Liv and the fairy have a falling-out.
Subplot Climax	This comes from the closing image in book three. Jaz and her friend create a secret community for those with the ability.	In each novel, there must be a romantic gesture where Liv gets a little closer to the fairy.

Chapter Twenty-Seven: Where to Next after This Book?

First, let us say, "You rock!" You've made it this far, and that means you have a strong foundation for your series. It means you have series unity. And it also means you've started writing your series. That's amazing.

When you started off reading this book, you came to it with an open mind, with a hope that it would help you start your journey to writing a series.

The want, the need, to write a series is because you have a connection to a series. This book has shown you not only your connection but also the connections you need to make to your series reader-ready reality.

Because writing a series is your dream. And the process we have given you in this book will make your dreams come true.

What You Have Learned

A book series is a gold mine for both the series reader and the series writer.

When a reader reads a book they love that is part of a series, they get goose bumps and feel they have found their series. What does a reader do when they find their series? They become loyal readers.

We all want to write a series that resonates with readers and makes them want to return to the world you have created, over and over again.

Merely creating a series is not what you want. We hope you came to this book because you wanted to write a series that resonated with readers. And the excitement is that you now have a process to create a story.

The critical part of getting a reader to love your series comes from structure. We believe readers fall in love with your structure at the first story arc scene.

Getting a reader to fall in love with your series all comes down to creating a well-structured series.

Your series will be structurally strong because the series structure is something you as the reader of this book have strong knowledge of.

You Have Made Artistic Decisions

You have learned how to make structural decisions that will make your series strong. These artistic decisions gave you a foundation to work from. In fact, these artistic decisions form the backbone of your series creation process.

Whether it is a closed series, with a single series level story arc, or an open series, with the series patterns built in, you know which path to take.

Using the process in this book, you can make sure that the reader finds the first book, and every book in your series, unputdownable.

You have learned to trust your series-writing voice to create series unity.

Whether you chose to write a closed or open series, this book taught you a process for both.

Your Series Structure Test

Using the Series Structure Test, you can then test whether your series idea is strong enough to support a series.

Your Series Vault

Your series vault is part of the key to your success. In this book, you have learned how to create your series vault so you can start writing the next book in your series and have total control.

Time for a Celebration Dance

And we hope that by using this book over and over again, you can write as many series as you want.

Time for a celebration dance. And keep tapping out those words on your keyboard.

Where to Next?

This is a glorious moment. If you did your fun series tasks while reading this book, you'll already have written one structurally sound scene. Now it's time to write the rest of the scenes.

If you want to outline each novel in more depth, read *Secrets to Outlining Your Novel: The Creative Story Outlining Method* by K. Stanley and L. Cooke.

If your writing style is just to get going, then write your series. Go on. We'll be cheering you the whole way.

Now you have your series, perhaps you want to make decisions about the following:

- A prequel
- A sequel
- A character spin-off
- A setting spin-off

Whatever you decide, you have a process to create your series.

Go and have fun. Be creative. Love what you write.

Glossary

Act 1

The first quarter of the novel, where the characters, the main story goal, and the stakes are all shown to the reader. This is Aristotle's beginning.

Act 2

From plot point 1 to plot point 2, and everything in between. This is Aristotle's middle.

Act 3

Everything after plot point 2 through to the climax and the resolution. This is Aristotle's end.

Backstory

Events that happen prior to a novel's opening image that explain a character's motivation to reach the story goal.

Blurb

Readers buy a book on its promise. This promise is the description of the story that includes who the protagonist is, what their main story goal is, and what's at stake if they don't achieve the main story goal.

Blurb Promise

The reason a reader buys the book. They want the book to be about what the blurb says. Successful books keep this promise.

Character

A person or animal or other being who is in a story.

Climax

The scene at the end of the story where the story goal is addressed. It is the scene with the most emotion and highest word count compared to those close by it.

Combined Protagonist

A combined protagonist comprises two main characters who both want the same thing, meaning their goal for the story is the same. In their struggle to achieve the goal, they will both suffer or benefit from the same events.

Conflict

Action that pits two or more characters against each other.

Closed Series

A series containing a fixed number of novels that tell one story.

Closed Series Single Novel

An individual novel that belongs to a closed series.

External Story Goal

What a character wants in the story, not what they want in life. This will be written in the story skeleton blurb for each novel in the series. There will also be a series story goal written in the series skeleton blurb.

Fiction

Stories based on made-up events.

Group Protagonist

The protagonist entity is a group of characters, a world, or a society.

Inciting Incident

The inciting incident contains the action that changes or disrupts the protagonist's ordinary life.

Main Event

The key action that takes place in a scene.

Middle Plot Point

The middle plot point scene should have something terrible or life-changing happen to the protagonist.

Narrative Strategy

How you write each scene in first-, second-, or third-person tense.

Novel

Book-length narrative prose that represents a fictitious story.

Open Series

A series containing an unlimited number of single novels that are connected by characters, plot, or settings.

Open Series Generic Skeleton Blurb

A skeleton blurb that can work for each book in an open series.

Open Series Single Novel

An individual novel that belongs to an open series.

Opening Image

The first scene in a novel.

Placeholder

When you have not decided on a decision, you write a memo with the title "placeholder." You can then come back to all placeholders when the inspiration strikes.

Plot

What happens in the story.

Plot Point 1

The moment in the story when the protagonist accepts the story goal.

Plot Point 2

The moment in the story when the protagonist is at their lowest emotional or physical state.

POV

The story or scene is filtered from one character's perspective. This means the reader is experiencing a scene through that character. They see, hear, feel, smell, and taste what that character does.

POV Character

A POV character is the character telling the story at any given time. This may or may not be the protagonist.

POV Strategy

How you use POV across the series.

Protagonist

The protagonist is the main character or main entity in the story. The protagonist is the character who has the most to lose. They are not always the character who changes the most, but they can be.

Protagonist Entity

A protagonist made up of one or more characters.

Protagonist Strategy

How you use a single, a combined, or a group protagonist across the series.

Resolution

This is everything after the climax scene and up to the last word.

Scene

A portion of a story where characters do something. A scene will have a beginning, a middle, and an end.

Series

A series is a group of novels connected by common characters, plot, or setting.

Series Climax

The climax scene in the final novel of a closed series.

Series Inciting Incident

The inciting incident of a closed series.

Series Middle Plot Point

The middle plot point of a closed series.

Series Outline

The main events for the story arc scenes across all novels in a closed series or across each novel in an open series.

Series Plot Point 1

Plot point 1 of a closed series.

Series Plot Point 2

Plot point 2 of a closed series.

Series Skeleton Blurb

Shows the protagonist, their story goal, and what's at stake if they don't achieve their goal for a closed series.

Series Story Arc

The story arc that starts in book one of a closed series and ends the final book of the series.

Series Type

A series is either a closed series or an open series.

Series Unity

A series is a group of novels that are connected in some way. Series unity means there are elements of story that make a group of novels a series.

Series Vault

A place to keep track of the decisions you make for the series.

Skeleton Blurb

Shows the protagonist, their story goal, and what's at stake if they don't achieve their goal.

Skeleton Blurb Template

A template for an open series that can be applied to each book in the series.

Stand-Alone Book Story Arc

A story arc that starts and ends in the same book.

Stand-Alone Novel

An individual book that does not belong in a series.

Story

A narrative that has a beginning, a middle, an end, plus an inciting incident, a plot point 1, a middle plot point, a plot point 2, a climax, and a resolution.

Story Arc

A diagram showing the location of the inciting incident, plot point 1, middle plot point, plot point 2, and climax in a story.

Story Goal

What the protagonist is trying to achieve in the story. This is stated in the novel's skeleton blurb.

Story Stakes

These are the consequences for the protagonist if they do not achieve the story goal in a single novel.

Subplot

A storyline that supports the main external plot.

Trilogy

A closed series containing three novels.

Appendix: Recap of Outlining a Novel

Every story needs three acts. The first act sets up the ordinary world and shows what the story is about. Every story needs an ending. This is act 3. And something must happen between the story setup and the ending. This is act 2.

We wrote *Secrets to Outlining a Novel: The Creative Story Outlining Method* by breaking the story into three acts, and then breaking act 2 into two parts. We did this to make it easier to outline and write a novel. Doing smaller parts and achieving something is motivating.

If a novel is sixty to ninety scenes, the main story will have at least twenty-six scenes:

1. Opening Image
2. Lead-Up to the Inciting Incident
3. Inciting Incident
4. Reaction to Inciting Incident
5. Resistance to Story Goal
6. Lead-Up to Plot Point 1
7. Plot Point 1
8. Reaction to Plot Point 1
9. Goal Attempt 1
10. Goal Attempt 2
11. Goal Attempt 3
12. Lead-Up to Middle Plot Point
13. Middle Plot Point
14. Reaction to Middle Plot Point
15. External Pressures 1 on Protagonist
16. External Pressures 2 on Protagonist
17. External Pressures 3 on Protagonist
18. Lead-Up to Plot Point 2

19. Plot Point 2
20. Reaction to Plot Point 2
21. Protagonist Understands the Story Goal
22. Lead-Up to Climax
23. Climax
24. Reaction to the Climax
25. Resolution
26. Closing Image

Once you create the main story outline, you can outline the subplots and fit the scenes in the appropriate places in the story.

Acknowledgments

K. Stanley:

Thank you to L. Cooke for working with me on our third book. Your knowledge and enthusiasm amaze me every day.

Thank you to our copyeditor, James Gallagher.

Thank you to our beta readers: Brandi Badgett, Lisa Taylor, Laura Pritchard, Mrs. G, Linda O'Donell, Hope Douglas, and Debbie Frank.

Jean McAuliffe, your comments on structure and consistency made this a better book.

Fictionary, the company, deserves a shout-out.

Mostly, thank you to Mathew, my husband and lifelong partner in everything. Without him, none of this has meaning.

L. Cooke:

Thank you to K. Stanley, writing with you is such fun —your story insights, energy and kindness may book creation an absolute joy.

James Gallagher of Castle Walls Editing. You make our writing stronger. Thank you.

Thank you to our generous beta readers: Brandi Badgett, Hope Douglas, Lisa Taylor, Laura Pritchard, Mrs. G, Linda O'Donell, and Debbie Frank.

Thank you to Jean McAuliffe, a very special ARC reader.

Thank you to the Fictionary Community—my daily tonic of inspiration.

Thank you to my parents, for your patience with my passions.

Thank you to my children, keep asking all the questions, I love you both. And to my husband, I love you, my Scottish hero.

About the Authors

K. Stanley

Combining her degree in computer mathematics with her success as a best-selling, award-winning author and fiction editor, K. Stanley founded Fictionary and is the CEO. Fictionary helps writers and editors create better stories faster with software, an online community, and training.

Her novels include *The Stone Mountain Mystery Series* and *Look the Other Way*. Her first novel, *Descent*, was nominated for the 2014 Arthur Ellis Unhanged Arthur for excellence in crime writing. *Descent* is also published in Germany by Luzifer-Verlag.

Blaze was shortlisted for the 2014 Crime Writers' Association Debut Dagger.

Her short stories are published in *The Ellery Queen Mystery Magazine*, and *Voices from the Valleys*. Her short story *When a Friendship Fails* won the Capital Crime Writer award.

Secrets to Editing Success: The Creative Story Editing Method, *Secrets to Outlining a Novel: The Creative Story Outlining Method*, *The Author's Guide to Selling Books to Non-Bookstores*, and *Your Editing Journey* are her non-fiction books.

L. Cooke

L. Cooke is a Fictionary Certified StoryCoach Editor and Head of Community and Training at Fictionary. Lucy is the co-author of *Secrets to Editing Success: The Creative Story Editing Method* and *Secrets to Outlining A Novel: The Creative Story Outlining Method* and *Secrets to Writing a Series: The Creative Series Writing Method*

She is writing her first novel, *My Fairy Assassin*.

© 2024 K. Stanley and L. Cooke

www.ingramcontent.com/pod-product-compliance
Lightning Source LLC
Chambersburg PA
CBHW030516230426
43665CB00010B/640